Affluence, Austerity and Electoral Change in Britain

Affluence, Austerity and Electoral Change in Britain investigates the political economy of public support for British political parties since Tony Blair led New Labour to power in 1997. Using valence politics models of electoral choice and marshalling an unprecedented wealth of survey data collected in the British Election Study's monthly Continuous Monitoring Surveys, the authors trace forces affecting support for New Labour during its 13 years in office. They then study how the recessionary economy has influenced the dynamics of party support since the Conservative–Liberal Democrat Coalition came to power in May 2010 and factors that shaped voting in Britain's May 2011 national referendum on changing the electoral system. Placing Britain in comparative perspective with cross-national survey data gathered in the midst of the worst recession since the 1930s, the authors investigate how the economic crisis has affected support for incumbent governments and democratic politics in over 20 European countries.

PAUL WHITELEY is Professor of Government at the University of Essex.

HAROLD D. CLARKE is Ashbel Smith Professor in the School of Economic, Political and Policy Sciences at the University of Texas at Dallas, and Adjunct Professor in the Department of Government at the University of Essex.

DAVID SANDERS is Professor of Government at the University of Essex.

MARIANNE C. STEWART is Professor in the School of Economic, Political and Policy Sciences at the University of Texas at Dallas.

Affluence, Austerity and Electoral Change in Britain

PAUL WHITELEY
Department of Government, University of Essex

HAROLD D. CLARKE
School of Economic, Political and Policy Sciences, University of Texas at Dallas, Department of Government, University of Essex

DAVID SANDERS
Department of Government, University of Essex

MARIANNE C. STEWART
School of Economic, Political and Policy Sciences, University of Texas at Dallas

CAMBRIDGE
UNIVERSITY PRESS

CAMBRIDGE
UNIVERSITY PRESS

University Printing House, Cambridge CB2 8BS, United Kingdom

Published in the United States of America by Cambridge University Press, New York

Cambridge University Press is part of the University of Cambridge.

It furthers the University's mission by disseminating knowledge in the pursuit of education, learning and research at the highest international levels of excellence.

www.cambridge.org
Information on this title: www.cambridge.org/9781107641167

© Paul Whiteley, Harold D. Clarke, David Sanders and Marianne C. Stewart 2013

First published 2013

Printed in the United Kingdom by Clays, St Ives plc

A catalogue record for this publication is available from the British Library

Library of Congress Cataloguing in Publication data
Clarke, Harold D.
Affluence, austerity and electoral change in Britain / Harold D. Clarke.
  pages cm
Includes bibliographical references and index.
ISBN 978-1-107-02424-3 (hardback)
1. Elections – Great Britain – History.   2. Voting – Great Britain – History.
3. Recessions – Great Britain – History.   4. Great Britain – Economic
conditions – 1997–   5. Great Britain – Economic conditions – 21st century.   I. Title.
JN956.C53   2013
324.941 – dc23   2013016801

ISBN 978-1-107-02424-3 Hardback
ISBN 978-1-107-64116-7 Paperback

Cambridge University Press has no responsibility for the persistence or accuracy of URLs for external or third-party internet websites referred to in this publication, and does not guarantee that any content on such websites is, or will remain, accurate or appropriate.

Most, probably, of our decisions to do something positive ... can only be taken as the result of animal spirits – a spontaneous urge to action rather than inaction, and not as the outcome of a weighted average of quantitative benefits multiplied by quantitative probabilities.

John Maynard Keynes, The General Theory of Employment, Interest and Money, 1936

The curious task of economics is to demonstrate to men how little they really know about what they imagine they can design.

Friedrich Hayek, *The Fatal Conceit*, 1988

The first point of recapitalisation was to save banks that would otherwise have collapsed. And we not only saved the world ...

Gordon Brown, 10 December 2008

We can't go on with the same irresponsible economic policies that gave us the biggest boom, the biggest bust ... and now threaten our recovery with higher debts, higher instability, higher taxes, higher interest rates and higher unemployment.

David Cameron, 2 January 2010

This can't go on. The world badly needs a change of course .... We need a new deal based on the understanding that collective austerity risks catastrophe.

Ed Balls, 27 October 2011

I have no illusions that there is a big task to turn round Labour's economic credibility and show – even as George Osborne's plans deliver unemployment rising, growth stagnating and long-term reform stalling – that Labour can be trusted again.

Ed Balls, 16 January 2012

Growth has been weaker than originally expected .... But the arguments for deficit reduction have become stronger, not weaker, over the last year.

George Osborne, 27 January 2013

Contents

Figures

Tables

Acknowledgments

Writing *Affluence, Austerity and Electoral Change in Britain* has been an enjoyable challenge. A large number of individuals and organizations assisted us in our efforts and we wish to take this opportunity to thank them. First and foremost is the Economics and Social Research Council. The ESRC provided major funding for the 2001, 2005 and 2010 British Election Studies (BES) that generated data for the vast majority of the analyses that we discuss in the pages that follow. ESRC funding enabled us to conduct the Rolling Campaign Panel Surveys (RCPS) and monthly Continuous Monitoring Surveys (CMS) as well as the traditional BES pre-campaign and post-election in-person surveys. The RCPS and CMS surveys permit us to track the short- and long-term dynamics of political attitudes and behaviour in the British electorate over a now lengthy period characterized by protracted prosperity followed by the most serious economic crisis since the Great Depression of the 1930s. The recession and the Coalition Government's imposition of stringent austerity policies to restore Britain's economic good health constitute an important, if very painful, real-world political economy experiment. Leveraging the data-generating power of the CMS, we investigate the dynamics of party support in a major mature democracy in a time of acute economic distress.

The CMS project builds on national monthly surveys initiated in April 2004 with a research grant provided by the National Science Foundation (US). We are pleased to acknowledge the generous assistance and sage advice of former NSF Political Science Program Director, Frank Scioli, in getting the CMS project underway. We also thank current NSF Political Science Program Director, Brian Humes, for assisting the Political Support in America and Political Support in Canada surveys that have been carried out in conjunction with the BES.

Since 2001, the fieldwork for the BES in-person surveys have been conducted by three highly capable survey houses, NOP in 2001,

NATCEN in 2005 and BMRB in 2010. Here, we wish to thank Nick Howat and his colleagues at BMRB for their first-rate work on the 2010 in-person surveys. We really appreciate their help. The RCPS and CMS national internet surveys were carried out by YouGov under the supervision of Project Director, Joe Twyman. Joe and the YouGov team have done a superb job in providing us and the election study community with an unparalleled array of high-quality survey data covering what has become an important period in British political-economic history. We owe Joe and others at YouGov a deep debt of gratitude. In addition, we are pleased to thank Pippa Norris, Ron Johnston, Charles Pattie and their colleagues for generously providing aggregate data on campaign spending, election results, and sociodemographics that we have merged with BES survey data.

The BES project has received substantial assistance from others as well. Over the past decade, the University of Texas at Dallas has provided research assistance that has greatly facilitated the assembly and processing of the BES data. In particular, we wish to thank UTD Provost, Hobson Wildenthal, for his continuing interest and support. We also thank Karl Ho and Russell Hoffman for their expertise in constructing the website used for disseminating BES survey data, graphics and research reports to user communities in the UK and around the world. We are very pleased to take this opportunity to recognize their generous assistance. In addition, we thank our energetic research assistant, Eddie Feng, for his quick and careful coding of masses of BES open-ended 'most important issue' responses and Cheryl Berry, UTD Administrative Assistant, for her invariably accurate and timely processing of the paperwork needed for Clarke and Stewart to travel to the UK and purchase the computers and software needed to analyze a large and valuable array of survey data.

In addition to those who have helped us with the BES project per se, there are many people we wish to recognize for helping us to develop our ideas about the science of electoral choice, the conduct of survey research and the analysis of survey data. The list is too long for complete enumeration – over the years we have accumulated many intellectual debts! However, we especially wish to thank Alan Acock, Jan Box-Steffensmeier, Ian Budge, Russ Dalton, Ray Duch, Justin Fisher, Jim Gibson, Jeff Gill, Jim Granato, Simon Jackman, Bill Jacoby, Rob Johns, Richard Johnston, Ron Johnston, Mike Lewis-Beck, Skip Lupia, Allan McCutcheon, Bill Mishler, Helmut Norpoth,

Charles Pattie, Jason Reifler, Doug Rivers, Brian Schaffner, Norman Schofield, Peter Schmidt, Tom Scotto, Paul Sniderman, Randy Stevenson, Lynn Vavreck, Herb Weisberg, Guy Whitten and Chris Wlezien. Special thanks go to Allan Kornberg, Larry LeDuc and Jon Pammett for many conversations where they communicated their insights about valence politics and implications for understanding public support for authorities, regime and community in democratic polities. Larry also deserves special recognition for developing and sharing his ideas on the politics of national referendums and the psychology of political choice in these important events.

Research is one thing, writing is another, and publication still another. We are privileged to publish *Affluence, Austerity and Electoral Change in Britain* with Cambridge University Press. We appreciate the continuing interest our editor, John Haslam, has shown in the project and his patience as we completed the manuscript. Clarke first broached the idea for the book to John at a Tower Center luncheon at Southern Methodist University a few years ago. We were gratified when he responded enthusiastically. Like all good editors, he then encouraged his authors to see the project through to completion. Thanks, John!

Last, certainly not least, we wish to thank Gill and Sue for their unflagging patience and very cheerful support over the several years we have been working on this project. Yes, studying voting and elections is fun, but we recognize that other things are too!

Paul Whiteley
Harold D. Clarke
David Sanders
Marianne C. Stewart

1 | The politics of affluence and austerity

In the May 1997 general election 'New Labour' won a landslide victory. The roots of the New Labour project lay in four successive, traumatic election defeats experienced by the party over the period from May 1979 to April 1992. The gradual transformation of Old Labour during these years came to fruition in 1997 and it produced a spectacular electoral success under the leadership of Tony Blair. Two more victories followed in 2001 and 2005, making Blair the only Labour leader in history to win three successive general elections. In May 2010, the New Labour era ended. Although the 2010 general election produced a hung parliament, Labour's much reduced share of seats made it very difficult – virtually impossible – for the party to continue in power as part of a viable coalition government. After five days of intensive interparty negotiations, Gordon Brown resigned as prime minister and Conservative Leader, David Cameron, was invited to form a government. The result was the Conservative–Liberal Democrat Coalition, Britain's first such government in over half a century.

In previous books, *Political Choice in Britain* (Clarke *et al.*, 2004b) and *Performance Politics and the British Voter* (Clarke *et al.*, 2009b), we have investigated alternative explanations of voting behaviour that have been proposed to account for the fates of British political parties both in the 'New Labour' era and more generally. We have provided a theoretical account of electoral choice which applies not only to Britain but also to other contemporary mature democracies such as Canada, France, Germany and the United States (see e.g. Clarke *et al.*, 2009a; Clarke and Whitten, 2013; Lewis-Beck *et al.*, 2012). According to this account, electoral choice in these countries is best understood as the product of the process of 'valence' or 'performance' politics. In a world of valence politics – where stakes are frequently high and risk is often better described as uncertainty – voters make choices primarily on the basis of evaluations of rival parties' perceived abilities to deliver policy outcomes on salient issues involving broad consensus about what government should do.

In this new book, the overarching theme of valence politics is extended both theoretically and empirically to explain, for the first time, the rise and fall of New Labour during its 13 years in office, and, in particular, the dynamics of party support since 2005 and why the New Labour era came to an end in 2010. Although several books and 'insider' accounts have been published on various aspects of the New Labour story,[1] a comprehensive analysis of the electoral politics of New Labour has not been told. Marshalling valence politics concepts and using an unprecedented wealth of survey data collected in recent British Election Studies (BES) enable us to investigate factors affecting support for New Labour in depth. We also conduct an in-depth analysis of the forces affecting the evolution of party support since the Conservative–Liberal Democrat Coalition came to power in May 2010 and factors that shaped the choices voters made in the May 2011 national referendum on adopting the Alternative Vote electoral system. In addition, recognizing the importance of voters' reactions to policy delivery as a core theme in the valence politics model, we investigate how those reactions have influenced the dynamics of people's subjective sense of well-being in the current era of austerity.

The valence politics model provides theoretical guidance for these investigations. Within a broadly defined rational choice framework, the valence politics model competes with spatial rivals as an explanation of electoral choice and party competition. Key ideas leading to the development of the valence politics model were advanced 50 years ago by Donald Stokes (Stokes, 1963; see also Stokes, 1992). As part of his insightful critique of spatial models of party competition, Stokes argued that voters rely heavily on their evaluations of rival parties' perceived capacities to deliver policy outcomes in issue areas on which there is broad consensus about what government should do. A classic example is the economy. Virtually everyone wants vigorous, sustainable economic growth coupled with low rates of unemployment and inflation. Similarly, a vast majority wish to live in a society that is not vulnerable to personal and national security threats posed by criminals, terrorists and miscellaneous miscreants. Again, almost everyone wants affordable, accessible and effective public services in areas such as education, health, transportation and environmental protection. Persistent public concern with such valence issues means that they typically dominate the political agenda in Britain and other mature democracies. These issues are important in emerging democracies as well (Ho *et al.*, 2013). Although the mix of valence issues varies over time, their continuing overall salience works to focus political debate on 'who can do the job' rather than on 'what the job should be'. As a consequence, evaluations of which party and which leader are best able to deliver on consensually agreed-upon policy goals are key drivers of voting in successive elections and do much to account for the dynamics of party support in inter-election periods.

The major alternative theoretical account of electoral choice, the spatial model of party competition, was developed in work by Duncan Black (1958) and Anthony Downs (1957). The key assumption underpinning this model is that *position or spatial issues* are the dominant factors governing voting decisions. Unlike valence issues, for spatial issues there is widespread *disagreement* in the electorate and among political parties regarding policy goals associated with these issues. For example, the Conservatives differ from Labour and the Liberal Democrats on the desirability of cutting taxes as a goal of government policy. Similarly, although both Labour and the Conservatives supported the invasion of Iraq in 2003, the Liberal Democrats openly opposed it, reflecting widespread public disagreement about British involvement in the conflict. According to spatial theories, voters have exogenously determined preferences and they attempt to 'maximize their utilities' by supporting a party that is closest to them in a policy space defined by one or more position issues or more general ideological orientations. For their part, parties are strategic actors who try to maximize electoral support in light of knowledge of voters' distributions in the commonly shared issue/ideological space. Although spatial models have been imaginatively elaborated in various ways, they have retained the core assumption that salient *position* issues are what matter for choices made by utility-maximizing voters (e.g. Adams *et al.*, 2005; Merrill and Grofman, 1999).

Academic theorizing about electoral choice, especially in the formal theory tradition, has been dominated by spatial models. In contrast, with the notable exception of the literature on 'economic voting' (e.g. Clarke *et al.*, 1992; Duch and Stevenson, 2008; Lewis-Beck, 1988; Norpoth *et al.*, 1991), less attention has been accorded to valence issues – despite abundant evidence of the central role that they have played in successive general elections in Britain and elsewhere. We have compared the explanatory power of spatial and valence models of electoral choice in *Political Choice in Britain* and *Performance Politics and the British Voter* (see also Clarke *et al.*, 2009a). In the present volume we consider the relevance of these rival accounts of voting behaviour for understanding the rapidly changing economic and political context that has characterized Britain in recent years. A key difference from our earlier books is a focus on the dynamics of party support on a month-by-month basis throughout the entire 2005–10 Parliament and the first two years of the Conservative–Liberal Democrat Coalition. Using multivariate statistical procedures we estimate dynamic models of party support containing valence and spatial variables and a variety of sociodemographic measures. The aim is to explain the evolution of party support in Britain's fast-changing post-2005 political-economic environment.

Taking account of the volatile post-2005 context is crucial for understanding contemporary electoral politics, since the most serious economic crisis since the Great Depression of the 1930s occurred during this period. Foreshadowed by the failure of the Northern Rock bank in autumn 2007, the crisis defined the political agenda in the run-up to the 2010 election and its effects have continued to reverberate strongly since then. A massively disruptive intervention, the crisis constitutes a natural experiment for testing the robustness of rival valence and spatial models for explaining electoral choice in good times and bad. An analysis of cross-level interactions between individual-level predictors of voting and contextual variables, capturing the political and economic dimensions of the crisis, enables us to investigate the explanatory power of rival valence and spatial models as the political-economic context has shifted from prosperity and stability to recession and turmoil. This could not be done in our earlier analyses of voting in the 2001 and 2005 general elections since the political-economic context in which voters made their choices was one of relatively uninterrupted 'good times'.

A second innovative feature of the present book concerns how voters try to make sense of, and hence make sensible choices in, politics. The development of our theoretical and empirical analyses draws on important insights from related fields. In particular, a key finding in political psychology is that many voters have low levels of political knowledge and lack coherent ideological frameworks that would enable them to make sense of political issues and events (Converse, 1964). The long-standing puzzle is to determine whether such voters can make sensible political decisions and, if so, how they do it. Recent research addresses this puzzle by showing that many people are 'cognitive misers' who use heuristics, that is, information cues or cognitive shortcuts, as guides. These heuristics help them avoid the costs of gathering and processing large amounts of complicated and oftentimes contradictory information required to understand issues and events in a complex and uncertain political world (see e.g. Lupia and McCubbins, 1998; Lupia *et al.*, 2000; Popkin, 1991; Sniderman *et al.*, 1991).

In particular, the use of 'fast and frugal heuristics' (Gigerenzer, 2008; Gigerenzer *et al.*, 2011) allows people to make effective decisions while at the same time greatly reducing the costs and extent of information processing. These findings are relevant to an aspect of the long-standing paradox of participation – the fact that voters have little incentive to invest heavily in learning about the complexities of politics prior to casting their vote since, acting as individuals, they have little influence over the outcome of an election. Fast and frugal information processing greatly minimizes decision-making costs. Analyses in this book develop and extend these ideas by considering how people use leader images, partisan attachments and other types of information to make electoral choices.

A third feature of the book is its focus on the roles of interpersonal and impersonal communications during the 'long' and 'short' campaigns preceding polling day. The 'Ground War', that is, the election campaign at the constituency level, and the 'Air War', the election campaign at the national level, are modelled using very large-scale, internet-based surveys and variables that index the influence of the media during the campaign. Leadership debates are an important innovation in British election campaigns and in 2010 the first-ever leaders' debate had a major impact. The impact of the debates and other developments in the campaign are analyzed using the 2010 BES Rolling Campaign Panel Survey (RCPS) data which enable us to monitor the evolution of key political attitudes on a daily basis.

A fourth feature of the book is the use of data gathered in monthly BES Continuous Monitoring Surveys (CMS) to study factors affecting the popularity of the new Coalition Government over the June 2010–August 2012 period. This very large data set enables us to investigate the explanatory power of competing accounts of party support in a dynamic context where the new Coalition Government has taken bold actions to stabilize Britain's finances. Reacting to the Government's large-scale cuts in public spending and public-sector employment coupled with substantial increases in taxes and fees, critics have blamed Prime Minister Cameron and his colleagues for derailing an incipient recovery and promoting rising unemployment, a 'double-dip' recession and extensive, unnecessary misery. Whether the Coalition will pay a heavy price in terms of diminished support in the next general election remains to be seen – but the stage is set.

A fifth feature is a thorough analysis of various forces – particularly levels of political knowledge, risk orientations and cues provided by the major political parties and their leaders – that influenced voting in the May 2011 AV ballot referendum. Very large surveys conducted as part of the BES CMS enable us to study the evolution of support/opposition for the AV ballot at both the aggregate and individual levels. In the event, the AV proposal was soundly defeated, thereby effectively settling the issue of reform of the Britain's voting system for the foreseeable future. Analysing forces affecting the choices voters made in the referendum is thus an interesting and important topic in its own right.

A sixth innovative feature of the book is an analysis of the political economy of subjective well-being in Britain. Stimulated by the utilitarian theories of Bentham (e.g. Mill, 1987) and the work of subsequent political reformers, the promotion of public well-being has been cited as a major goal of democratic politics and it is a major underlying theme in the valence politics model of electoral choice. In recent years, scholars and politicians (including Prime Minister David Cameron) have recognized the importance of learning about factors that influence citizens' sense of subjective well-being. In the present volume, we employ multilevel modelling procedures to investigate how salient contextual events and conditions (the economic crisis and recession, large-scale retrenchment in public-sector programmes and spending, tax increases) have influenced the public's sense of well-being over and above the nonpolitical factors considered in previous research.

In the next section we describe survey components of the 2010 British Election Study employed in this volume.

BES surveys

The 2010 British Election Study gathered data using representative national in-person and internet surveys. In this book, we make extensive use of the data gathered in the 2010 Rolling Campaign Panel Survey (RCPS), as well as data collected in monthly national Continuous Monitoring Surveys that began in April 2004. All of the RCPS and CMS data were gathered via the internet by YouGov, plc. The RCPS was very much larger than traditional in-person surveys with an initial sample size of nearly 17 000 respondents, approximately 4000 of whom had been interviewed earlier as part of the 2005 RCPS. This inter-election panel feature of the 2010 RCPS makes it possible to track the attitudes and behaviour of a large sample of respondents from just before the 2005 general election all the way through to the 2010 election and beyond. The large 2010 RCPS sample also enabled us to resurvey over 500 respondents each day during the 30 days of the official campaign, thereby providing a daily tracking record of the impact on public opinion of the leader debates and other events. A third wave of interviews was conducted with 2010 RCPS respondents immediately after the general election took place, thereby yielding a national three-wave panel survey with pre-campaign, campaign and post-election components.

The monthly national Continuous Monitoring Surveys (CMS) are a third feature of the 2010 BES. These monthly surveys began in April 2004 with funding provided by a grant from the National Science Foundation (US). They now extend through December 2012, and the total sample size is nearly 120 000 cases. The aim of the CMS is to track trends in public opinion in inter-election periods, since many key events which influence election outcomes occur months or years before polling day. The CMS has focused on monitoring public reactions to policy delivery, and data gathered in the project are utilized extensively in the present volume. In spring 2011 the CMS was adapted to the task of monitoring public opinion dynamics in the run-up to the referendum on the Alternative Vote in May 2011 and voting in that event. We also employ CMS data to study public reactions to the economic crisis and the austerity policies implemented by the Coalition Government.

The research design facilitated by these internet surveys is considerably more complex than the single post-election in-person survey which was the staple feature of the BES in earlier periods. Party support is subject to ongoing dynamics and consequential shifts in public opinion can occur years before an election is called, as well as during the official campaign period. The design of the 2010 BES enables us to capture changes in important variables that determine how individuals vote and it facilitates modelling effects of the context in which these changes occur. Survey data gathered frequently and regularly are required for empirical analyses of these dynamic processes – hence the RCPS and CMS.

The year 2013 represents the 50th anniversary of the first national election study in Britain, conducted by David Butler and Donald Stokes in 1963 (Butler and Stokes, 1969). The present book investigates political support in the New Labour and post-New Labour eras, but in view of this anniversary it is appropriate to look over this lengthy period and ask what changes have occurred in our understanding of forces driving voting and election outcomes and methodological approaches that facilitate investigation of these topics. A long-run perspective also shines light on theoretical implications of the valence model which extend beyond electoral politics. We examine these issues next.

Studying electoral politics in the long run

There have been major changes in electoral politics in Britain over the 50 years since David Butler first visited Ann Arbor and Donald Stokes first sampled claret at the Nuffield high table. Turnout in successive general elections from 1945 to 2010 are displayed in Figure 1.1, and it is clear that there has been a long-term decline in electoral participation over this 65-year period. The highpoint of postwar turnout occurred in 1950, a contest that was arguably the first real peacetime election after the Second World War. The 1945 election was something of an outlier since it took place only a matter of weeks after the Second World War ended in Europe with all of the disruption that implied. With many voters in the armed forces still scattered across various theatres of war we would not expect turnout to be high. However, in 1950 fully 84 per cent voted – a sharp contrast to the 2010 election when just over 65 per cent cast a ballot.

In fact, Figure 1.1 probably overestimates participation, since the percentages are calculated as the ratio of people who voted to those on the electoral register. If individuals are not on the register, this

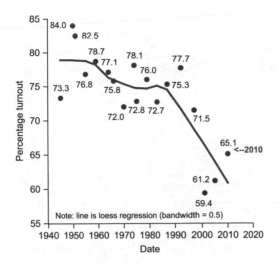

Figure 1.1 Turnout in British general elections, 1945–2010.
Source: Kavanagh and Cowley, 2010: 351.

will disqualify them from voting, regardless of their desire to do so. In the 2010 BES post-election in-person survey nearly 7 per cent of the respondents reported that they were not on the electoral register where they currently lived and a further 1 per cent said that they did not know. Expressed in terms of the potential electorate in 2010, these groups represent nearly 3.5 million people.[2]

Figure 1.1 shows that, since its high point in 1950, electoral participation gradually declined with the occasional rally in the early 1970s and 1990s. However, the trend was remorselessly down and the decline accelerated dramatically after 1997. The low-point was in 2001 when just over 59 per cent cast a ballot and turnout has revived only modestly in the two most recent elections. It is also the case that low turnout has been a feature of recent elections for the European Parliament, the Scottish Parliament and Welsh Assembly, as well as London mayoral elections. Similarly, turnout in the 2011 AV referendum was a dismal 42 per cent. Overall, electoral participation in Britain has declined quite significantly since its heyday in the 1950s.

Figure 1.2 reports percentages voting for the three main parties plus the combined vote for various minor parties in general elections from 1945 to 2010. These percentages are calculated in terms of the eligible electorate rather than as percentages of those voting, in order

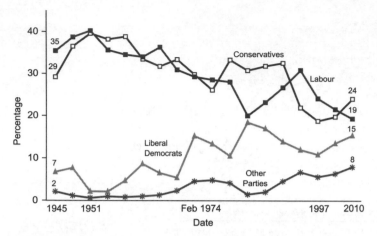

Figure 1.2 Parties' vote shares as percentages of the electorate, 1945–2010 British general elections.
Source: Kavanagh and Cowley, 2010: 351.

to highlight the effects of declining turnout on party support. The overall picture conveyed in Figure 1.2 is one of a party system eroding over time. The process has not been linear; rather it has accelerated when particularly unsuccessful governments were in power, and it has responded to shocks generated by important events.

The Conservatives and Labour dominated the political arena between 1945 and 1974, although as Figure 1.2 shows a relatively gentle decline occurred in both parties' shares of the electorate during this period. The February 1974 general election saw a dramatic increase in support for the Liberals following the unsuccessful Conservative administration of Edward Heath between 1970 and 1974. This was an era of rising inflation, industrial unrest and the three-day working week. Together with significant U-turns in government policies, the bad economy and the sour public mood did much to ensure the government's defeat (Hennessey, 2000: 331–56). The Liberals received a second boost to their electoral fortunes following the split in the Labour Party in December 1981 and the formation of the Social Democratic Party (SDP). The subsequent Liberal–SDP Alliance came very close to pushing Labour into third place in the 1983 general election and this eventually led to the creation of the Liberal Democrats in 1988 (Whiteley *et al.*, 2006). These traumatic events for Labour set the party on the road leading to the eventual creation of New Labour (Seyd and Whiteley, 2002). The process unfolded slowly, as party traditionalists battled modernizers to determine the party's future course.

Figure 1.2 shows that Labour lost the 1951 general election with just over 40 per cent of the electorate and it won a landslide victory in 1997 with just under 30 per cent. In fact, Labour lost in 1951 with a larger share of the electorate than the Conservatives and Liberal Democrats combined received in 2010. These figures illustrate the extent of change that has occurred in voting behaviour over the long run. The Liberals and subsequently the Liberal Democrats have been major beneficiaries of the long-run trend, but there has also been a sizable increase in support for minor parties. These parties include the Scottish National Party (SNP), Plaid Cymru in Wales, the United Kingdom Independence Party (UKIP), the Greens and radical-right parties including the National Front and the British National Party (BNP). Collectively, minor parties were supported by only 2 per cent of the electorate in 1945 but by 8 per cent in 2010. In the latter year, they garnered fully 12 per cent of the votes cast.

The implication of these substantial changes in voting behaviour is that we require theoretical accounts that can explain the large-scale temporal dynamics and methodological approaches that can gather the data needed to test these accounts empirically. With this point in mind we review the origins of the study of voting in Britain and discuss how theoretical and methodological approaches have responded to the mandate of explaining the dynamics of electoral choice.

Changing theoretical perspectives

When *Political Change in Britain* was first published in 1969, it was a seminal contribution to the study of voting and elections (Butler and Stokes, 1969). The book placed a heavy emphasis on the sociology of partisanship, a concept introduced in the British context by Donald Stokes, one of the creators of the famous 'Michigan' model of voting behaviour (Campbell *et al.*, 1960). Partisanship – what the Ann Arbor social psychologists called party identification – played a central role in Butler and Stokes's analysis. They argued: 'most electors think of themselves as supporters of a given party in a lasting sense, developing what might be called a "partisan self-image"' (Butler and Stokes, 1974: 39).

Butler and Stokes proposed that partisanship in Britain is primarily a product of enduring social cleavages, particularly social class, and it is transmitted across the generations by socialization processes in the family, social networks and local communities. The implication is that electoral politics is driven ultimately by social class. Peter Pulzer captured this idea in an often-quoted phrase: 'in British party politics, class is everything, all else is embellishment and detail' (Pulzer, 1967). The class environment, within which people were reared, created and subsequently reinforced their partisan attachments and, in turn, those durable attachments largely explained how people voted in successive general elections.

In 1960s Britain most middle-class individuals identified with and voted for the Conservative Party and most working-class individuals identified with and voted for Labour. The first of the British Election Study surveys conducted in 1963 showed that 79 per cent of respondents who thought of themselves as middle class were Conservative identifiers and 72 per cent of those who viewed themselves as working class were Labour identifiers (Butler and Stokes, 1974: 77).[3] At the same time 86 per cent of Conservative identifiers voted for the party, and 91 per cent of Labour identifiers cast a ballot for their party (Butler and Stokes, 1974: 46). The Liberals were discussed but not in any great detail, and the minor parties hardly figured in this analysis because they received only a very small proportion of the vote. There were exceptions to the general pattern, prompting research on working-class Tories on the one hand (McKenzie and Silver, 1968), and middle-class Labourites on the other (Parkin, 1968). However, these deviations from the 'class voting rule' were regarded as curiosities – remnants of an earlier age scattered on the class-ridden political landscape of mid-twentieth-century Britain. 'Electoral Anoraks' might enjoy studying curiosities not on the main diagonal of the famed 2 × 2 social class and voting table, but they were of no practical importance.

It can be argued that the gentle decline in Labour and Conservative support during the 1950s and 1960s, together with the modest reduction in turnout in elections in this period, did not constitute a serious challenge to the class-partisanship model. At the same time, Butler and Stokes were aware that there is considerable turnover in the electorate. They believed that demographics – the arrival of a large group of weakly socialized young partisans in the 1960s, coupled with the departure of strongly socialized older partisans, taken together with immigration patterns – could explain the resulting changes in party support. To wit: 'The scale of these demographic changes is sufficient to yield a 10 per cent turnover of the electorate within a five year Parliament' (Butler and Stokes, 1974: 211).

It is readily apparent that from the 1970s onwards the argument that generational replacement explains electoral change is increasingly implausible. There is simply too much short-term volatility for socio-logical explanations to handle. Interestingly enough, Butler and Stokes accepted this point in their analysis of the inter-election panel sur-veys they conducted as part of their early studies. In discussing these findings they noted that: 'in the five intervals of change that we have examined in the 1960s, there were never as much as two thirds of the public positively supporting the same party at two successive points of time' (Butler and Stokes, 1974: 268). Turnover in party support by one-third of the electorate in one Parliament is difficult to reconcile with a 10 per cent turnover arising from generational replacement.

This meant that from the beginning, the theoretical argument was flawed, even though *Political Change in Britain* was clearly a landmark study and a major contribution to the growing body of international research on elections. Awareness of these problems is perhaps the rea-son why Butler and Stokes concluded their book on a note of theoret-ical agnosticism: 'We have shunned the adoption of any single model of change, trying instead to distinguish in the system we are studying some persistent processes that give partial clues to change' (Butler and Stokes, 1974: 406).

Given the evidence in Figures 1.1 and 1.2, much subsequent work on voting behaviour in Britain necessarily has focused on the dynamics of party support, with the emphasis on explaining change rather than continuity. In the next section we discuss the theoretical and method-ological consequences of the large-scale dynamics apparent in electoral choice in contemporary Britain.

Fifty years of research: theoretical and methodological lessons

Voting theories have evolved since the Butler-Stokes era and, as our previous research shows, the valence model provides the best expla-nation of electoral choice and change in Britain (Clarke *et al.*, 2004b, 2009b). However, it is not the only account, since the spatial model also makes a contribution to understanding voting behaviour, although repeated testing shows it is a secondary contribution in comparison with the one made by the valence model. This is largely because the valence model takes a more realistic view of the psychology of voters. The model emphasizes the use of 'fast and frugal' heuristics (Gigerenzer, 2008; Gigerenzer *et al.*, 2011) in situations where voters lack the incentive and ability to be well informed about politics and government. This reality-oriented psephological anthropology distinguishes the valence model from its spatial competitor, where Laplacean omniscience and rational ignorance are locked in tight recursion.

The discussion of Figure 1.2 hints at the fact that the valence model has wider implications for how citizens' react to the practice of democracy in their country. At the core of modern democratic politics is a relationship – a contract – between governing elites and the general public which might be described as an 'invisible handshake' (Whiteley, 2012). That is, citizens look to the state to protect them from the risks inherent in modern life by providing social welfare, health care and protection from crime, terrorism and the mischief of unbridled markets (Beck, 1992). They also expect support from the state in terms of the provision of education, child-rearing assistance and income maintenance in old age. If this implicit bargain is to work, citizens have to acknowledge their obligations to the state in return (Kornberg and Clarke, 1992). This principally takes the form of being willing to pay taxes, obey the law and serve in the armed forces in times of national emergency. Norms supportive of these obligations are quite strong in Britain, although they are eroding over time (Whiteley, 2012: 15–33). Citizens have other important obligations to the state as well, including a willingness to participate in elections both to choose governments and to legitimate the larger political order. If this balance of rights and responsibilities gets out of alignment, for example, if large numbers of citizens demand big cuts in taxation while calling for big increases in spending on public services, then the system can break down.

This is a real danger in the present period of austerity for the existing major parties because of the impact of the worst recession since the 'dirty 30s'. This huge and thus far enduring shock to democratic political order is, if anything, more significant than the shocks which occurred in the 1970s and early 1980s. Turmoil on the scale experienced in that period had a significant impact on the party system and the present experience may do the same. The present 'great recession' is a major challenge to the relatively tranquil environment of British electoral politics which prevailed throughout much of the post-Second World War era, and it is likely to have implications well beyond the electoral process.

Our analysis of the valence model has focused almost exclusively on the electoral consequences of performance politics, but if the performance is bad enough this has the capacity to influence the contours of the party system itself. Effects may extend further, threatening the configuration of major political institutions and even the integrity of the political community (Easton, 1965; Kornberg and Clarke, 1992). Instead of merely opting for one party rather than another as a choice of government-of-the day, the electorate might decide to dispense with one or more of the major parties. When Labour replaced the Liberals as the main party of opposition after the First World War, this 'Strange Death of Liberal England' was explained largely in sociological terms (Dangerfield, 1935). However, a more convincing case can be made that it was the product of valence politics. A combination of a badly managed war effort by the Liberal Government, a civil war in the party over the leadership, together with the relentless pursuit of austerity policies by the party in the postwar era, eventually put paid to its hopes of ever returning to power on its own (Whiteley *et al.*, 2006).

A similar point can be made about the referendum on independence in Scotland which is scheduled for autumn 2014. The referendum is the product of Labour's failure to sustain its support in Scotland, coupled with the rise of the Scottish Nationalists and their narrative that Scotland will be better off independent from the rest of the United Kingdom. It is possible, although not inevitable, that Scots will be persuaded to vote for independence if they see nothing but continuing austerity and stagnation by remaining attached to Westminster. More generally, if partisan dealignment can happen in periods of relative prosperity, then it could have major consequences for existing political parties in a period of sustained economic crisis. The valence model thus has theoretical implications which go well beyond electoral choice per se.

The emphasis on the need to model political choice in a dynamic setting has implications for methodological approaches to the study of elections. The post-election face-to-face probability survey has been a feature of the British Election Study since 1963, and the Economic and Social Research Council mandated a face-to-face probability survey in its 2012 call for bids for a new study. What has become increasingly apparent is that, as the sociological model becomes increasingly marginal for understanding electoral choice, so do in-person surveys rooted in sociological explanations of political phenomena. This type of survey continues to be important for studying sociological questions such as changes in family structures or shifts in employment patterns in the economy, because these processes typically change only slowly. But in the rapidly changing world of electoral politics in-person surveys are inadequate for gathering the data needed to understand the individual- and aggregate-level dynamics that drive voting behaviour and political change.

This conclusion is warranted for several reasons. First, although many researchers regard face-to-face probability samples as a 'gold standard' for studying sociopolitical phenomena, it is important to remember that the sampling frames they utilize are lists of potential interviewees, not achieved interviews. Given such a list, it is easy to draw a random sample – achieving it is something else entirely. In this regard, response rates have been declining rather steeply for in-person surveys across the social sciences. The first American National Election Study (ANES), a face-to-face survey conducted in 1948, had a response rate of 84 per cent (Luevano, 1994). In contrast, the response rate for the 2008 US presidential election study was 60 per cent. The first British Election Study conducted in 1963 had a response rate of 79 per cent (Butler and Stokes, 1974: 435), whereas the 2010 face-to-face study response rate was 56 per cent. The response rate in the latter survey was low despite the fact that financial incentives were provided for participants, something unheard of in 1963. With declining response rates the likelihood of the achieved sample differing systematically from the target sample increases. It cannot be assumed that respondents are simply a random subsample of those chosen from a list to be interviewed. Interviewees in election studies clearly tend to be more psychologically and behaviourally engaged in politics than are those who fail, for whatever reason, to be interviewed.

However important, increasing 'unit nonresponse' is not the most difficult problem for contemporary in-person election surveys. Easily the biggest scientific problem is the time taken to collect the data. In 2010 the fieldwork for the BES post-election survey started immediately after the general election on 7 May and was finally completed on 5 September, four months later. During that period huge changes occurred in the political context in which respondents were interviewed, as the new Coalition Government began to institute its stringent austerity policies. The effects can be illustrated with one example, that of public feelings about Liberal Democrat leader, Nick Clegg.

In Chapter 4 we document that the Liberal Democrat leader enjoyed a high level of popularity coming into the 2010 campaign, and this increased substantially after his well-received performance in the first debate. As a result, his average rating on the 0–10 affect scale, where 0 means 'strongly dislike' and 10 means 'strongly like', was 5.6 in the RCPS post-election internet survey, which was conducted in the week immediately after the balloting. Clegg's rating was considerably higher than those for David Cameron and Gordon Brown, which were 4.6 and 3.6, respectively. However, many people viewed the Coalition Agreement as a 'sellout' by Clegg because he abandoned widely publicized promises he had made during the election campaign. Particularly damaging was his U-turn on university tuition fees, something he had pledged to oppose, and his popularity fell sharply in the months following the election.

Specifically, Clegg's affect scores, as measured in the Continuous Monitoring Survey, dropped to 5.1 in June 2010, to 4.7 in July, and to 4.6 in August. By the end of the year, feelings about him had fallen to a dismal 3.7 points. In contrast, his score in the BES in-person post-election survey was 5.0, which is based on scores provided by all of the face-to-face respondents interviewed over the period between May and early September. Because face-to-face surveys take a very long time to collect, they effectively ignore contextual conditions and events – like Clegg's policy reversals – that may have major effects on the dynamics of political attitudes and opinions, including feelings about party leaders. The analyst using these surveys (including the 2010 BES) will be unable to capture the dynamics of support for the Liberal Democrat leader in the post-election period or, equally important, to obtain an accurate measure of public opinion about him when voters cast their ballots. Sorting the in-person data by date of interview will not suffice. Since in-person surveys make no attempt to gather random sub-samples on a daily, weekly or monthly basis, temporal disaggregation is apt to produce highly unrepresentative 'convenience samples in time'.

There are other problems with in-person probability surveys. They have become extraordinarily expensive, with the face-to-face component of the 2010 BES costing just short of £1 million. Since they are so expensive there are strict limits on the number of panel waves which can be collected and, again, study of dynamic processes is severely inhibited. In this regard, the situation is much worse than when Butler and Stokes began the BES project in the 1960s. In addition, space limitations in the survey mean that only a very limited number of questions can be included in the survey instrument by outside research groups wishing to work with a BES team. Again, budget limitations prevent inter-election surveys being conducted with this method and there is limited technical facility for conducting anything but very rudimentary survey-based experiments. The conclusion is clear – face-to-face surveys are not cost effective and have limited utility for studying the dynamics of political support.

The main alternatives to in-person surveys, namely telephone and internet surveys, also have problems. Telephone surveys often have extremely low response rates, sometimes 20 per cent or less (see Sanders *et al.*, 2007). With telemarketing, answering machines, mobile phones and telephone preference restrictions, interviewers may have to call a multitude of potential respondents to find anyone willing and available to be interviewed. In addition, although telephone surveys originally were quite cost effective when they first became popular a quarter-century ago, they are now expensive. Currently, telephone surveys also have very limited capacity for performing survey experiments and data quality is often problematic.

The internet is a more promising methodology, since, as the 2010 BES RCPS study illustrates, internet studies are highly cost-effective and large numbers of people can be surveyed in very short periods of time. Internet surveys conducted for the BES in 2010 used quota samples rather than probability samples and this is a limitation. So is coverage: not everyone has access to the internet. But, internet penetration in Britain already is high (84 per cent circa December 2011),[4] and it is very likely that the coverage problem will effectively disappear over the next decade. Everyone will be online. Matching individuals in online panels with randomly sampled persons (Vavreck and Rivers, 2008), developing sophisticated interactive experimental tools (Sanders *et al.*, 2008) and administering questions in innovative ways that engage respondents and generate high-quality data mean that the internet is likely to become the most important vehicle for studying the dynamics of party support in the years ahead. In this regard, recent

research in Britain and the United States shows that for modelling purposes internet data provide an accurate and high-quality alternative to
face-to-face data (Ansolabehere and Schaffner, 2011; Sanders *et al.*,
2007). In this book, we exploit the advantages of the BES internet surveys to study the dynamics of electoral choice as Britain moved from
an era of affluence to one of austerity.

Plan of the book

Affluence, Austerity and Electoral Change in Britain begins by focusing
on the politics of the New Labour era. In Chapters 2 and 3 we tell the
story of New Labour – how it gained power and eventually lost it – up
to the beginning of the 2010 election campaign. In Chapter 2 we study
the Blair years, showing that factors affecting party choice remained
remarkably similar across the 1997, 2001 and 2005 general elections.
In all three elections the valence model dominated as an explanation
of party choice, with voters being motivated by their perceptions of
which of the rival parties could deliver effective policies, particularly
in relation to the economy. What changed over time were distributions on fundamental variables such as party identification, evaluations
of parties' managerial capabilities and reactions to party leaders. In
Chapter 3 we analyze changing party fortunes under Blair's successor
and long-time rival, Gordon Brown. We find remarkable continuity
across the Blair and Brown years, with valence forces dominating and
spatial considerations playing a secondary role.

Chapter 4 shifts the analysis to the campaigns the political parties
waged in the run-up to the 2010 general election. After describing
events over the year leading up to polling day and the dynamics of
party support during the 2010 campaign, the chapter examines the
'Ground War' – campaigns at the constituency level. The 'Air War' –
the national campaign waged through the mass media – is also analyzed. This analysis focuses on the impact of the party leader debates.
Leader debates are a major innovation in British electoral politics and
they dominated the national campaign in 2010.

Chapter 5 investigates the explanatory power of competing models
of voting in the 2010 general election. Analyses demonstrate the dominance of the valence politics model and thereby confirm the results
in our previous studies of electoral choice in Britain (Clarke *et al.*,
2004b, 2009b). However, an important question that remains largely

unanswered is the extent to which competing models provide a stable explanation of voting behaviour over time. Given the very different contexts of the 2005 and 2010 general elections, it is possible that the explanatory components in voting models would play different roles depending on the changed circumstances. The effects of varying contexts on electoral choice are estimated using a multilevel model specification and data gathered in the BES CMS from April 2004 to April 2010. The results show that there were systematic changes in the effects over time, but they were more complex than a simple 'increasing emphasis on the economy in hard times' hypothesis might suggest. There is also evidence to suggest that voters are increasingly disillusioned with both Labour and the Conservatives when it comes to judgments about the state of the economy influencing their voting behaviour.

Chapter 6 analyzes the dynamics of political support in the era of coalition politics following the 2010 general election. After describing the negotiations leading to the formation of the Conservative–Liberal Democrat Coalition Government, the chapter considers factors affecting party support after the new government took office. Immediately after the election there was a nascent consensus that the Coalition's bitter austerity medicine must be swallowed if the economy was going to return to good health. However, monthly CMS surveys document that public attitudes have evolved, with increasingly sharp disagreements emerging about the effectiveness and fairness of the austerity programme. With Labour's reputation for managerial competence tarnished by the economic crisis, minor parties, particularly UKIP, have profited from growing disillusionment with the Coalition's failure to achieve a vigorous recovery. Chapter 6 also considers relationships among elements of the 'objective' and 'subjective' economies. Analyses reveal that inflation and unemployment affect economic expectations in predictable ways but, importantly, expectations also affect inflation and indirectly, unemployment. Echoing Keynes, we find voters' 'animal spirits' are important, economically as well as politically.

Chapter 7 focuses on the May 2011 national referendum on a proposed change in Britain's electoral system. Assessments of the 'pros' and 'cons' of AV and FPTP and the broader political reform agenda had very strong effects on referendum voting. Partisan and leader image cues were also influential, with analyses revealing theoretically interesting interaction effects involving leader images and knowledge of leaders' positions on AV. Contradicting a familiar conjecture, statistical techniques developed for analyzing interaction effects in nonlinear models show that more knowledgeable voters placed greater weight on leader image cues than did less knowledgeable ones. Additional analyses document that valence politics considerations would continue to dominate the calculus of electoral choice if the AV electoral system had been in place at the time of the 2010 general election.

Chapter 8 poses the basic, but hitherto largely ignored, question: 'Why is performance politics important to voters?' Reactions to policy delivery are central to the valence model of electoral choice. Using CMS survey data that enable us to control for several other prominent explanatory variables in the literature on subjective well-being, analyses demonstrate that successful policy delivery increases voters' happiness or life satisfaction and failed policies have the opposite effect. The strongest effects of policy delivery stem from reactions to personal experience rather than more global assessments of policy success or failure. Chapter 8 also demonstrates that feelings of subjective well-being are influenced by macroeconomic contextual effects. When the run on Northern Rock in autumn 2007 heralded the imminent arrival of the global financial crisis and subsequent recession, subjective well-being responded rapidly. This effect weakened once the worst of the recession was past, suggesting that voters gradually adjusted to heightened joblessness. In an era of austerity, high unemployment was becoming the 'new normal'.

Chapter 9, the concluding chapter, revisits the political economy of austerity by investigating the political consequences of the economic crisis in a comparative European context. After reviewing major findings in earlier chapters, Chapter 9 uses European Social Survey (ESS) data to study how the recession has affected government performance evaluations in 23 countries. Analyses reveal that performance politics, exemplified by public attitudes to the state of the economy and other policy issues, play a dominant role in explaining confidence in governments. However, other factors, including voters' positions on spatial issues and their leadership evaluations, matter as well. Chapter 9 also presents CMS evidence showing that the British public is very pessimistic about prospects for solving the economic crisis in the foreseeable future. The dynamics of these 'bearish' attitudes have been strongly affected by the real economy, especially unemployment rates, with the Coalition Government's austerity policy pronouncements enhancing the dark public mood. The chapter concludes by considering the implications of Britain's new political economy of austerity for the outcome of the next general election.

2 | *Tony's politics*

Prosperity and performance

Tony Blair propelled New Labour to power in May 1997, campaigning with the slogan 'New Labour – New Britain'. From the time he became party leader in July 1994, he took full advantage of the difficulties encountered by John Major's weak and divided Conservative government. Blair had two core objectives, both of which reflected reactions to his party's lack of success in four successive elections held since 1979. He aimed to position what he called 'New Labour' as a responsible, slightly-left-of-centre party that would strive to achieve Labour's traditional goal of protecting the vulnerable and enhancing the life chances of the disadvantaged. At the same time, however, New Labour would not threaten the interests of Britain's increasingly prosperous middle class. Mr Blair and his colleagues believed that they could achieve these ends by demonstrating that their party was capable of managing the economy effectively – indeed, more effectively than their Conservative rivals. The resulting prosperity would provide the revenue needed for greatly enhanced social policy investment. New Labour thereby would deliver a highly attractive confluence of compassion and competence to government policy. During much of its long sojourn in the political wilderness Labour had been widely regarded as too great a risk to be trusted with the reigns of power. The party might care deeply about increasing public welfare, but it was incompetent to do much, if anything, about it. Blair aimed to change that longstanding perception and keep it changed.

Basking in the glow of his 1997 landslide victory, Blair's government got off to a terrific start. Labour experienced an extended honeymoon, enjoying enormous opinion polls leads over the demoralized Conservatives. By sticking firmly to the Conservatives' spending plans for the first two years, as it had promised to do during the 1997 election campaign, New Labour demonstrated fiscal responsibility and consolidated a reputation for managerial acumen that it had begun to acquire almost by default in the wake of the 1992 Exchange Rate Mechanism crisis. By handing control of interest rates to the Bank of England's Monetary Policy Committee, Blair displayed his determination to run monetary policy in the service of controlling inflation, rather than as a handmaiden of party interests and the exigencies of the electoral calendar. Political business cycles would give way to sound economic stewardship in the national interest.

Bolstered by the buoyant world economy of the late 1990s, Labour's political 'fundamentals' were in excellent shape. The party claimed to have devised a 'third way' – somehow different from both liberal capitalism and democratic socialism – that would combine fiscally responsible macroeconomic management that encouraged enterprise with gentle but continuous attempts to redistribute income and wealth towards the disadvantaged. Enjoying the support of key sections of the popular press, New Labour was viewed by voters, journalists and dominant opinion in the City of London as a competent and compassionate manager of the country's economic affairs.

Mr Blair's party had other advantages as well. Labour's new leader was a fresh face on the national political scene and his image resonated positively with much of the electorate, especially when compared to his Conservative counterparts – first, John Major and William Hague, and subsequently, Iain Duncan Smith and Michael Howard. In addition, and also very significantly, Blair's party had a substantial 'partisan edge' – it had considerably more identifiers than either the Conservatives or the Liberal Democrats. Policy moderation paid dividends as well. New Labour was seen by many voters as close to the ideological centre-ground – the terrain where the fabled median voter resided and, more important, where much of the British electorate located themselves. These were enormous assets that the prime minister and his government were keen not to squander.

Freed of the need to focus on recalcitrant economic difficulties – the bugbear of the Wilson and Callaghan governments in the 1960s and 1970s – Blair's New Labour government was able to pursue a wide range of policy initiatives designed to solve long-standing problems and modernize the British polity. Building on work begun by John Major, huge and ultimately successful efforts were made to bring about a peace accord in Northern Ireland. Scotland was offered, and embraced, devolution and a Scottish Parliament. Wales was granted its own Legislative Assembly. The Human Rights Act of 1998 incorporated the European Convention on Human Rights into UK law. The

Freedom of Information Act opened up all areas of British public life to greater scrutiny. In the international arena Blair was active as well, playing a crucial role in persuading NATO to take difficult military action in conflicts in Kosovo and Bosnia aimed, again successfully, at protecting the lives of civilians. With these accomplishments and a solid political base provided by sustained economic growth and apparently sound public finances, New Labour proceeded to win two further general elections, in 2001 and 2005.

Yet, despite these successes, New Labour's popularity – and especially that of its embodiment, Tony Blair – gradually faded. From the time of John Smith's death in 1994, there had been persistent rumours of serious disagreements and jockeying for power between Blair and his Chancellor of the Exchequer, Gordon Brown. These rumours were subsequently confirmed as fact in various memoirs published after Blair's exit and Labour's subsequent defeat in the 2010 election. Enoch Powell is famously said to have observed that all political careers end in failure. By May 2007, Blair was regarded as a failure by enough of his parliamentary colleagues to submit to the growing pressures that he should step down as prime minister. His resignation prompted the uncontested acclamation of Gordon Brown as his successor.

In this chapter and the next, we trace the story of New Labour – how it gained power and gradually lost it – up to the beginning of the 2010 election campaign. In this chapter we focus on the Blair years. We show that factors affecting party choice remained remarkably similar across the 1997, 2001 and 2005 general elections. In all three instances, voters were decisively motivated by valence considerations – by their perceptions of the capacities of the rival parties to deliver effective policy solutions, particularly in relation to the economy. What changed over time was how people distributed themselves on the political-economic fundamentals – their party identifications, their judgments about the economic management capabilities of the parties and their evaluations of the party leaders. The first section of the chapter presents individual-level analyses of voting in the 1997, 2001 and 2005 general elections that document the overall stability of the calculus of party support during this period. In the second section aggregate time-series analyses demonstrate how a pernicious combination of declining confidence in Labour's ability to manage the economy, increasingly negative assessments of Blair's performance, growing public unhappiness with the Iraq War and a mix of adverse events progressively weakened Labour's standing with the electorate. The end result was that by 2007, even though he had only recently led his party to its third successive general election victory, Blair was obliged to take his leave.

Making political choices, 1997–2005

Scholars have been attempting to explain why voters make the choices that they do for over well over half a century.[1] A diverse range of competing theories have been offered. We have engaged extensively with these theories in our previous research and it is clear that a valence politics model of party choice dominates its rivals (e.g. Clarke, 2004b; 2009b). A spatial model makes lesser, although nontrivial, explanatory contributions. In contrast, models that emphasize social class or other sociodemographic characteristics are much less important. Overall, we find that, despite its richer parameterization, a composite model which combines valence, spatial and demographic variables generally provides the best fit to the data, although a pure valence model performs almost as well. We reprise these theories briefly here and then deploy them in analyses of party choice in the 1997, 2001 and 2005 general elections.

The first set of variables in our composite model comprises various sociodemographic characteristics. The central idea here, articulated most famously by Butler and Stokes (1969) in their classic study *Political Change in Britain*, is that since particular parties tend to represent the interests of some groups in society more effectively than others, party choice is rooted in people's sociodemographic characteristics, with social class being especially important in the British case. According to this account, Labour support enjoyed its strongest support among male, working-class voters, particularly in the north of England and in Scotland and Wales. This was supplemented by strong support among Britain's growing ethnic minority communities, as Labour emerged in the 1960s and 1970s as the party that was prepared to legislate to protect them from discrimination and disadvantage. In contrast, the Conservatives received disproportionate support from middle and upper-class voters, from women, from older people, and from the south of England and East Anglia. The Liberal Democrats, for their part, had no distinctive demographic profile, other than a relatively strong historical base in the South West.

A key hypothesis flowing from models emphasizing social class and other demographics was that since social change was slowly paced, patterns of party support would remain quite stable over lengthy periods of time. If social class really was 'everything' in mid-twentieth-century British party politics as many claimed (e.g. Pulzer, 1967), stability – not change – in parties' vote shares was what should be expected. But, *pace* Butler and Stokes and other proponents of the class politics thesis, change, not stability, became the watchword of British electoral politics in the 1970s, with the inadequacies of the social class model and its relatives being dramatized by the sizable swings in parties' fortunes that characterized most general elections in the decade (e.g. Sarlvik and Crewe, 1983).

Butler and Stokes also placed considerable emphasis on *party identification* or *partisanship*, the idea that people feel a psychological attachment to a party, which disposes them to vote for that party in successive elections. Although typically measured with a single standard battery of survey questions, partisanship has been conceptualized in two very different ways. Butler and Stokes and other advocates of the social-psychological or 'Michigan' approach (e.g. Campbell *et al.*, 1960; Converse, 1969; Green *et al.*, 2002) regard party identification as a long-term *affective* attachment that is typically acquired in adolescence or early adulthood and which the individual tends to carry through life. In contrast, advocates of the rational choice approach regard party identification as a cumulative 'running tally' of evaluations of party performance. Updated continuously over time with older evaluations progressively discounted in favour of newer ones, these tallies are subject to change (e.g. Achen, 1992; Clarke and Stewart, 1994; Fiorina, 1981; Franklin, 1992).

We have engaged with this debate in our previous research where we present statistical evidence documenting substantial ongoing dynamics in party identification in Britain and several other contemporary mature democracies (e.g. Clarke and McCutcheon, 2009; Clarke *et al.*, 2004b; Clarke *et al.*, 2009a; see also Neundorf *et al.*, 2011). This evidence weighs heavily in favour of a cognitive-evaluative interpretation of partisanship that allows individual- and aggregate-level partisan change over time in reaction to changing evaluations of party performance. Accordingly, we regard party identification as part of our broader valence politics model of electoral choice that emphasizes the importance of performance judgments for understanding the individual- and aggregate-level aetiology of party support.

The *valence politics model* has its origins in Stokes's path-breaking critique of spatial models of party competition (1963, 1992). According to the valence politics model, voters focus on parties capacities to deal with what Stokes called valence issues – those issues where there is widespread agreement on the desirability of particular policy outcomes, for example low rates of unemployment and inflation coupled with vigorous, sustainable rates of economic growth; efficient, cost-effective health and educational systems; and security from threats posed by terrorists and common criminals. Although voters agree on the policy outcomes they want, there may be, and often is, substantial disagreement about the capacity of rival parties and leaders to deliver these outcomes.

Three main factors drive voters' assessments. First, since party identifications are conceptualized as cumulative evaluations of party performance, partisanship itself represents a major, predisposing, influence on electoral choice. The second factor involves party leader images. Since leaders are key political decision-makers, voters' perceptions of their demonstrated and anticipated performance represent a crucial aspect of valence calculation: the more highly a voter thinks of a particular leader the more likely that voter is, *ceteris paribus*, to support that leader's party. As described in the language of experimental economics and cognitive psychology, leader images constitute a 'fast and frugal' heuristics (Gigerenzer, 2008; Gigerenzer *et al.*, 2011) for voters seeking guidance in a political world characterized by high stakes and abundant uncertainty.

Assessments of the capacities of competing parties to deal with most important issues facing the country are the third factor. Quite simply, voters will tend to support the party that they consider best able to deal with the issues they deem to be the most important. Typically – not invariably – these are valence issues as described above. Given the pivotal importance of the economy as end and means, valence models sometimes include a specific economic component.[2] There are generally two sorts of economic mechanisms at work: judgments of the economic management capacities of the rival parties and evaluations of the past and future state of the country's and one's own personal finances. Regarding the former, the basic proposition is that voters tend to support the party that is seen as most capable of managing the economy effectively. As for the latter, the basic claim is that people who believe the economy (either national, personal or both) is performing relatively well typically want to preserve the political status quo that has produced their sense of prosperity – and they therefore tend to support the incumbent government. In contrast, if national or personal economic conditions are judged negatively, voters are prepared to abandon an incumbent government for one of its opposition rivals.

In contrast to the valence politics model, spatial models of party competition emphasize position issues and proximities between voters and parties on those issues. Having their origins in rational choice accounts of political behaviour advanced over half a century ago (Black, 1958; Downs, 1957), spatial models focus on issues where there is a clear divergence of desirable policy alternatives – such as whether the state should play an extensive or a limited role in the country's economic affairs or whether a liberal or an authoritarian approach should be adopted in dealing with criminals – and where both voters and parties can in principle adopt different positions in some well-defined and commonly understood uni- or multidimensional issue space.[3] Spatial theory contends that voters will opt for the party they consider closest to them on the position issues about which they care most. An overarching 'left–right' ideological continuum is often used as a global measure for summarizing these positions; on other occasions, analysts attempt to determine what the key issue dimensions are and then to measure where voters place themselves and major parties on those dimensions. In the present analyses, we employ a survey measure which assesses preferences for the extent to which the state should devote more resources to public services, although this entails a rise in taxation. This variable is supplemented with additional spatial measures, depending on their availability in the 1997, 2001 and 2005 BES datasets.

A final set of factors relevant for a composite model relate to the specific *electoral context* at hand. In Britain, this often means that some voters, convinced that their preferred party stands no chance of winning in their local constituency, may behave tactically – opting for a 'second-best' party that has a realistic chance of capturing the seat. Accordingly, models of the vote need to take this possibility into account. A second sort of contextual effect relates to the possibility that there may be an issue, or set of issues, that arise in a particular election and that at least in principle are capable of affecting the votes of a significant number of people. For example, in the 2005 general election, the issue of Britain's involvement in the Iraq War was fiercely debated, even though most people did not regard it as the most important issue of the day, and it was certainly thought at the time to have led some voters, particularly left-leaning Labour partisans, to decide against casting a Labour ballot. Some of these erstwhile Labour supporters voted for another party, and others decided not to vote at all (Clarke *et al.*, 2009b, ch. 5). Again, this sort of issue needs to be incorporated into models of the vote to ensure that they are correctly specified.

There are broadly two ways of testing the competing claims of these various accounts of electoral choice. One approach is to estimate each model separately and to compare the outcomes using model selection criteria such as the Akaike Information Criterion that discount explanatory power by the number of parameters specified in various models (Burnham and Anderson, 2002). A second approach is to combine explanatory variables in competing models in a single 'joint nesting model' to assess which effects are the most significant determinants of vote choice (e.g. Charemza and Deadman, 1997). In our previous work we have followed both strategies and repeatedly found that they suggest similar inferences regarding the explanatory power of rival models. Given that the second strategy can be more parsimoniously reported, we adopt it here.

For each election considered, model specification and estimation consist of two strands. For the incumbent party, we assume that the key decision facing voters is whether to continue to support it or to opt for one of its competitors. Accordingly, we estimate a binomial logit model (e.g. Long and Freese, 2006) of incumbent party vote. In 1997, with the Conservatives as incumbents, this entails a binomial estimation of Conservative-other party voting; in 2001 and 2005, it involves binomial estimations of Labour-other party voting. For the opposition parties, we assume that the key choice is which party is most attractive in comparison with the governing party. Accordingly, we estimate opposition voting as a multinomial logit model, with the incumbent party as the base category. Throughout, because of low numbers of survey respondents supporting various minor parties, we group all parties other than Labour, the Conservatives and the Liberal Democrats as 'Other'.

For each election, then, our model specification is:

Vote = f (Demographic Characteristics –

Gender, Age, Ethnicity, Region;

Party Identification –

Labour, Conservative, Liberal Democrat, Other;

Party Leader Affect –

Blair, Major/Hague/Howard, Ashdown/Kennedy;

Party Best Most Important Issue –

Labour, Conservative, Liberal Democrat, other;

Economic Calculations –

Economic Evaluations, Conservative *versus*

Labour Economic Management Capabilities;

Party-Issue Proximities –

Proximity to Labour, Conservatives, Liberal Democrats;

Context Specific Factors –

Evaluations of Iraq war (2005 only); Tactical Vote).   (2.1)

Table 2.1 summarizes the results of estimating Eq. (2.1) for the 1997, 2001 and 2005 general elections. For each election, Panel A reports the results of a binomial logit analysis of incumbent party support and Panel B reports the results of multinomial logit analyses of voting for the main opposition party (Labour or Conservative, as appropriate), with the incumbent as base category. Results are not reported for the Liberal Democrat or 'other' party support, although these additional categories were included in the analyses. The 2001 results are taken from table 4.10 in Clarke *et al.* (2004b: 109–11), in which additional controls (not reported here) were also applied for home ownership, occupational sector, and emotional reactions to national and personal economic conditions. The results for 2005 are taken from table 5.4 in Clarke *et al.* (2009b: 166–7), where additional controls (not reported here) were applied for emotional reactions to the economy, the NHS and the Iraq War.

The independent variables used for 1997 are the closest to those for 2001 and 2005 that can be derived from the 1997 BES data. The

Table 2.1 Binomial and multinomial logit analyses of voting in 1997, 2001 and 2005 general elections

	1997 Panel B Labour β	1997 Panel A Conservative β	2001 Panel A Labour β	2001 Panel B Conservative β	2005 Panel A Labour β	2005 Panel B Conservative β
Sociodemocratics:						
Gender	0.05	−0.10	0.01	−0.07	−0.26	−0.18
Age	−0.01	0.01	0.01	0.01	−0.01**	0.02**
Ethnicity	1.32*	−0.82	−0.75*	2.03*	−0.97****	0.43
Country/region:						
North	1.22**	−0.82*	0.68*	−1.62**	0.28	0.31
Midlands	0.34	−0.06	0.65*	−0.82	0.12	0.28
SE	0.18	−0.00	0.08	−0.18	−0.04	0.52
SW	−0.25	−0.33	−0.33	−0.28	0.16	0.15
Wales	1.47*	−0.90	0.06	−0.92	−0.12	−0.01
Scotland	0.95**	−1.22**	0.44	−0.92	−0.04	0.21
Social class	−0.23	0.27	−0.04	0.09	−0.38*	0.85***
Party identification:						
Conservative	−3.20***	2.84***	−1.50***	1.46***	−1.09***	1.56***
Labour	2.52***	−2.07***	1.14***	−2.45***	0.91**	−1.72***
Liberal Democrat	−0.12	−1.05*	−0.99**	−0.69	−1.51***	0.25
Other parties	0.13	−0.39	−1.11*	−0.79	−0.98**	0.51
Party leader images:						
Blair	0.19***	−0.04	0.46***	−0.52***	0.41***	−0.50***
Major/Hague/Howard	−0.33***	0.30***	0.01	0.32***	−0.13***	0.58***
Ashdown/Kennedy	0.03	−0.10*	−0.28***	−0.09	−0.31***	0.04

Party best most important issue[a]:

	(1)	(2)	(3)	(4)	(5)
Conservatives	−0.26	0.22	−0.97**	0.73	1.42***
Labour	0.38	−0.03	0.38*	−0.92**	−0.84***
Liberal Democrat	0.18	−0.25	−0.78*	−1.40*	−1.21*
Economic judgments:					
Evaluations	0.02	−0.04	0.19*	−0.38*	−0.55***
Management: Conservatives worst / Labour best	0.51***	−0.52***	0.54*	−1.29***	−1.28***
Party–issue proximities:					
Conservative proximity	−0.24***	0.23***	−0.04	0.17**	0.20***
Labour proximity	0.41***	−0.18	0.07	−0.13*	−0.14***
Liberal Democrat proximity	−0.30*	0.13	−0.07	0.11	−0.03
Iraq War				0.02	0.05
Tactical voting	−0.63	0.11	−0.85***	0.77*	−0.13
Constant	0.79	−2.66		2.53*	−2.95
McFadden R^2	0.60	0.74	0.58	0.61	0.60
N	2049		3025		3962

*** $p \leq 0.001$; ** $p < 0.01$; * $p < 0.05$; one-tailed test.

Note: Panel A is binomial logit analysis of incumbent party support; Panel B is multinomial logit analysis of Opposition parties using incumbent party as base category. Multinomial logit analyses also included Liberal Democrat and other party choices; results for Liberal Democrats and other parties not reported.

[a] Best party on most important issue measures are not available in 1997 survey. Measures used here derived from questions regarding the extent to which parties are capable of strong government. For other differences between 1997 and 2001/2005, see text.

main differences for 1997 relate to party best on the most important
issue and economic evaluations. Regarding 'party best', which measures judgments about party policy competence, no direct questions
were asked in 1997. The closest questions in the 1997 survey were
in a battery that elicited respondents' views regarding how far each
of the major parties were 'capable of strong government'. Accordingly, these measures are used in the 1997 model instead of the 'best
party' measures. Regarding economic evaluations, no direct question
was asked about economic management competence in the 1997 survey. However, there was a series of questions about whether economic
conditions (in terms of jobs, prices and taxes) had deteriorated and
whether the Conservative government was to blame. The 1997 measure accordingly reflects the extent to which respondents considered
the Conservatives to be poor economic managers, whereas the 2001
and 2005 measures directly capture judgments about Labour's managerial skills. Although these differences in the measurement of some
explanatory variables are unavoidable, as discussed below their impact
on the results of our analyses do not appear to be important.

The models reported in Table 2.1 are all well-determined, with
impressive goodness-of-fit (McFadden R^2) statistics. To make sense of
the results reported, we discuss each horizontal segment of the table in
turn and then reflect on its general lessons. Consider first the sociodemographic segment. Most of the coefficients across all three election
years are nonsignificant, although there are occasional exceptions. For
example, in 1997 Labour did disproportionately well in the north of
England (see the positive coefficient for North, $\beta = 1.22$, $p \leq 0.01$).
Again, in 2001, the Conservatives performed relatively poorly in the
North ($\beta = -1.62$, $p \leq 0.01$) but made gains among ethnic minority
voters ($\beta = 2.03$, $p \leq 0.05$). In 2005 Labour lost support among ethnic
minority voters ($\beta = -0.97$, $p \leq 0.001$), presumably a reflection
of opposition among British Muslims to the Iraq War. Much more
interesting is the general lack of significant demographic effects in
Table 2.1, particularly those for social class. This variable features significantly only in 2005, when middle-class voters were more likely to
support the Conservatives ($\beta = 0.85$) and less likely to support Labour
($\beta = -0.38$). An 'other things equal' qualification is appropriate here.
The demographic effects reported in Table 2.1 are what are left when
various psychological characteristics of voters are taken into consideration. Nonetheless, the results strongly indicate that there is only

a very limited direct role for sociodemographic factors in explaining party choice. However, it also bears emphasis that if only sociodemographic characteristics are included in the models, their explanatory power is extremely weak.[4]

The *party identification* segment of Table 2.1 produces a large number of significant effects, all of which are in the expected direction. For example, in all three elections, Conservative voting is positively affected by Conservative identification and negatively affected by Labour identification. The reverse is true for Labour support, which is invariably positively and significantly affected by Labour partisanship and negatively affected by Conservative partisanship. The negative effects of identification with a rival party do not always attain statistical significance but all relevant coefficients are correctly signed, suggesting that partisanship generally behaves as hypothesized.

A similar conclusion emerges regarding *leader images*. We use leader affect scores as a summary for leader images, as previous analyses have shown that most of the variation in leader evaluations across a range of dimensions can be conveniently captured by these affective responses (Clarke *et al.*, 2009b: ch. 5). As Table 2.1 documents, positive assessments of a party's leader have positive, and generally highly significant, effects on that party's vote (see e.g. the positive coefficient for Major, $\beta = 0.30$, $p \leq 0.001$ in 1997) and negative effects on voting for the main rival party (see the negative coefficient, $\beta = -0.33$, $p \leq 0.001$, for Major in the Labour column for 1997).

Results for the party best on the most important issue segment of Table 2.1 are more ambiguous. In 1997, variable this rarely achieves statistical significance – in contrast to the strong, consistent pattern of correctly signed, significant coefficients in 2001 and 2005. We strongly suspect that this inconsistency is a result of the imperfect measuring instrument used to capture 'best party' in 1997.

The economic evaluations segment also provides mixed results. Here, however, we suspect that this result genuinely reflects mixed effects. The measures for economic evaluations are all fairly consistent over time – and yet their effects are generally nonsignificant (with the highly significant negative effect for Conservative support in 2005 being the obvious exception). However, in terms of economic management capabilities, the picture is more reassuring. In 1997, people who thought the Conservatives had done a poor job in managing the economy were significantly less likely to vote for that party ($\beta = -0.52$, p ≤ 0.001) and significantly more likely to vote for one of its rivals (see the positive significant coefficients for the other parties). Similarly, in 2001 and 2005 those who considered Labour best at managing the economy were significantly more likely to vote for that party and significantly less likely to support the Conservatives.

The party-issue proximities segment of Table 2.1 supports the hypothesis that there are spatial effects on Labour and Conservative voting. Across all three elections, proximity to the Conservatives consistently encourages Conservative voting and discourages support for Labour. In complementary fashion, proximity to Labour is positively associated with Labour voting and negatively associated with casting a Conservative ballot. In 2005, the effects of spatial voting were pronounced, with proximity to Labour or the Conservatives consistently being significantly associated with a reduced probability of voting for the respective rival party.

Finally, the context-specific segment of Table 2.1 indicates that reactions to British participation in the Iraq War – potentially relevant only in 2005 – exerted no direct effect on support for any of the parties. However, this is not to say opinions about Iraq were irrelevant for electoral choice. The effects of reactions to the war operated primarily through voters' assessments of Tony Blair (see also Clarke *et al.*, 2009b: ch. 4). Finally, the effects of tactical voting are inconsistent over time. Tactical considerations appear to have been insignificant in 1997. In 2001, Labour suffered marginally in favour of the Conservatives, Liberal Democrats and miscellaneous other parties. In 2005, there was a small positive effect for the Liberal Democrats but no significant negative effect on either of its two main competitors.

What general lessons can be drawn from these findings? The first conclusion is that the effects of sociodemographic and election-specific factors are very limited. Although it is appropriate to include these terms in models of the vote as statistical controls, they do not appear to contribute much to explaining how people cast their ballots. A second conclusion, and one that bears emphasis for understanding the motors of electoral choice in contemporary Britain, is that valence forces dominate in the three elections. Party identification, leader evaluations, party best on most important issue (in 2001 and 2005) and economic management evaluations generally yield statistically significant and correctly signed coefficients. In essence, voters support the parties that they think are best able to deliver successful policy outcomes; they eschew parties about which they have serious policy delivery doubts. The third conclusion is that there is a subordinate, but nontrivial, role for spatial considerations – voters tend to vote for the party that is closest to them on position issues and to reject parties that take a stance that is distant from their own on such issues.

Since the coefficients in Table 2.1 are generated by analyses of non-linear (binomial and multinomial logit) models, the magnitudes of the effects of various predictor variables are difficult to discern (Long and Freese, 2006). In this regard, it is helpful to calculate the change in the probability of voting for a particular party when each predictor variable is varied from its minimum to its maximum value – while holding all other predictor variables constant at their respective means. The consequences of calculating these probability shifts are reported in Table 2.2, where we now include results for the Liberal Democrats which were estimated but not reported in the models in Table 2.1. Table 2.2 shows the probability changes (Δp) for the three core valence measures that were available across all three elections – partisanship, leader evaluations and judgments about Conservative versus Labour economic management competence. Table 2.2 also documents the corresponding changes for the spatial proximity measures. To keep the exposition reasonably parsimonious, we restrict the presentation to effects of Labour identification on Labour voting; Conservative identification Conservative voting and Liberal Democrat identification on Liberal Democrat voting.

The entries in Table 2.2 are easily interpreted. For example, the figure of 0.47 for the effect of Labour identification on Labour support in 1997 means that a Labour identifier was $\Delta p = 0.47$ more likely to vote Labour than someone who was not a Labour identifier but who was otherwise similar in all other respects. Some important conclusions are suggested by the numbers in Table 2.2. First, as the first row of the table indicates, across all three major parties and across all three elections, party identification exerted a fairly consistent set of effects, reflecting its enduring importance. For example, the Δp values for Conservative identifiers are 0.20 in 1997, 0.21 in 2001 and 0.20 again in 2005. Second, across all three parties the effects of leader images increased over time. In 1997, the Blair effect was 0.40; by 2005 it was 0.67. Similar increases were experienced for the effects on support of Conservative leader images ($\Delta p = 0.81$ by 2005) and Liberal Democrat leader images ($\Delta p = 0.78$ by 2005). This might

Table 2.2 *Change in probability of voting Labour, Conservative and Liberal Democrat associated with key predictor variables, 1997, 2001 and 2005 general elections*

	Labour voting				Conservative voting				Liberal Democrat voting		
	1997	2001	2005		1997	2001	2005		1997	2001	2005
Labour partisanship	0.47	0.27	0.21	Conservative partisanship	0.20	0.21	0.20	Liberal Democrat partisanship	0.41	0.38	0.30
Blair image	0.40	0.76	0.67	Major/Hague/ Howard image	0.16	0.37	0.81	Ashdown/ Kennedy image	0.25	0.64	0.78
Poor Conservative versus good Labour economic management	0.04	0.13	0.16	Poor Conservative versus good Labour economic management	−0.06	−0.11	−0.15				
Labour issue-proximity	0.67	0.00	0.39	Conservative issue-proximity	0.12	0.16	0.35	Liberal Democrat issue-proximity	0.38	0.24	0.51

Note: Changes in probabilities calculated using Clarify (Tomz *et al.*, 1999).

reflect a secular trend, involving the increasing presidentialization of British party politics, or it might stem from Blair's dominance of the political scene up to 2005, which was in turn reflected in larger leader effects for all parties. This is a theme to which we return in later chapters. Third, although Liberal Democrat support – unsurprisingly – was not strongly influenced by perceptions of Conservative versus Labour economic managerial capacity, these perceptions affected the probabilities of voting Labour or Conservative in fairly symmetrical ways. The changing patterns of Labour (0.04 in 1997; 0.13 in 2001; 0.16 in 2005) and Conservative Δp values (respectively, -0.06, -0.11 and -0.15) are very similar, suggesting an increasingly important role for judgments about economic management as the period progressed.

Finally, the Δp pattern for the spatial proximity variables tells an interesting story. Spatial considerations became more important over time for both the Conservatives and Liberal Democrats: the Δp value for the effect of Conservative issue proximity on Conservative voting increased from 0.12 in 1997 to 0.35 in 2005; the corresponding figures for the effect of Liberal Democrat proximity on Liberal Democrat voting were 0.38 in 1997 and 0.51 in 2005. However, Labour's case was rather different. Being positioned close to Labour on key issues was a major factor in Labour support in 1997 ($\Delta p = 0.67$), but by 2001 the effect had disappeared – a possible reflection of Tony Blair's effort to present Labour as ideologically neutral party of the 'third way'. In any event, the effect had been partially restored by 2005.

Our discussion so far has consisted in demonstrating the continuing importance of four politico-economic fundamentals to the individual calculus of party support between 1997 and 2005 – party identification, leader evaluations, economic management perceptions and spatial proximities. To study the larger canvas of British electoral politics over this period, the remainder of the chapter links movements in these fundamentals to the aggregate evolution of party support from Blair's first electoral victory in May 1997 to his replacement as prime minister in June 2007.

The dynamics of party support, 1997–2007

In this section we focus primarily on aggregate monthly time series data. These data enable us to describe the evolution of party support patterns and most of the fundamentals on a continuous basis for the

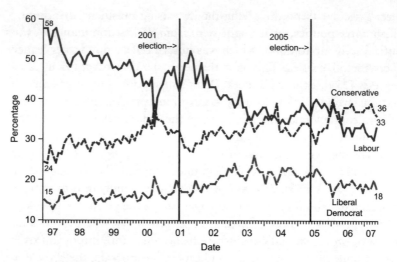

Figure 2.1 Labour, Conservative and Liberal Democrat vote intentions, June 1997–May 2007.
Source: Monthly average poll-of-polls, percentage intending to vote for each party reported by MORI, ICM, Gallup, YouGov, ComRes and BPIX.

entire 1997–2007 period. Figure 2.1 describes the changing pattern of major party support, measured as the percentage intending to vote for each party (actual vote is recorded in the months when elections occurred). As the figure shows, Labour enjoyed a huge lead over its rivals until 2000. There was a sharp, but temporary, downward spike in Labour support at the time of the September/October 2000 fuel crisis, when the Conservatives very briefly took the lead. Then, the status quo ante was restored – and Labour's commanding lead with it. However, the most interesting general feature of Figure 2.1 is the trends that are described. Liberal Democrat poll numbers moved slightly upwards over the period but the really clear trends are the progressive decline in Labour support – from well over 50 per cent in 1997 to the mid-30s by 2007 – and the gradual (although still limited) recovery in Conservative fortunes, which rose from the mid-20s in 1997 to the mid-30s by 2007.

What produced these changes? What was happening to the fundamentals described above? Figure 2.2 displays the dynamics of identification with the three major parties until the middle of 2007. The pattern is similar to, yet subtly different from, that for the dynamics

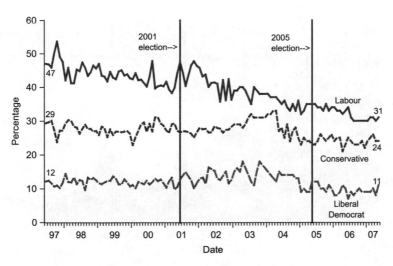

Figure 2.2 Labour, Conservative and Liberal Democrat party identification, June 1997–May 2007.
Source: Gallup Dynamics of Party Support Project, Democracy and Participation Project, BES monthly CMS surveys.

of vote intentions documented in Figure 2.1. Whereas for vote intentions, there are points where the Labour and Conservative lines cross each other, Labour is always ahead of the Conservatives in terms of party identification. Although Conservative voting intentions were at times higher than those of Labour, the Conservatives never succeeded in overtaking Labour in terms of partisan attachments. This 'partisan edge' was a hugely valuable electoral resource for Labour – and a real obstacle for the Conservatives – and it persisted right through to the 2010 general election.

Figure 2.3 illustrates how opinion about Tony Blair changed after 1997 by depicting the percentage of voters who thought he was 'doing a good job as prime minister'. There are a few obvious short-term fluctuations (which we discuss briefly below), but the central message from the graph is the clear long-term decline in Blair's approval rating over time (the simple correlation between his approval rating and time is very impressive, $r = -0.92$). The implication is that although Blair was a huge electoral asset for Labour in the early years, by the end of the period he was becoming a liability. This conclusion is reinforced by the evidence presented in Figure 2.4. This figure plots the

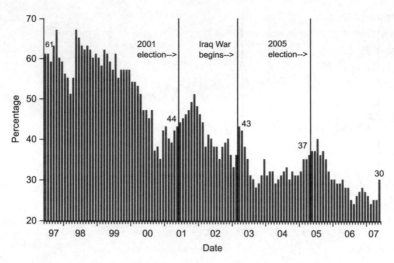

Figure 2.3 Tony Blair's approval ratings, June 1997–May 2007.
Source: Gallup and YouGov surveys.

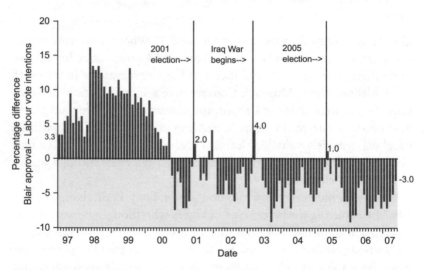

Figure 2.4 Difference between Blair's approval ratings and Labour vote intentions, June 1997–May 2007.
Source: Figure 2.4 shows differences between Blair approval and Labour vote intention percentages presented in Figures 2.2 and 2.3.

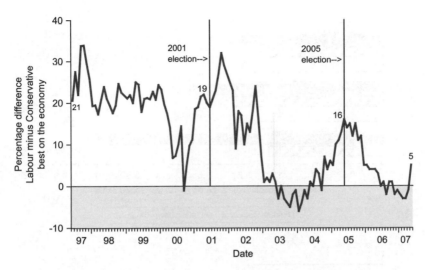

Figure 2.5 Labour versus Conservative economic competence, June 1997–May 2007.
Note: figure displays the percentage who consider Labour would handle the situation best if Britain were in economic difficulties minus percentage believing Conservatives would handle the situation best.
Source: Gallup and YouGov monthly surveys.

difference between Blair's approval ratings and Labour vote intentions each month between June 1997 and May 2007. Until the 2001 general election, Blair typically ran well ahead of his party. Thereafter, with one of two brief exceptions, he ran behind it – as we shall see shortly, tending to pull down Labour support rather than boosting it.

The third fundamental described earlier relates to voters' views of the relative economic management capabilities of the two major parties – Labour and the Conservatives. Figure 2.5 shows the balance of support for Labour versus the Conservatives in terms of being able to 'handle the situation best' if Britain were in economic difficulties. Points on the graph above the zero line indicate that more people favour Labour than the Conservatives; below it, that they favour the Conservatives than Labour. The story is straightforward. Until December 2002, Labour almost always enjoyed a sizable competence lead over their principal rival. Thereafter, the picture became more ambiguous, although Labour still enjoyed a substantial lead on some occasions – especially, and critically, in the run-up to the 2005 election. Afterwards, Labour's competence lead gradually evaporated.

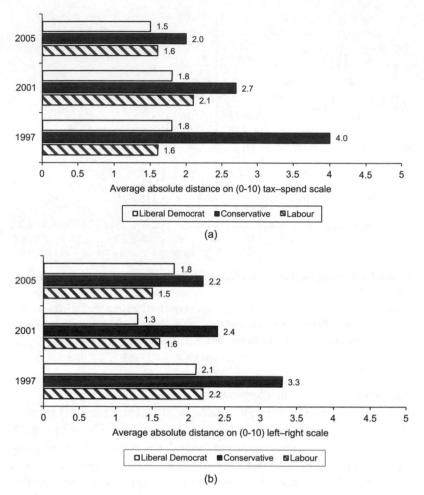

Figure 2.6 Issue–party proximities on tax–spend and left–right scales, 1997, 2001, 2005.
A. Tax–spend scale B. Left–right scale
Source: 1997, 2001 and 2005 BES in-person surveys.

For the final fundamental – spatial positioning – no suitable time series data exist. However, we can determine the relative positions of the parties in terms of issue-position proximities at the time of the 1997, 2001 and 2005 general elections. Figure 2.6 reports the relevant information. Data on two sets of issue positions are presented: (a) beliefs about the desirability of spending more on better public services even if it means higher taxation, and (b) positions on the venerable left–right ideological continuum. These are the only scales available for which comparable data are available across all three elections. The cell entries in the table represent the average absolute distances between voters' self-locations on the scales and their perceptions of where each of the parties stands on the given dimension. Thus, a higher score means that a party is perceived as being further away from the average voter; a lower score means it is perceived as being closer.

The message conveyed by these numbers is straightforward. Voters generally perceived themselves as being fairly close to both Labour and the Liberal Democrats across all three elections. On tax–spend, Labour was on average the closest party in 1997 (1.6 points) and only slightly more distant than the Liberal Democrats in 2001 and 2005. On left–right, Labour was seen as getting progressively closer to voters – an average distance of 2.2 in 1997, 1.6 in 2001 and 1.5 in 2005. However, the big change that the table demonstrates concerns the Conservatives. In 1997, on tax–spend, their score of 4.0 suggests they were more than twice as distant from the average voter than was either Labour (1.6) or the Liberal Democrats (1.8). However, the Conservative scores for 2001 and 2005 are 2.7 and 2.0, respectively. Similarly, the Conservatives' proximity scores on left–right fell from 3.3 in 1997 to 2.4 in 2001 and to 2.2 in 2005. The latter two numbers put them much closer to the scores recorded by their competitors. Although we do not report the detailed figures here, the main reason for these reductions was that most voters perceived that the Conservatives, even before David Cameron became party leader, had moved towards the centre-ground on these two scales. Since this is where most voters are located, this perceived movement reduced the average distance between them and the Conservatives. As a result, the spatial advantage enjoyed by Labour over their principal rival in 1997 had been significantly reduced by 2005. The advantage remained, but it was less of a resource than it had been. Yet another fundamental had shifted away from Labour.

Explaining the decline in Labour support

The dynamic data summarized above are suggestive, but they convey only limited information about possible causal relationships between variables of interest. In this section we develop and test a series of

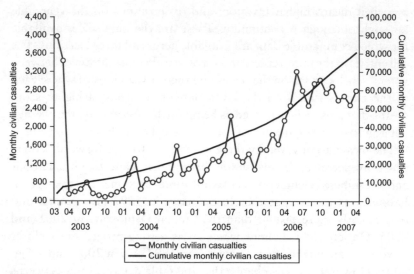

Figure 2.7 Monthly and cumulative civilian casualties in Iraq, March 2003–
May 2007.
Source: www.iraqbodycount.org

statistical models that analyze Labour's changing electoral fortunes
during the Blair years. Ideally, we would have specified time series
models that considered the effects of all four of our fundamental variables on Labour support. However, as noted above, we cannot include
spatial proximity measures because the relevant data are unavailable.

We also omit measures of party identification. This is not because
we believe it to be unimportant. On the contrary, as our individual-
level analyses demonstrated, partisanship has sizable effects on party
preferences. The difficulty is that at the aggregate level, party support
and party identification are highly collinear,[5] and as a result including
party identification variables in vote intention models risks obfuscating
the effects of other predictors. As a practical result, we consider the
effects on Labour support of two of the fundamentals outlined above –
assessments of Tony Blair as prime minister and judgments about
Labour versus Conservative economic management competence. We
also include variables measuring civilian casualties in Iraq (see Figure
2.7). We have shown elsewhere (Clarke *et al.*, 2009b: ch. 4) that the
rising toll of civilian deaths eroded Labour support in the run-up to
the 2005 election. Here, we assess these negative effects up to Blair's

resignation as prime minister in June 2007. We consider the continuing effects of Iraqi civilian casualties up to 2010 in Chapter 3.

In addition to these explanatory variables, we also analyze the consequences of a series of political events that occurred between 1997 and 2007. Previous research has shown that such events can have both short-term and longer-lived effects on party popularity. The events considered here include: (a) the September 2000 fuel crisis, which as we saw earlier caused a downward spike in Labour support; (b) the passage of the December 2001 Terrorism Bill, which represented Blair's response to 9/11 and which generated a considerable negative response from liberal media commentators – which in turn saw a second brief downward movement in Labour support; and (c) the start of the government's involvement in the Iraq War in March 2003, which generated a brief 'rally round the flag' spurt in Labour support. We also apply a statistical control for the state of the objective economy in the form of changes in the level of unemployment.[6]

Statistical tests reveal that Labour support, Blair's approval ratings and perceptions of economic management competence travel together in dynamic equilibrium.[7] Starting in March 2003, civilian casualties in Iraq also begin their upward trajectory. Accordingly, we employ the following error correction specification:

$$
\begin{aligned}
\Delta \text{Lab}_t = {} & a + \beta_1 \Delta \text{LabEcManage}_t + \beta_2 \Delta \text{Blair}_t + \beta_3 \text{Fuel Crisis}_t \\
& + \beta_4 \text{Terrorism Bill}_t + \beta_5 \text{IraqWar-Start}_t \\
& + \beta_6 \Delta \text{IraqCasualties}_t + \beta_7 \Delta \text{Unemployment Rate}_t \\
& + \alpha_1 (\text{Lab}_{t-1} - c_0 - c_1 \text{LabEcManage}_{t-1} - c_2 \text{Blair}_{t-1} \\
& - c_3 \text{IraqCumCasualties}_{t-1}) + \varepsilon_t
\end{aligned}
\tag{2.2}
$$

where Lab_t is Labour vote intentions at time t; LabEcManage is Labour versus Conservative economic management competence; Blair is Blair's PM approval ratings; Fuel Crisis and Terrorism Bill are respectively dummy variables for September 2000 and December 2001; IraqWar–Start is a dummy for March 2003; IraqCasualties measures the monthly number of civilian deaths deriving from the Iraq War and subsequent occupation; IraqCumCasualties measures cumulative Iraqi civilian casualties; Unemployment Rate is the percentage of the working age population unemployed each month; the expression in parentheses represents the error correction mechanism; Δ is the difference operator; and ε_t is a stochastic error term ($N(0,\sigma^2)$).

Table 2.3 *Error correction model of the dynamics of Labour vote intentions, July 1997–June 2007*

Dependent variable: ΔLabour vote intentions$_t$	β	s.e.
Δ Labour economic management competence$_t$	0.22***	0.04
Δ Blair's approval rating$_t$	0.11*	0.06
Fuel crisis	−7.10***	1.50
Terrorism bill	−4.37***	1.41
Iraq War begins	2.46*	1.40
Iraq War – civilian casualties	−0.03	0.11
Δ Unemployment rate$_{t-1}$	−3.97**	1.58
Error correction mechanism$_{t-1}$	−0.47***	0.06
Labour economic management competence in ECM $_{t-1}$	0.27***	0.04
Blair's approval rating in ECM $_{t-1}$	0.19***	0.06
Iraq War cumulative civilian casualties in ECM $_{t-1}$	−0.22***	0.06
Constant	13.44***	1.85
Adjusted R^2	0.65	
N	120	

*** $p \leq 0.001$; ** $p \leq 0.01$; * $p \leq 0.05$; one-tailed test

Table 2.3 reports the result of estimating Eq. (2.2) using data for July 1997 to May 2007 period. The model is well-determined (adjusted $R^2 = 0.65$) and passes a battery of standard diagnostic tests. The expressions for the error correction terms all produce correctly signed and significant coefficients. The long-run effects of Labour economic management perceptions ($c = 0.27$) and prime ministerial approval ratings ($c = 0.19$) are both positive whereas the long-run effects for cumulative civilian casualties in Iraq ($c = -0.22$) work to reduce Labour support. The substantive results tell an important story about the impact of the two fundamentals and various events. First, both Blair's approval ratings ($\beta = 0.11$) and perceptions of Labour's managerial competence ($\beta = 0.22$) were crucial in determining Labour support over the 1997–2007 period. Both coefficients are significant, positive and sizable. Second, the fuel crisis ($\beta = -7.10$) and the passage of the terrorism bill ($\beta = -4.57$) both damaged Labour's standing. However, both of these effects were ephemeral. The model specification entails that they were discounted at the rate defined by the adjustment parameter for the error correction mechanism ($\alpha = -0.47$). This parameter is sizable, and it indicates that both effects had virtually disappeared within two quarters after they occurred.[8]

However, the third conclusion concerns a variable that does not influence Labour support, that is, a variable that does not have a statistically significant effect in the analysis summarized in Table 2.3. The results indicate that although there was a brief boost to Labour support at the start of the Iraq War ($\beta = 2.46$), as the conflict developed the monthly toll of civilian casualties exerted *no* short-term effect (see the nonsignificant $\beta = -0.03$ for the Iraq War–civilian casualties term). Finally, the results in Table 2.3 show that the measure of the objective economy – unemployment – had only a modest direct impact on Labour support ($\beta = -3.97$). This does not mean that unemployment was unimportant. As we demonstrate in Chapter 3, unemployment also exerted an indirect impact on Labour support – operating by influencing economic management competence perceptions.

Explaining changing fundamentals

The results reported in Table 2.3 agree with the individual-level account of electoral choice in the Blair era presented earlier. The two key fundamentals in the time series analysis – Blair's approval ratings and Labour's economic management credentials – exert powerful effects on the dynamics of Labour support between 1997 and 2007. The graphs presented above (Figures 2.4 and 2.6) show that these two fundamentals weakened over the same period. Inevitably, however, the question arises as to *what drives the fundamentals*. We answer this question by analysing a model of the dynamics of Blair's ratings between 1997 and 2007. In the next chapter we analyze analogous models of Gordon Brown's approval ratings during his premiership 2007–10. We also present a model of Labour versus Conservative economic management competence perceptions that covers the period of both premierships, that is, from July 1997 through to April 2010.

Paralleling analyses of Blair's approval ratings from 1997 through 2005 presented in Clarke *et al.* (2009b: ch. 4), we model the dynamics of these ratings using an error correction model with an autoregressive conditional heteroskedasticity (ARCH) component to capture the growing consensus in public opinion that he was not performing well (Enders, 2009: ch. 3). As in that model, we hypothesize that the variance in Blair's approval rating is a function of growing civilian casualties in Iraq – a simple, but powerful, cue that that protracted and bloody conflict was not going well. Thus, our model of Blair's approval ratings is:

$$\Delta \text{Blair}_t = a + \beta_1 \Delta \text{LabEcManage}_t + \beta_6 \Delta \ln(\text{IraqCasualties})_{t-3}$$
$$+ \beta_3 \text{Princess}_t + \beta_4 \text{GoodFriday}_t + \beta_5 \text{IraqWar-Start}_t$$
$$+ \beta_6 \Delta \text{Unemployment Rate}_t$$
$$+ \alpha_1 (\text{Lab}_{t-1} - c_0 - c_1 \text{LabEcManage}_{t-1}) + \varepsilon_t \qquad (2.3a)$$

and the model for the ARCH process in the error variance of this model is:

$$\sigma_t^2 = \omega + \lambda \varepsilon_{t-1}^2 + \gamma \ln(\text{IraqcumCasualties})_{t-1}, \qquad (2.3b)$$

where in Eq. (2.3a) Blair, LabEcManage, IraqCasualties, IraqWar–Start, IraqCumulativeCasualties and Unemployment Rate are defined as in Eq. (2.2); Princess is a dummy variable for Blair's 'People's Princess' speech at the time of Princess Diana's death in September 1997; GoodFriday is a dummy for the Good Friday peace accord in Northern Ireland in April 1998; the expression in brackets represents the error correction term involving Labour support and evaluations of Labour's economic managerial competence; Δ is the difference operator; and ε_t is a stochastic error term $\sim N(0, \sigma^2)$.

In the ARCH model (2.3b) for the variance at time t, σ_t^2, ε_{t-1}^2 is the innovation variance at time t-1, $\ln(\text{IraqCasualties})_{t-1}$ is the log of civilian casualties at time t-1, λ, γ, and ω are parameters to be estimated. The expectation is that λ and ω will be positive, λ and γ will be negative. The negative sign on γ reflects how growing civilian casualties in Iraq were helping to build a (negative) consensus about Blair's performance as prime minister. Models (2.3a) and (2.3b) are estimated simultaneously using maximum likelihood procedures.

The results reported in Table 2.4 show that the model is reasonably well determined (adjusted $R^2 = 0.37$) and passes a standard battery of diagnostics. The conclusions suggested by the estimated coefficients are straightforward. The positive and significant coefficients for the two economic competence terms indicate that judgments about Labour's managerial acumen exerted both short-term ($\beta = 0.38$) and long-term ($c = 0.96$) effects on Blair's approval ratings. There were also brief upward surges in his popularity associated with the People's Princess

Table 2.4 *Error correction ARCH model of the dynamics of Tony Blair's approval ratings, July 1997–June 2007*

Dependent variable: ΔBlair approval$_t$	β	s.e.
Predictor variables: mean equation		
ΔLabour economic management competence$_t$	0.38***	0.05
Iraq War – civilian casualties$_{t-3}$	−0.23**	0.11
People's Princess speech$_{t-1}$	4.74***	1.67
Good Friday Accord$_t$	9.04***	0.95
Iraq War begins$_t$	3.90*	2.10
Δ Unemployment rate$_{t-1}$	−6.99***	1.72
Error correction mechanism$_{t-1}$	−0.11***	0.03
Labour economic management competence in ECM$_{t-1}$	0.96***	0.17
Constant	2.90***	0.87
Predictor variables: ARCH 1 process		
Innovation variance $\varepsilon^2{}_{t-1}$	0.50**	0.18
Iraq War – cumulative civilian casualties$_{t-1}$	−0.16**	0.07
Constant	2.99***	0.66
Adjusted R^2	0.37	
N	120	

*** $p \leq 0.001$; ** $p \leq 0.01$; * $p \leq 0.05$; one-tailed test.

speech ($\beta = 4.74$), with the signing of the Northern Ireland peace accord ($\beta = 9.04$) and the start of the Iraq War ($\beta = 3.90$). These effects decayed, albeit slowly as indicated by adjustment parameter ($\alpha = -0.11$) for the error correction mechanism.

The model suggests there were two other major, continuing short-term drivers of Blair's popularity. One was the objective condition of the economy. Changes in unemployment ($\beta = -6.99$) exerted a strong negative effect, significantly damaging his standing. The second was the growing toll of civilian casualties in Iraq. We saw in our analysis of Labour support that cumulative casualties did not have a direct effect on Labour support. However, the significant negative coefficient for the civilian casualties term in Table 2.4 ($\beta = -0.23$) indicates that the war corroded Blair's reputation and this indirectly inflicted additional damage on Labour.

The ARCH portion of the model also performs as anticipated. All of the parameters in the ARCH process are statistically significant (p < 0.01) and correctly signed – both the intercept term and the lagged value of the innovation variance carry positive signs, whereas the impact of lagged casualties is negative. Again, the latter result testifies that over the long haul, Blair's continuing support for British participation in the war worked not only to reduce his approval ratings but also to make them less variable. The mounting carnage in the conflict helped to forge a consensus that Blair's performance left something – much – to be desired.

As noted above, we leave the analysis of assessments of Labour's relative economic management competence to Chapter 3. However, anticipating those findings, we can report here that, regardless of short-term shocks to competence perceptions that derive from specific events, over the 1997–2010 period these assessments were driven by three key factors. These are: changes in people's expectations about the financial prospects of their households; the condition of the UK stock market as summarized by the FTSE index of 100 leading shares; and changes in the level of unemployment. Not surprisingly, given the findings reported in previous studies,[9] competence perceptions were influenced positively by personal financial optimism and stock market confidence, and they were negatively affected by changes in unemployment. Perceptions of Labour's competence on the economy were driven primarily by voters' sense of economic optimism, by investor confidence in the UK economy, and by the condition of the objective economy as reflected in unemployment.

Conclusion: Tony's politics reconsidered

The story told in this chapter is straightforward. Analyses of voting in the 1997, 2001 and 2005 general elections revealed that the same set of factors – the fundamentals – consistently exerted the most powerful effects on party support. Labour voting was governed primarily by identification with that party, images of party leader Tony Blair, beliefs about Labour's economic management competence vis-à-vis the Conservatives and the extent to which Labour was seen as close to voters on major position issues. Similarly, Conservative support was strongly influenced by Conservative partisanship, evaluations (in turn) of John Major, William Hague and Michael Howard, judgments about the Conservatives' economic management competence and proximity of the party to voters on position issues. Finally, Liberal Democrat support was influenced most by Liberal Democrat partisanship, evaluations of Paddy Ashdown (in 1997) and of Charles Kennedy (in 2001 and 2005), and perceptions of Liberal Democrat proximity on important position issues. These effects were relatively stable across elections. There were other minor effects on voting choice that operated in specific cases, but none compared in magnitude with the effects of the 'big beast' fundamentals.

The critical question addressed in the second part of this chapter focused on what changed in these fundamentals between 1997 and 2007 to produce a situation where Labour support was in decline and Blair was obliged to resign as prime minister in the wake of sagging approval ratings. Our answer is straightforward. First, in addition to the short-term effects of events such as the 2000 fuel crisis and the introduction of the 2001 terrorism bill, New Labour's popularity was damaged by the image that Blair projected. An asset until 2001, Blair's ratings thereafter ran behind those of his party. As the model of Labour support shows, Blair's declining approval ratings pulled his party down. Second, Labour's reputation for superior economic management gradually faded, particularly after the 2001 election. However, the Labour support model on its own is not sufficient to explain why both Blair's ratings and his party's managerial reputation declined. The answers lie partly in the Iraq quagmire and partly in rising unemployment. Analyses document that Blair's ratings suffered long-term erosion as a result of his continuing advocacy of British involvement in the Iraq War, a conflict that many people viewed as an ill-considered, even immoral, venture. Labour's reputation for managerial competence – which was clearly beginning to falter in the run-up to the 2005 general election – was damaged by dwindling economic confidence among both consumers and investors and the growth in unemployment that ensued after 2004. In sum, Blair's weakening position after May 2005 derived from two key sources: the Iraq War and the incipient economic decline that had begun in 2004 but which was to accelerate significantly after his departure.

Throughout this chapter one name has been given scant attention – that of Blair's Chancellor and successor, Gordon Brown. In many respects, Labour's economic failures were in reality Brown's – although it was not seen that way by his many supporters inside the Labour Party who contributed to his rapid and largely unchallenged succession as party leader and prime minister. In the next chapter, we continue the story with Gordon Brown's premiership and the run-up to the 2010 general election.

3 | Gordon's politics

Economic crisis and political change

Leadership succession is never easy in British party politics, particularly if the outgoing leader is an incumbent prime minister. When Anthony Eden succeeded Winston Churchill as prime minister in April 1955, he had been waiting in the wings as leader-designate for almost a decade. Within two years he was forced to resign because of his inept handling of the Suez crisis. Jim Callaghan, who unexpectedly succeeded Harold Wilson in 1976, managed to survive until 1979, but his premiership was plagued by successive economic crises and backbench rebellions that were especially difficult to manage, given Labour's small parliamentary majority. John Major took over from Margaret Thatcher in November 1990. Against almost all expectations given the grim state of the national economy, Major took his party to a narrow victory in the 1992 general election. However, his subsequent tenure as prime minister was a tortuous one, punctuated by a major economic crisis within months of his election victory (the Exchange Rate Mechanism fiasco of September 1992) and a series of backbench rebellions that sought to take advantage, as with Callaghan, of the prime minister's small Commons majority.

When Gordon Brown succeeded Tony Blair on 27 June 2007, he appeared to be in a very different position from those of his postwar counterparts. Like Eden, he had been waiting expectantly for over a decade for his predecessor to make way. However, unlike Eden, Brown was not faced with the sort of major challenge to Britain's global role that was occasioned by the demands for political independence that were sweeping through Britain's current and former colonies in the 1950s. And, unlike Callaghan and Major, Brown was not taking over in conditions of economic crisis. When he became prime minister, Britain had enjoyed a 15-year period of uninterrupted good times – since 1993 the annual GDP growth rate had not fallen below 2 per cent. Unlike Major, Brown was elected unopposed as party leader, and by implication as prime minister. As Chancellor of the Exchequer since New Labour's initial victory in 1997, he had overseen the extended period of prosperity that preceded his premiership and as a result had established a reputation for highly competent economic management. He had consolidated this reputation by his dour rhetorical claims, widely believed at the time, that his budgets were invariably models of fiscal prudence. He asserted that under New Labour Britain had followed a cautious and responsible strategy for public finances – his 'golden rule' – in which public borrowing and spending would never again exceed tax receipts during the course of the (unspecified) 'economic cycle'. According to Brown, the era of 'boom and bust' that long had bedevilled British political economy was a thing of the past. In addition, he enjoyed a 66-seat parliamentary majority as a result of the disproportionate way Britain's electoral system translated popular votes into parliamentary seats (see e.g. Farrell, 2011; Johnston *et al.*, 1999). Although Labour had received only 35 per cent of the popular vote in the 2005 general election, it had obtained fully 55 per cent (355) of seats in the House of Commons.

But if Brown's position in summer 2007 looked quite rosy for an incoming prime minister, there were also dark clouds on the horizon. There had been recurrent rumours in the press about Brown's temper and, notwithstanding his confident performances at the despatch box as Chancellor, his indecisiveness when it came to major issues, especially those outside his Treasury remit. He was often criticized for being absent from the House when contentious votes were being held and for failing to establish a clear position on major issues when his party and public opinion needed to be both informed and 'led'. There was also a widespread view that Brown and his followers had been manoeuvring to remove Blair almost since the time of their supposed Granita restaurant deal in 1994 when, following John Smith's death, Brown had agreed to allow Blair to assume Labour's leadership unopposed on the understanding that Blair would eventually cede the leadership. This view obviously had been strengthened by Blair's promise prior to the 2005 general election (assumed to be the price of the Brownite faction's full participation in the 2005 campaign) that, if elected, he would not serve a full third term as prime minister.

After a brief burst of popularity in the summer of 2007 following his appointment as prime minister, Brown's indecisiveness rapidly came to the fore. As an incoming prime minister who had not led his party to victory in a general election, there was no constitutional requirement for him to ask the people for an explicit mandate for his premiership.

Nonetheless, Brown seriously considered calling an autumn 2007 election since a victory at this point would secure a personal mandate and keep Labour in office until at least 2012. Various signals from Downing Street led journalists, party activists and the public to expect that parliament would be dissolved any day. However, in late September, in the wake of David Cameron's public challenge to Brown that the Conservatives would relish an early election, Brown's indecisiveness found expression in his decision to delay calling one. Shortly afterwards, the first real signs of the looming 'credit crunch' and global economic crisis began to appear following the collapse (and subsequent nationalization) of the Northern Rock bank. The failure of Northern Rock had been preceded by a widely publicized public panic and the first run on a British bank in 150 years. By November 2007, Labour's and Brown's popularity ratings were beginning to nosedive and all thoughts of an early election call were rapidly dispelled.

The story of Gordon Brown's premiership thereafter was one of declining popularity, punctuated by occasional but invariably short-lived triumphs and widely publicized rumours of attempted coups by his rivals. Things improved briefly in autumn 2008 when Brown made a determined move to persuade other OECD leaders to move decisively to prop up the ailing global banking sector to pre-empt a further loss of confidence in international financial markets. The respite proved temporary and the erosion in public confidence began again – a situation that was not helped by the MPs' expenses scandal in spring 2009. By the start of the official election campaign in April 2010, Labour's popularity had fallen below 30 per cent and bad poll numbers were to plague Brown and his party throughout the ensuing campaign.

In this chapter we analyze the changing fortunes of the parties and Prime Minister Brown. Why did New Labour falter after Blair gave way? In what ways did voters change their views of the parties? Did the individual calculus of party support change in significant ways after 2007? Or was it simply a matter of the political 'fundamentals' changing, which, in turn, produced significant changes in support for the governing party? And if the fundamentals changed, were they driven by the same factors depicted in Chapter 2 in our analysis of changing party fortunes in the Blair years? We begin with a discussion of factors affecting party support over the May 2005–April 2010 period. We find remarkable continuity across the periods of the Blair and Brown governments, with valence forces dominating and spatial considerations playing a secondary role. Against the backdrop of these general findings, we employ individual-level panel data to investigate how valence and other issues operated at different stages of the electoral cycle. Then, we specify a set of time series models to analyze the dynamics of party support. We demonstrate that a variety of discrete events influenced party popularity in the Brown era but that, as with support during Blair's premiership, rising unemployment also mattered.

Party choice, 2005–2010

In Chapter 2 we considered several theoretically motivated rival models of electoral choice. Analyses documented that although there were some statistically significant sociodemographic correlates of party support between 1997 and 2005, their effects were very weak. The main drivers of voting behaviour involved valence judgments and spatial calculations. By far the most important determinants of voting in the 1997, 2001 and 2005 general elections – the key *valence fundamentals* – were party identification, leader images and judgments about rival parties' policy competence. We also found that spatial considerations were influential, with voters tending to support the party that they perceived to be closest to them in terms of the desirability of state provision of public services and the way that the state should deal with criminal behaviour.

The individual-level analyses presented here differ from those in Chapter 2. There, we examined cross-sectional survey data gathered in the 1997, 2001 and 2005 British election studies. Here we employ individual-level panel data across the period from April 2005 to April 2010. As part of the 2005 and 2010 British Election Studies we surveyed subsets of the same respondents on eight different occasions between these dates. We use these data to construct a five-wave panel that maps the dynamics of key political attitudes over time. Wave 1 contains questions that were asked either in the pre-campaign, campaign or post-election surveys conducted at the time of the May 2005 general election. Wave 2 was conducted in June 2006; Wave 3 in July 2008; Wave 4 in July 2009; and Wave 5 in March/April 2010. Taken together, these data enable us to assess changes in party preference from before the 2005 election to the beginning of the 2010 election campaign.[1]

There are many different ways of analysing individual-level panel data to identify factors governing changing party preferences. Here we use what has become a standard approach to panel model specification – the inclusion of lagged endogenous variables. These models take explicit account of the fact that, in trying to understand why voters make particular choices at time t, we know what their preferences were at time t-1. Note that this is not the same as asking people how they voted 'last time', since we know that recalled preferences are often influenced by current ones. With panel data, we actually have an uncontaminated record of past preferences that can be compared with current preferences. With the multiwave BES data, we have a series of such preferences over the interval involving the two most recent British general elections.

The particular model specified here enables us to investigate how political fundamentals affected individual-level changes in party preferences across the 2005–10 period. Specifically, the model is:

Preference for party X_t = f (preference for party X_{t-1}
+ sociodemographic characteristics – gender, age, ethnicity, region
+ party identification – Labour, Conservative, Liberal Democrat
+ party leader affect – Blair/Brown, Howard/Cameron, Kennedy/Campbell/Clegg
+ party best on most important issue – Labour, Conservative, Liberal Democrat
+ economic calculations – Conservative versus Labour economic management capabilities
+ party-issue proximities – proximity to Labour, Conservatives, Liberal Democrats
+ context specific factor – evaluations of Britain's involvement in the Iraq War)   (3.1)

Although this specification is very similar to the one employed in Chapter 2, it differs in an important way. The present model includes party preference at t-1 on the right-hand-side of the equation. Including this lagged endogenous variable (LEV) means that it is the *dynamics* of support for party X between t-1 and t that are being modelled on the basis of the right-hand-side independent variable set – rather than simply party preference at time t.

We analyze models of the form outlined in Eq. (3.1) following the practice established in our previous research and in Chapter 2.

Table 3.1 *Rival binomial and multinomial logit panel models of party support, 2005–10*

| | Opposition parties | | | |
Rival models	McFadden R^2	AIC	McFadden R^2	AIC
Party support t-1	0.45	2205	0.41	5251
Party support t-1 + demographics	0.46	2182	0.42	5170
Party support t-1 + demographics + attitudes towards Iraq War	0.50	2132	0.43	5104
Party support t-1 + party identification	0.63	1471	0.58	3773
Party support t-1 + valence calculation	0.71	1163	0.67	2969
Party support t-1 + spatial calculation	0.57	1745	0.51	4331
Composite model	0.76	1012	0.73	2587

N = 3467; clusters = 1416
Note: binomial logit model of Labour support; multinomial logit model of Conservative, Liberal Democrat and Other party support with Labour as the reference category.
AIC – Akaike Information Criterion.

This involves estimating a binomial logit model for governing party (Labour) support and a multinomial logit model for opposition party (Conservative, Liberal Democrat, Other Parties) support using Labour as the reference category. Results of these analyses are displayed in Table 3.2. However, Table 3.1 first reports comparative fit statistics for several rival models: (i) the lagged dependent or endogenous variable (LEV) on its own; (ii) the LEV plus key sociodemographics; (iii) the LEV plus sociodemographics plus attitudes towards Britain's military intervention in Iraq; (iv) the LEV plus party identification; (v) the LEV plus valence factors; (vi) the LEV plus spatial variables. Specifically, Table 3.1 reports two summary statistics: the (McFadden) R^2 and the Akaike Information Criterion (AIC). For purposes of model comparison, larger McFadden R^2 values denote a better fit, whereas lower AIC values indicate superior performance controlling for the number of estimated parameters.[2]

These statistics clearly demonstrate that the LEV-plus-demographics model barely improves upon the baseline LEV-only model: the McFadden R^2 increases by only 0.01 for both the binomial and multinomial models and the AIC statistic experiences only a very modest reduction. Adding attitudes towards the Iraq War makes a small improvement in fit, that is, the McFadden R^2 rises to 0.50 in the Labour-all other parties model and to 0.43 in the opposition model. However, the biggest increases in R^2 and largest reductions in the AIC are apparent for the spatial, party identification and valence models. In the Labour case, the McFadden R^2 rises to 0.57 for LEV-plus-spatial calculation, to 0.63 for LEV-plus partisanship and to 0.71 for the LEV-plus-valence model. Similar improvements are evident in the AIC for these models. Echoing observations in Chapter 2, these results suggest that valence considerations have the largest effects on voters' choices, although other factors make explanatory contributions of varying importance. This conclusion is reinforced by the McFadden R^2 and AIC values reported for the composite model that includes all predictor variables. The R^2 value for this model is larger, and the AIC values smaller, than for any of the separate rival models reported in the table. This finding clearly indicates that changes in party preferences between 2005 and 2010 were driven by a combination of the explanatory factors outlined in Eq. (3.1). Similar to results reported in earlier studies of political choice in Britain (Clarke *et al.*, 2004b, 2009b), we find that valence models dominated but did not formally encompass (Charemza and Deadman, 1997) their rivals between 2005 and 2010.

Table 3.2 reports estimates of the effects of various predictors on Labour and Conservative support in the composite models. Although the effects of these predictor variables on support for the Liberal Democrats and other parties were considered in the analysis, in the interest of parsimony these results are not reported here.[3] Estimation is by clustered binomial logit for the Labour model and by clustered multinomial logit for the Conservative model. Predictor variables are grouped under headings defined by the models outlined above.

As Panel A of Table 3.2 shows, changes in Labour support are driven primarily by key valence fundamentals. Labour partisanship has a strong positive effect ($\beta = 0.91$), whereas Conservative partisanship exerts negative effects. Regarding other valence variables, Labour support is positively affected by Labour leader evaluations ($\beta = 0.22$), by perceptions that Labour is best on the most important issue ($\beta = 1.13$) and by the belief that Labour is best able to manage the economy ($\beta = 0.67$). Labour support is negatively affected by perceptions that the best party on the most important issue is either

Table 3.2 *Binomial and multinomial logit panel models of Labour and Conservative voting intentions, 2005–10*

Predictor variables	Labour		Conservative	
	β	s.e.	β	s.e.
Voting intentions$_{t-1}$:				
Labour$_{t-1}$	1.96***	0.19		
Conservative$_{t-1}$			2.23***	0.34
Liberal Democrat$_{t-1}$			1.05**	0.35
Other party$_{t-1}$			1.45***	0.46
Demographics:				
Age	−0.01	0.01	0.02	0.01
Gender	−0.28	0.21	−0.19	0.28
Ethnicity	0.06	0.43	0.89	0.61
Scotland	−0.40	0.33	0.25	0.46
Wales	0.88**	0.31	−1.07	0.64
Social Class	−0.15	0.20	0.27	0.26
Attitudes towards Iraq War$_{t1}$	0.19**	0.08	−0.11	0.10
Party identification:				
Labour$_t$	0.91***	0.11	−1.19***	0.19
Conservative$_t$	−0.23	0.29	0.20	0.33
Liberal Democrat$_t$	−0.76*	0.32	−0.51	0.50
Party leaders:				
Blair/Brown$_t$	0.22***	0.04	−0.30***	0.06
Cameron$_t$	−0.07	0.05	0.44***	0.06
Kennedy/Campbell/Clegg$_t$	−0.09	0.05	−0.08	0.06
Party best most important issue:				
Labour$_t$	1.13***	0.25	−1.93***	0.53
Conservative$_t$	−1.20***	0.37	1.39***	0.37
Liberal Democrat$_t$	−0.95**	0.41	−1.45**	0.62
Performance on economy:				
Labour best$_t$	0.67***	0.13	−0.64***	0.18
Conservatives best$_t$	0.08	0.15	0.52***	0.18
Party-issue proximities:				
Labour closest on tax/spend$_t$	0.09	0.06	−0.14	0.08
Conservatives closest on tax/spend$_t$	−0.03	0.04	0.20***	0.07
Liberal Democrats closest on tax/spend$_t$	−0.04	0.06	−0.01	0.08
Labour closest on crime/rights$_t$	0.13**	0.05	−0.17**	0.06
Conservatives closest on crime/rights$_t$	0.01	0.04	0.08	0.06
Liberal Democrats closest on crime/rights$_t$	−0.03	0.06	−0.04	0.06

Table 3.2 (cont.)

	Labour		Conservative	
Predictor variables	β	s.e.	β	s.e.
Constant	−5.29***	0.81	−0.92	1.12
McFadden R^2	0.76			0.72
Number of cases (clusters)	3467 (1416)		3467 (1416)	

*** p ≤ 0.001; ** p ≤ 0.01; * p ≤ 0.05; one-tailed test, robust standard errors.
Note: binomial logit model of Labour voting intentions; multinomial logit model of Conservative, Liberal Democrat and Other voting intentions with Labour as the reference category; coefficients for Liberal Democrat and Other party voting intentions in the multinomial model not reported.

the Conservatives (β = −1.20) or the Liberal Democrats (β = −0.95). Regarding other predictors, the only significant spatial effect is proximity to Labour on the crime/rights scale (β = 0.13). Again echoing previous results, demographics are relatively unimportant, with the only significant (positive) effect being residence in Wales (β = 0.88). The context-specific Iraq variable is statistically significant, although as discussed below, relatively minor in its consequences.

Panel B of Table 3.2 reports the equivalent coefficients for Conservative support. Here, neither the demographic nor the context-specific variables have significant effects. However, the fundamentals continue to behave largely as expected. Although Conservative identification is nonsignificant, Labour partisanship exerts a sizable and significant negative effect (β = −1.19). Regarding other valence variables, the leadership, party best and economic management terms all have significant positive coefficients in the Conservative analyses and significant negative effects in the Labour ones. Similarly, the spatial measures indicate that Conservative support was stronger among those who were closer to the party on the tax/spend scale (β = 0.20) and more distant from Labour in terms of crime/rights (β = −0.17).

As observed in Chapter 2, the magnitudes of the coefficients in logit models are difficult to interpret. Accordingly, Figures 3.1 and 3.2 report the results of converting statistically significant coefficients in Table 3.2 into changes in probability (Δp) of voting Labour and Conservative that result from moving each predictor variable from its minimum to its maximum value while holding all others constant at

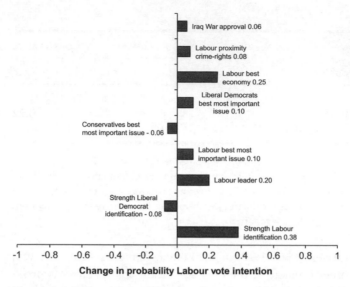

Figure 3.1 Effects of significant predictor variables on probability of Labour vote intentions.
Note: Changes in probability as predictor variables vary from minimum to maximum values holding other predictors constant at their respective means.

their means. The story told by the two figures is straightforward. The key movers of Labour and Conservative party preferences between 2005 and the start of the 2010 campaign were partisanship, evaluations of party performance on important issues, leader images and, to a lesser extent, spatial considerations. The biggest influence on Labour voting was Labour partisanship ($\Delta p = 0.38$), although there were also substantial effects for Labour leader evaluations ($\Delta p = 0.20$) and Labour economic management competence ($\Delta p = 0.25$). The largest influence on Conservative voting was associated with views of the Conservative leader ($\Delta p = 0.70$), an effect almost certainly related to replacing Michael Howard with David Cameron in December 2005. Perceptions of Conservative economic management competence ($\Delta p = 0.38$) and spatial proximity to the Conservatives on the tax/spend scale ($\Delta p = 0.26$) also exerted substantial effects on support for the party.

Key findings from these analyses can be easily summarized. Although the results presented here concern the dynamics of party preference among the same group of individuals over time, we find that the major

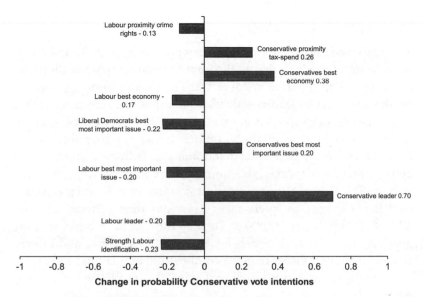

Figure 3.2 Effects of significant predictor variables on probability of Conservative vote intentions.

Note: Changes in probability as predictor variables vary from minimum to maximum values holding other predictors constant at their respective means.

predictor variables are the same as those for the cross-sectional analyses presented in Chapter 2. Controlling for prior preferences, current preferences are still affected overwhelmingly by valence fundamentals – partisanship, leader images, and party performance evaluations – with spatial calculations exerting lesser, albeit nontrivial effects. Bearing in mind that previous analyses have demonstrated that partisanship has dynamic properties and can be regarded as an integral part of the valence model (Clarke *et al.*, 2004b, 2009b; Clarke and McCutcheon, 2009), it is clear that valence factors play a hugely important role in explaining why voters shifted their preferences away from Labour and towards the Conservatives between 2005 and the start of the 2010 campaign. Between 2005 and 2010, there was a growing tendency to believe that the Conservatives rather than Labour could deliver the most effective solutions to policy problems confronting the country. The next section investigates the dynamics of party support between 2005 and 2010 in greater depth to see if various factors weighed differently in the calculus of party choice at different stages of the electoral cycle.

Party support, 2005–2010

To understand the evolution of party support between 2005 and 2010, we provide an analysis that both simplifies and temporally disaggregates the models reported in Table 3.2. The simplification involves: (i) *relative* measures of leader evaluations and policy competence rather than separate measures for each party and (ii) a summary measure of spatial proximity of voters and parties. Also, the simplified model focuses on the three issue areas that dominated political discourse after 2005 – the economy, the NHS and Britain's protracted intervention in Iraq. The temporal disaggregation consists in estimating separate models for changes in preferences over four time periods: 2005–6, 2006–8, 2008–9, and 2009–10. To keep the analysis simple, we estimate separate binomial models for Labour, Conservative and Liberal Democrat support rather than the combination of binomial and multinomial estimation that we used in Table 3.2.[4] The basic form of the model is:

Support for party X_t = f (support for party X_{t-1}
  + party X leader ratings minus (party Y + party Z leader
    ratings/2) at time t
  + proximity to party X, averaged across the tax/spend and
    crime/rights scale at time t
  + assessment of Labour competence minus
    Conservative competence on the economy at time t
  + assessment of Labour competence minus
    Conservative competence on the National Health Service at
    time t
  + approval of UK involvement in the war and occupation in
    Iraq at time t_1)   (3.2)

Note that measures of partisanship are excluded from the specification because with only two waves of data in each estimated model, the effects of partisanship are largely picked up by the lagged endogenous variable, X_{t-1}. Theoretical expectations for various effects are that party X's relative leader ratings and party X's proximity will have positive effects on party X's support; relative Labour versus Conservative competence on the economy and on the NHS will have positive effects on Labour support, negative effects on Conservative support and no effects on Liberal Democrat support;[5] approval of the Iraq intervention will have positive effects on Labour and Conservative support (both parties supported British involvement) and negative effects on Liberal Democrat support (the Liberal Democrats were the only major party to oppose the intervention).

Table 3.3 reports the results of estimating model (3.2) for Labour support. Several conclusions are suggested. First, the overall pattern of coefficient signs and significance levels confirms both the importance of valence and spatial calculations in the determination of party support. All of the relevant coefficients in each of the models are positively signed and statistically significant. Second, the consistency of leader effects over time indicates that, notwithstanding the change in prime minister from Blair to Brown in June 2007, voters continued to emphasize party leader images in their vote choice calculations.

A third noteworthy set of coefficients in Table 3.3 concerns reactions to involvement in Iraq. The variable of interest measures approval/disapproval of Britain's role in that wartorn country as recorded in the 2005 pre-election survey. Figure 3.3 reports the distribution of attitudes in that year, both for all of the 2005 respondents and for those respondents who participated in the 2005–10 panel. As the figure illustrates, not only was public opinion quite critical of the war and occupation in 2005 (60 per cent disapproved or strongly disapproved), but the panel respondents' opinions (62 per cent disapproved or strongly disapproved) were very similar to those of the general population.[6]

The BES inter-election panel surveys did not repeat the question about Iraq in waves conducted after 2005. However, the attitudes that respondents expressed in the 2005 pre-election survey – as well as the Iraq War itself – cast a long shadow. We saw in Chapter 2 that attitudes towards the war eroded Labour support in the 2005 general election, with an important avenue of influence being the damage that negative attitudes towards the conflict inflicted on Tony Blair's leadership ratings. It is clear from the Wave 2 model in Table 3.3 that attitudes towards Britain's participation in Iraq were still affecting Labour support in 2006 ($\beta = 0.14$, $p \leq 0.05$). Yet as the table also shows, the Iraq effect lost its power in the Wave 3 and Wave 4 models. Other more pressing concerns about party competence with respect to the economy and NHS came to the fore. However, in the Wave

Table 3.3 *Binomial logit models of Labour voting intentions,*
2005–10 panel surveys

	β	s.e.
Wave 2 model: Labour supporter at t_2 (2006)		
Labour supporter t_1 (2005)	2.30***	0.21
Labour leader affect relative to affect for Conservative and Liberal Democrat leaders t_2	0.27***	0.04
Proximity to Labour on tax/spend and crime/rights t_2	0.32***	0.07
Labour minus Conservative competence on economy t_2	0.52***	0.11
Labour minus Conservative competence on NHS t_2	0.29***	0.09
Approval Britain's involvement in Iraq War t_1	0.14*	0.08
McFadden $R^2 = 0.64$ N $= 1496$		
Wave 3 model: Labour supporter t_3 (2008)		
Labour supporter t_2 (2006)	3.17***	0.28
Labour leader affect relative to affect for Conservative and Liberal Democrat leaders t_3	0.37***	0.05
Proximity to Labour on tax/spend and crime/rights t_3	0.25***	0.07
Labour minus Conservative competence on economy t_3	0.18*	0.11
Labour minus Conservative competence on NHS t_3	0.34***	0.10
Approval of Britain's involvement in Iraq at t_1	−0.08	0.10
McFadden $R^2 = 0.67$ N $= 1437$		
Wave 4 model: Labour supporter t_4 (2009)		
Labour supporter t_3 (2008)	2.94***	0.27
Labour leader affect relative to affect for Conservative and Liberal Democrat leaders t_4	0.30***	0.06
Proximity to Labour on tax/spend and crime/rights t_4	0.21**	0.08
Labour minus Conservative competence on economy t_4	0.32**	0.11
Labour minus Conservative competence on NHS t_4	0.19*	0.11
Approval Britain's involvement in Iraq War t_1	0.16	0.10
McFadden $R^2 = 0.67$ N $= 1424$		
Wave 5 model: Labour supporter t_5 (2010)		
Labour supporter t_4 (2009)	2.97***	0.29
Labour leader affect relative to affect for Conservative and Liberal Democrat leaders t_5	0.27***	0.06
Proximity to Labour on tax/spend and crime/rights t_5	0.19*	10
Labour minus Conservative competence on economy t_5	0.34**	0.12
Labour minus Conservative competence on NHS t_5	0.18*	0.10
Approval of Britain's involvement in Iraq War t_1	0.29***	0.09
McFadden $R^2 = 0.65$ N $= 1393$		

*** $p \leq 0.001$; ** $p \leq 0.01$; * $p \leq 0.05$; one-tailed test, robust standard errors.

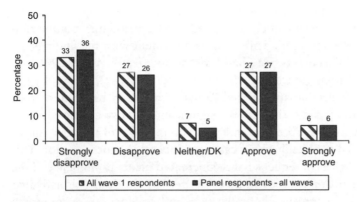

Figure 3.3 Attitudes towards Britain's involvement in the Iraq War.

5 model, the Iraq effect again becomes statistically significant (β = 0.29, p $\leq$ 0.01). The positive sign indicates that those who approved of the war were more likely to vote Labour – and that those who disapproved (a sizable majority) were less likely to do so. Although Britain withdrew its forces from Iraq in April 2009, the fact that US forces remained until December 2011 and civilian casualties continued to mount meant that Iraq stayed in the headlines until well after the 2010 general election. Indeed, as the election approached, judgments about Labour's handling of what many believed was a major foreign policy misadventure came back to bite it. Negative public reactions to the war that had tarnished Tony Blair's image in 2005 continued to reflect badly on Gordon Brown's government, lessening his party's chances of remaining in power as the 2010 election approached.

The results of estimating Eq. (3.2) for Conservative and Liberal Democrat party support show that the calculus of support for the Conservatives remained basically consistent over the 2005–10 period (data not shown in tabular form). As expected, the relative leader rating terms are always positive and significant while the Labour minus Conservative competence terms for both the economy and the NHS are always negative and significant. The spatial proximity term is nonsignificant in the Wave 3 model, suggesting that Cameron's efforts to position his party more closely to the centre-ground between 2006 and 2008 were less important than his efforts to convince the electorate that his party was the most competent to deal with Britain's economic difficulties and that the NHS was safe in Conservative hands. The behaviour of the Iraq variable is capricious – it is significant in the Wave 2 and Wave 4 models but appears to have no impact in the run-up to the election itself. This result is consistent with the findings for the Liberal Democrats. Iraq had little or no effect between 2006 and 2009 (it is nonsignificant in the models for Waves 2, 3 and 4), but as the 2010 election approached (Wave 5) it clearly began to matter, as it had five years earlier. As the significant negative coefficient ($\beta = -0.25$) in the Wave 5 model indicates, disapproval of Britain's role in Iraq boosted the likelihood of casting a Liberal Democrat ballot. This probably was a consequence of the increased media prominence of the Liberal Democrats in the run-up to the general election. This activated anti-Labour sentiment about the war and occupation, encouraging some voters to punish Labour by opting for the Liberal Democrats as the only mainstream party with well-established anti-Iraq War credentials. Finally, the Liberal Democrat results also reveal that perceptions of the relative policy competences of Labour and the Conservatives on the economy and the NHS generally had no effect on Liberal Democrat voting. There is one significant effect (for the economy in the Wave 2 model) but, this apart, none of the relevant coefficients achieves statistical significance.

Paralleling findings in Chapter 2, the present analyses strongly support the idea that calculus of party support was quite consistent throughout the Blair and Brown years. Overwhelmingly, voters looked to valence considerations – to judgments about who was best able to provide effective policy delivery – to help them decide which party they should support. Spatial or ideological positioning also played a role but it was very much a secondary one. However, as in Chapter 2, the assertion that leader evaluations and policy competence assessments were key drivers of changing patterns of party preferences does not tell us why these fundamentals changed over the 2007–10 period. We address this topic in the next section.

Party support dynamics, 2007–2010

Gordon Brown became prime minister in June 2007. Notwithstanding the fact that his predecessor had left office in mid-term – a relatively unusual event in British politics – Brown's accession occurred at a fairly tranquil time. There was no serious economic crisis making front page news although, as the British public was soon to learn, there was one

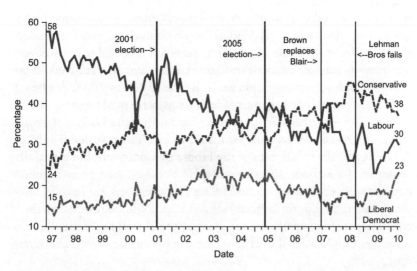

Figure 3.4 Dynamics of Labour, Conservative and Liberal Democrat vote intentions, July 1997–April 2010.
Source: Monthly average poll-of-polls, percentage intending to vote for each party as reported by MORI, ICM, Gallup, YouGov, ComRes and BPIX polls.

lurking around the corner. There was no obvious climate of political scandal or incompetence, although a major scandal would be revealed less than two years later. The governing Labour Party was not unduly divided nor its backbenchers particularly unruly. As noted above, there was an expectation that Brown might call a very early (autumn 2007) election to consolidate his position in the party and the country. His failure to do so, in the face of a strong rhetorical challenge from Conservative leader David Cameron, marked the beginning of a protracted and spasmodic decline in Labour fortunes that characterized the remainder of Brown's term in office.

Figure 3.4 illustrates dynamics in the three main UK political parties vote intention shares between July 2007 – Brown's first full month in office – and May 2010 when Labour lost the general election. The period began with a modest Labour lead in the polls, but this rapidly evaporated after September 2007 and declined immediately thereafter. There was a brief revival in the autumn of 2008 when Brown made a serious (and partially successful) attempt to persuade other key OECD leaders that the world economy was desperately in need of the kind of major fiscal stimulus that the British government was proposing in order to avoid the painful 'credit crunch' from degenerating into a worldwide 'double-dip' recession. The economic and political leadership that Brown provided at the time received favourable press coverage in many western countries and this fed through to a recovery in his party's standing in the opinion polls. By the spring of 2009, this boost to Labour popularity began to fade. Things were made worse – albeit temporarily – by the MPs' expenses scandal that the *Daily Telegraph* exposed between March and May 2009. The affair revealed that large numbers of MPs on all sides of the House of Commons, but especially those on the Labour and Conservative benches, had been claiming expenses for their work-related living arrangements far beyond anything anticipated in the official rules or that could be justified to their constituents. In a small number of cases the claims had actually been fraudulent and resulted in criminal charges being brought against the miscreants.

As Figure 3.4 shows, the expenses scandal temporarily reduced support for both Labour and the Conservatives. Labour fortunes thereafter gradually recovered – although not sufficiently for the party to mount a serious challenge to the Conservatives in the 2010 general election. Conservative popularity rapidly returned to trend after the scandal, thereafter continuing the very gentle decline that had begun in mid-2008. Liberal Democrat support appeared to be largely unaffected by the scandal – or indeed by other events during the 2005 parliament – but it did increase steadily from late 2009 as the election approached.

Figure 3.5 depicts the evolution of public attitudes towards the expenses scandal between June 2009 and April 2010. During this period the BES Continuous Monitoring Survey asked respondents a series of questions about their reactions to the emerging revelations about MPs' misbehaviour. The results reported in Figure 3.5 are typical of the responses. Close to half of those surveyed consistently agreed with the proposition that the scandal 'proves MPs are corrupt' with roughly only a fifth disagreeing. Interestingly, the sense of public outrage about the scandal did not diminish much over time – the distribution of opinion about how MPs had behaved was very little changed in April 2010 from what it had been in June 2009. So, here we have a puzzle. If outrage at the scandal remained fairly constant, why did the Labour and Conservative parties suffer only a temporary loss of support as a result of it? The answer lies in issue salience. As Figure 3.6 illustrates, before the expenses scandal erupted in April 2009, roughly

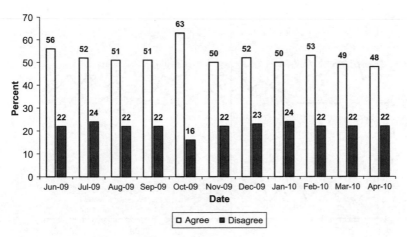

Figure 3.5 Percentages agreeing MPs are corrupt, June 2009–April 2010.
Source: BES monthly CMS surveys.

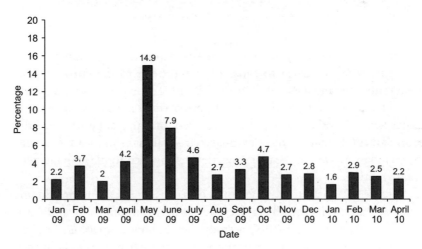

Figure 3.6 Dishonesty as most important issue, January 2009–April 2010.
Source: BES monthly CMS surveys.

2–4 per cent of the public considered 'dishonesty' to be the most important issue facing the country. In May this number increased to almost
15 per cent. Thereafter, the salience of dishonesty rapidly declined so
that by September it was back to around 3 per cent. After a slight
increase in October (the time of the party conferences when some

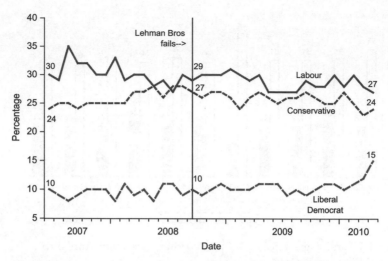

Figure 3.7 Dynamics of partisanship, June 2007–April 2010.
Source: Gallup Dynamics of Party Support Project surveys, Democracy and Participation Project surveys, NSF-BES CMS surveys.

voters were obviously reminded of the delinquency of some MPs), salience levels returned to those observed prior to the initial revelations about scandal emerged in early 2009. The expenses scandal only affected party support for the brief period when it was a salient political issue. At other times, the big drivers of party support were the fundamentals that we have emphasized – partisanship, leader images and judgments about the major parties' relative economic management capabilities.

Figure 3.7 illustrates the dynamics of party identification for Labour, Conservatives and the Liberal Democrats between June 2007 and April 2010. Unlike the 1997–2007 period when Labour's partisan share fell from 47 to 31 per cent, identifications with all three parties did not vary greatly from mid-2007 onwards. Labour partisanship remained almost continuously higher than that of the Conservatives, but the margin was not great – Labour's partisan share began at 30 per cent and ended at 27 per cent, whereas the Conservatives began and ended at 24 per cent. Liberal Democrat identification remained the prerogative of small minorities – it began at 10 per cent and increased to 15 per cent in the month immediately before the 2010 election. Clearly, if voters had made their choices in 2010 purely on the basis of partisan

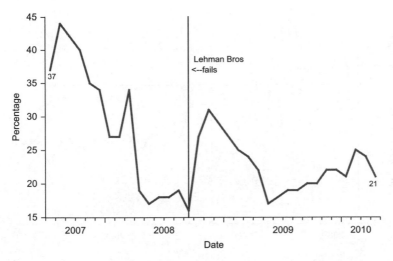

Figure 3.8 Gordon Brown's approval ratings, July 2007–April 2010.
Source: Monthly Gallup and YouGov surveys.

attachments, Labour would have come out ahead of the Conservatives and the Liberal Democrats would have run a distant third. The fact that the election produced a hung parliament with the Conservatives gaining some 36 per cent of the popular vote compared to Labour's 29 per cent and the Liberal Democrats' 23 per cent suggests that forces must have been operating on other fundamentals to yield such an outcome.

Figure 3.8 displays the percentage of respondents in monthly CMS surveys who approved of the job that Gordon Brown was doing as prime minister. After a brief bounce in the polls after taking office, Brown's approval ratings deteriorated, a decline that was obviously exacerbated by the growing sense of national and global economic peril that developed in the wake of the banking crisis and ensuing credit crunch. In April 2008 Brown's approval ratings collapsed to less than 20 per cent in the wake of his government's decision to abolish the 10p in the starting rate of income tax, a policy that was widely (and correctly) assumed to hit the very poorest wage-earners the hardest. Brown had announced the decision to abolish the 10p rate in 2007 when he was Chancellor of the Exchequer and he continued to defend it as prime minister. His insistence on following through with his plans engendered a sharp loss in public confidence. His ratings

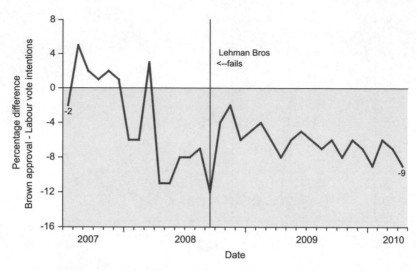

Figure 3.9 Difference between Brown's approval ratings and Labour vote intentions, July 2007–April 2010.
Source: Monthly CMS surveys.

plunged and remained low until autumn 2008 when his brief demonstration of global economic leadership, which as noted above was associated with a modest recovery in Labour's poll ratings, appears to have stimulated a temporary revival in approval of the prime minister himself. By summer 2009 Brown's appeal again had faded and his ratings remained relatively low through to the election.

Figure 3.9 reinforces this story. It shows the difference between Labour's popularity and the prime minister's approval ratings. Following a political honeymoon in summer 2007, Brown's approval – like that of Blair before him after 2001 – consistently trailed behind his party. Many of his parliamentary colleagues were conscious of the fact that the prime minister was likely to prove an electoral liability. Fears that yet another leadership change would both divide the party and sow confusion among voters as to what Labour stood for prevented them from taking decisive action. Although their imminent arrival was a recurrent rumour, the 'men in grey suits' never showed up at Number 10.

Figure 3.10 presents the movements in a third fundamental – judgments regarding Labour versus Conservative economic management capabilities. The story here resembles that for Brown himself. Given

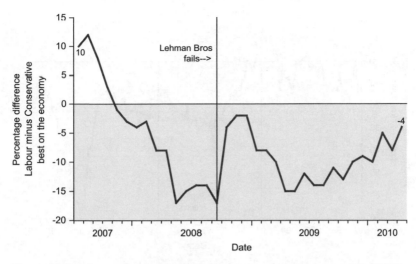

Figure 3.10 Labour versus Conservative economic competence, July 2007–April 2010.
Note: Scale measures the percentage who consider Labour would handle the situation best if Britain were in economic difficulties minus percentage believing Conservatives would be best.
Source: CMS monthly surveys.

the prime minister's long tenure as Chancellor, it is perhaps not surprising that his own popularity – and that of his party – was tied strongly to assessments of his economic performance. As the figure illustrates, public evaluations of Labour's economic management competence relative to the Conservatives declined sharply when the banking crisis struck in late 2007. Despite a partial recovery in evaluations at the time of Brown's display of global economic leadership in autumn 2008, Labour's economic reputation rapidly declined afterwards. Evaluations drifted in a pro-Labour direction in the year or so before the election, but they never exceeded the 'zero' point on the graph – the level at which more voters preferred Labour to the Conservatives as managers of Britain's economic destiny. In spring 2010, the Conservatives continued to enjoy a distinct, if modest, lead over Labour in terms of perceived managerial competence on the economy.

Clues about the sources of the Conservative edge on the economy are provided in Figures 3.11, 3.12 and 3.13. Figure 3.11 displays aggregate dynamics in personal financial expectations over the 1997–2010 period. These movements are measured using monthly variations in the

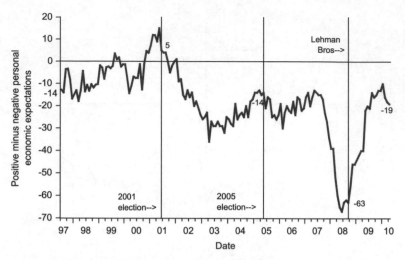

Figure 3.11 Balance of positive and negative personal financial expectations, July 1997–April 2010.

Note: The index subtracts the percentage of respondents who are pessimistic about the financial prospects of their household over the next year from the percentage who are optimistic.

Source: Gallup and YouGov monthly surveys.

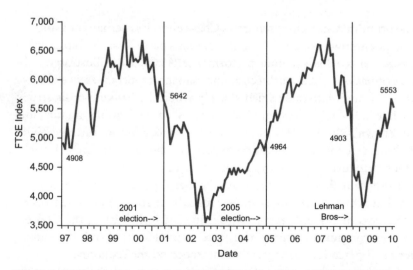

Figure 3.12 Dynamics of stock prices: FTSE index, July 1997–April 2010.
Source: UKfinance.yahoo.com.

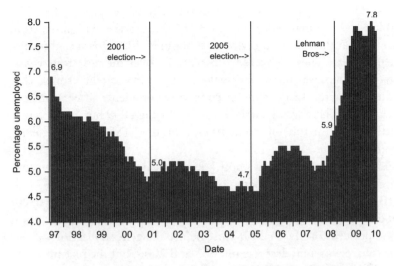

Figure 3.13 Dynamics of unemployment, July 1997–April 2010.
Source: www.tradingeconomics.com/united-kingdom/unemployment-rate.

percentage of people who are optimistic about the financial prospects for themselves and their household minus the percentage who are pessimistic. Previous research has documented that movements in this index are related to voters' assessments of parties' relative economic competence – the more that people feel optimistic about their own economic prospects, the more likely they are to view the economic management capacity of the incumbent party favourably. Although the expectations index trended upwards during Labour's first term in office 2001, reaching a peak at the time of the 2001 general election, thereafter it deteriorated, with the balance of expectations remaining negative through to the 2010 general election. Not unexpectedly, Figure 3.11 documents a steep plunge in optimism in autumn 2007 in the wake of the collapse of the Northern Rock bank. The resultant 'credit crunch' gradually transmuted into a more generalized crisis of confidence across the western industrialized economies and, although expectations recovered slowly through 2008 and 2009, they suffered a further decline in the first two quarters of 2010. Given that the public economic mood was decidedly bearish, it is not surprising that Labour found itself trailing the Conservatives on the economic competence scale in the run-up to the 2010 election.

A similar story is told by movements in UK share prices – the FTSE 100 index – summarized in Figure 3.12. Share prices had fallen from their peak at the time of the 'dotcom' boom in 2000 down to a trough in early 2003. They recovered substantially over the next four years, only to collapse again in the wake of the same credit crunch that produced the marked decline in consumer confidence after Northern Rock failed. There was a partial recovery during 2009 but, as the figure illustrates, by the time of the 2010 election the FTSE rally was clearly incomplete.

Finally, Figure 3.13 shows how a key indicator of the objective condition of the economy – unemployment – behaved between 1997 and 2010. In July 1997, shortly after Labour took office, unemployment stood at 6.9 per cent. Then, it steadily declined, reaching its low point of 4.6 per cent in March 2005, just before the general election of that year. There was a modest rise in 2005 and 2006, but the picture worsened markedly after April 2008, with the unemployment rate climbing from 5.1 to 7.9 per cent by July 2009. On the eve of the 2010 election, things had hardly improved. Joblessness remained at a dismal 7.8 per cent.

Taken together, Figures 3.11 to 3.13 illustrate the multiple economic difficulties confronting Labour as the 2010 election approached. Consumer expectations were low and falling. Business confidence was modest and faltering. Unemployment had just experienced the largest and most rapid rise in almost two decades. Not surprisingly, in April 2010 for a clear majority of voters the single most important issue facing the country was the state of the economy.[7] The key point at issue was which of the two major parties could convince the electorate that it was best able to handle Britain's economic problems. By spring 2010 it had become clear to most observers that the banking and credit crisis, which had been provoked by the collapse of Northern Rock in September 2007 and of Lehman Brothers in September 2008, had transmuted into a quasi-global sovereign debt crisis. The very instruments that most Western governments had used to prevent the banking crisis from degenerating into a more widespread economic collapse – increased government spending and borrowing – had produced a situation where many of those governments, Britain's included, were facing unsustainable levels of debt-servicing repayments.

Labour argued that its decisive action in responding to the credit crunch, by increasing its own spending and borrowing and encouraging other OECD governments to do the same, had avoided the mistakes of the 1930s. In that earlier era governments had failed to see that in times of falling consumer demand they need to spend money (financed, if necessary, by borrowing more) to jumpstart economic activity and growth. According to Labour, Britain's sovereign debt needed to be reduced sufficiently slowly to ensure that public spending cuts did not produce a spiral of declining economic activity and increased welfare spending as a result of rising unemployment.

For their part, the Conservatives contended that Britain's sovereign debt difficulties had been created by Labour's irresponsible economic management during the good times between 1997 and 2007. Instead of holding down public spending and paying off the country's debts, Blair and Brown had continued to expand welfare provision – redistributing income to less well-off groups almost by stealth – funded by steadily increasing levels of public borrowing. When the credit crunch struck, Labour's policy of increasing borrowing and spending to maintain economic activity had elevated UK public borrowing to unsustainable levels that urgently needed to be shrunk to maintain investor confidence. According to the Conservatives, the key policy priority was to reduce Britain's debt as rapidly as possible; the private sector would fill any employment gap left by reductions in public spending. As shown in Figure 3.10, the fact that voters generally tended to see the Conservatives as being better than Labour at dealing with Britain's economic problems suggests that on the eve of the 2010 general election it was the Conservatives' arguments that carried greater weight in voters' minds. It seems likely that the declines in consumer and business confidence and the sharp increase in unemployment played a part.

Building on the model of Labour support for the Blair years developed in Chapter 2, Table 3.4 presents a model of Labour support that covers the full period of Labour government between July 1997 and the start of the official general election campaign in April 2010. The specification follows the same structure as Eq. (2.2) in Chapter 2. The model contains exactly the same core variables as that reported in Table 2.3, but these are supplemented by several additional events – the switch from Blair to Brown in June 2007; the Northern Rock crisis

Table 3.4 *Model of the dynamics of Labour support during the Blair and Brown eras, July 1997–April 2010*

Dependent variable: change in Labour support$_t$	β	s.e.
Change in Labour economic management competence$_t$	0.21***	0.04
Change in prime minister's approval ratings$_t$	0.12**	0.04
Fuel crisis (September 2000)	−7.24***	1.47
Terrorism bill (December 2001)	−4.71***	1.40
Iraq War – start (April 2003)	2.82*	1.40
Iraq War – civilian casualties$_t$	−0.02	0.11
Change in percentage unemployed$_{t-1}$	−2.45*	1.20
Switch from Blair to Brown (June 2007)	2.42*	1.40
Northern Rock (September 2007)	1.51	1.40
Ten pence income tax abolished (April 2008)	0.30	1.43
Brown's global leadership post Lehman (October 2008)	2.37*	1.40
Expenses scandal – start (May 2009)	−5.18***	1.42
Error correction adjustment parameter$_{t-1}$	−0.47***	0.06
Labour economic management competence term in error correction mechanism$_{t-1}$	0.22***	0.05
Blair's approval ratings term in error correction mechanism$_{t-1}$	0.27***	0.04
Iraq War cumulative civilian casualties term in error correction mechanism$_{t-1}$	−0.23***	0.06
Constant	13.44***	1.70
Adjusted R^2	0.65	
N	154	
Sample: July 1997–April 2010		

*** $p \leq 0.001$; ** $p \leq 0.01$; * $p \leq 0.05$; one-tailed test.

of September 2007; the abolition of the 10p tax band in the April 2008 budget; Brown's global leadership role which he asserted in the wake of the Lehman Brothers collapse in September 2008; and the first full month of the MPs' expenses scandal in May 2009. Model coefficients are estimated using OLS regression.

The coefficients for the core variables are identical to those reported in Table 2.3 in terms of signs and significance levels, and they are very similar in terms of magnitude. These similarities reinforce the story that we told in Chapter 2 about direct influences on Labour popularity – throughout the 1997–2010 period, Labour support was driven primarily by changes in perceptions of economic management competence, changes in assessments of the prime minister's leadership and changes in unemployment, with an additional long-term negative effect exerted by the rising toll of civilian casualties in Iraq.

Over and above the effects of these variables, the direct effects of salient events during the Brown period were relatively modest. As Table 3.4 shows, the Northern Rock crisis and the 10p tax affair both failed to exert significant direct effects on Labour support. This said, the switch to Brown gave Labour a brief boost ($\beta = 2.42$) and Brown's global leadership posturing also briefly enhanced his party's poll standing ($\beta = 2.37$). In contrast, the expenses scandal temporarily reduced Labour's support by just over 5 points ($\beta = -5.18$). The adjustment parameter ($\alpha = -0.47$) associated with the error correction mechanism operating between Labour support, on the one hand, and Brown's approval rating and Labour's perceived economic competence, on the other, indicates that the effects of these events decayed fairly rapidly.

As observed in Chapter 2, knowledge that Labour support was driven primarily by perceptions of its managerial competence and attitudes towards its leaders does not tell us what was driving those variables. Accordingly, we develop models for Brown's approval ratings during his prime ministerial term and for Labour versus Conservative economic management competence for the period covering both the Blair and Brown premierships.

Our model of Gordon Brown's approval ratings is similar to the model of Blair's approval discussed in Chapter 2 (see Table 2.4). However, it differs in three respects. First we do not include a term for Iraq casualties in the Brown model. Although, as shown in Table 3.4 (and earlier in Table 3.2), Iraq casualties continued to damage Labour as a whole in the run-up to the 2010 election, Brown never experienced the same public identification with the Iraq occupation as did his predecessor. In this sense, there is no reason to expect that Iraq would have damaged Brown's ratings in the same way that it affected Blair's.[8] Second, we include a different set of events in the Brown model. Specifically, for Brown we include dummy variables for Northern Rock, the 10p tax band abolition, his global leadership stance after the failure of Lehman Brothers, and the start of the MPs' expenses scandal. Third, the Brown model is hypothesized to have a simple error

Table 3.5 *Model of the dynamics of Brown's approval ratings, August 2007–April 2010*

Dependent variable: change in Brown's approval ratings$_t$	β	s.e.
Change in Labour economic management competence$_t$	0.38**	0.13
Northern Rock (September 2007)	−1.71	2.57
Ten pence income tax abolished (April 2008)	−7.39**	2.85
Brown's global leadership post Lehman (October 2008)	6.91*	2.87
Expenses scandal – start (May 2009)	−1.03	2.46
Error correction adjustment term$_{t-1}$	−0.79***	0.18
Labour economic management competence term in error correction mechanism$_{t-1}$	−1.06***	0.08
Constant	26.06***	5.75
Adjusted R^2	0.75	
N	33	
Sample: August 2007–April 2010		

*** $p \leq 0.001$; ** $p \leq 0.01$; * $p \leq 0.05$; one-tailed test.

structure. This means that we that we do not estimate the ARCH process similar to that used in conjunction with Blair's approval model (see Chapter 2).

Table 3.5 reports coefficient estimates for the Brown approval model. Changes in voters' perceptions of Labour's economic management competence exerted a powerful positive effect (β = 0.38) on prime ministerial approval. This is hardly surprising. Brown had established his reputation as Chancellor prior to becoming prime minister. That his own fortunes as leader should be tied to his party's reputation for economic competence was only to be expected. However, similar to Labour support, events played relatively modest roles. Northern Rock and the expenses scandal left Brown's ratings unaffected. His demonstration of global leadership in the wake of the dramatic collapse of Lehman Brothers (β = 6.91) boosted his standing in voters' eyes, whereas the 10p tax affair (β = −7.39) had the opposite effect. Although these effects were initially quite substantial, the large adjustment rate for the error correction process (α = −0.79) – indicates that they were rapidly eroded by the error correction process involving Brown's approval ratings and perceptions of Labour's economic managerial competence. Effects associated with his '15 minutes of fame on the world stage' and the expenses scandal had evaporated well before the April 2010 general election.[9]

The model of economic management competence perceptions is based on our discussion of the dynamics of key economic conditions above and from a consideration of the key events between 1997 and 2010 that might have affected public perceptions of Labour's general policy competence and its economic competence in particular. The economic drivers in the model are aggregate personal financial expectations, business confidence as reflected in the FTSE index of share prices, and the unemployment rate. Given that Labour was the incumbent party, we anticipate that economic expectations and share prices will exert positive effects on perceptions of the party's economic management competence, whereas unemployment will have a negative effect. Dummy variables for the following events also are included:

- The September 2000 fuel crisis, where the government temporarily seemed unable to ensure fuel supplies across the country: a negative effect on competence perceptions is expected.
- The 9/11 attack in September 2001, where the government's reassuring and resolute response reinforced perceptions of capacity for resolute policymaking: a positive effect is expected.
- The Railtrack bailout in March 2002, when the government spent £9bn to save an ailing company: a negative effect is expected.
- The switch from Brown to Blair in June 2007: this is included for control purposes.
- The Northern Rock collapse in September 2007 signalling the start of the credit crunch: this is expected to exert a negative effect on competence.
- The abolition of the 10 tax band in April 2008, which was widely portrayed as increasing the tax burden on the lowest paid workers: a negative effect is expected.
- Brown's display of global leadership in October 2008: a positive effect is expected.
- The start of the MPs' expenses scandal in May 2009: although Labour MPs were not the only offenders, it is expected that generalized public anger would be targeted primarily at the incumbent

government: this would produce a drop in perceptions of Labour's competence to govern.

• Annual Labour Party Conferences: these stage-managed bursts of positive publicity should produce positive effects.

Thus, the Labour versus Conservative economic management judgments model is:

$$\Delta \text{LabEcManage}_t = a + \beta_1 \Delta \text{Expectations}_t + \beta_2 \Delta \text{FTSE}_t$$
$$+ \beta_3 \Delta \text{Unemployment Rate}_t + \beta_4 \text{Fuel Crisis}_t$$
$$+ \beta_5 \text{Attack}_t + \beta_6 \text{Railtrack} + \beta_7 \text{Switch}$$
$$+ \beta_8 \text{NorthernRock} + \beta_9 \text{TenPTax}$$
$$+ \beta_{10} \text{Glead} + \beta_{11} \text{Exp} + \beta_{12} \text{Conf}$$
$$+ \alpha_1 (\text{LabEcManage}_{t-1} - c_0 - c_1 \text{Expectations}_{t-1}$$
$$- c_2 \text{FTSE}_{t-1}) + \varepsilon_t \qquad (3.3)$$

where LabEcManage is Labour versus Conservative economic management competence; Expectations is the balance of (positive and negative) personal financial expectations; FTSE is the Financial Times Share Index; Unemployment is the monthly unemployment rate; Fuel Crisis, Attack, Railtrack, Switch, Northern Rock, TenPTax, Glead, Exp and Conf are dummy variables for the months identified above; the expression in brackets represents an error correction mechanism involving LabEcManage, Expectations and the FTSE index; β_1-β_{11} and c_0-c_2 are estimated effects of various predictor variables on Labour versus Conservative Economic Management Competence; Δ is the difference operator; and ε_t is a random error term.

The results of estimating Eq. (3.3) show that the model is well determined and all predicted relationships are correctly signed and statistically significant at conventional levels ($p \le 0.05$) (data not shown in tabular form). The only nonsignificant coefficient is for the switch from Blair to Brown, suggesting that the change in prime minister by itself did nothing to affect the public's assessment of the two main parties' economic management capabilities. The key economic variables behave exactly as predicted. Aggregate expectations ($\beta = 0.11$) and the FTSE index ($\beta = 13.09$) – consumer and business confidence – had positive effects on perceptions of Labour competence whereas unemployment had a negative effect ($\beta = -4.58$). Labour's failure to stimulate a sustained recovery in either consumer or business confidence in advance of the 2010 election, together with its failure to hold down unemployment, clearly damaged its competence ratings which, in turn, weakened its ability to secure re-election. In addition to these general effects, events also mattered, although their impacts were temporary. The fuel crisis, the Railtrack bailout, the Northern Rock failure, the abolition of the 10p income tax band and expenses scandal temporarily damaged Labour's economic reputation. The government's vigorous response to 9/11, Brown's display of global economic leadership post-Lehman Brothers and Labour's opportunity to grandstand each year at its annual conference all enhanced its reputation. However, the error correction mechanism involving perceived Labour economic competence, personal economic expectations and the FTSE index worked to erode the effects of these events. The small (but significant) coefficient for error correction mechanism ($\alpha = -0.19$) means that it operated slowly – discounting shocks at a rate of 19 per cent in every month after they occurred. The effect may have been slow, but it was inexorable. In most cases, the influence of various shocks had substantially or wholly dissipated before voters went to the polls in the 2001, 2005 and 2010 general elections.

Conclusions: economic blues for Mr Brown

This chapter has delineated the major considerations that British voters used to make their party support choices during the New Labour era that extended from the party's 1997 landslide victory to the eve of its 2010 defeat. We have established that the main factors affecting these changed very little over this period. The fundamental drivers of party choice in the Blair and Brown years remained the same – people's party identifications, their assessments of the merits of party leaders and their judgments of which party was best able to deal with the most important issues facing the country were what mattered most. Proximities to the main parties on key position issues played a secondary, but nontrivial, role.

This chapter has focused on the period of Gordon Brown's premiership. This was a time of deepening economic crisis – indeed, the most serious and protracted downturn since the Second World War. The crisis, unanticipated when Brown succeeded Blair, forced Brown and his Labour government to wrestle with multifaceted economic difficulties that affected the UK and much of the Western world. In addition, the prime minister and his party had to contend with a reinvigorated Conservative opposition whose new leader, David Cameron, was determined to modernize and shed the 'nasty' image that plagued it during the Thatcher–Major era. It was also a period when the reputation of British politicians in general was tarnished by the MPs' expenses scandal revealed in a protracted series of widely publicized and occasionally lurid *Daily Telegraph* articles in spring 2009.

Analyses of individual-level panel data gathered in BES-CMS surveys revealed that, although the voters' decision calculus generally remained constant over the 2005–10 period, there were times when some issues were more important than others. The effects of voters' assessments of the economy and of the NHS and their sense of the positioning of the rival parties on issues such as the tax–spend trade-off did not vary much over time. However, the influence of the Iraq War varied. People's assessments of Britain's military involvement in Iraq were important in the formation of party preferences in 2005 but in the period between the 2005 and 2010 elections they faded into the background. But, as the 2010 election approached, Iraq began again to affect people's thinking. Those who took a negative view of Britain's involvement in that strife-ridden country were significantly more likely to abandon Labour between mid-2009 and the start of the 2010 campaign. Elections, as often has been observed, concentrate minds. The re-emergence of Iraq as a driver of party support between 2009 and 2010 is a reminder to politicians of all hues that even when issues seem to be dead and buried, if they are important enough – as Iraq clearly was for some Labour supporters – they can reappear to inflict electoral damage at inopportune times.

The key conclusions about the political economy of the Brown era derive from our time series analyses of the dynamics of party support. Figure 3.14 summarizes the major elements of the story. The first, key, point is that Labour support was driven primarily by assessments of the prime minister himself, by perceptions of Labour economic management competence, by the condition of the objective economy as measured by unemployment and by the mounting toll of civilian casualties in Iraq. Chapter 2 has documented that these factors also had strong effects on Labour's popularity during Tony Blair's premiership. Second, Gordon Brown's approval ratings were determined in large part by views of his party's economic competence. This was in contrast

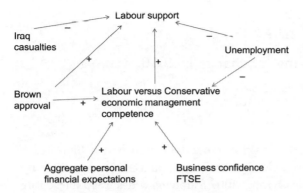

Figure 3.14 Sources of Labour party support in the Brown era.

to Blair whose ratings were also affected adversely by civilian deaths in Iraq. Finally, assessments of Labour versus Conservative economic competence were driven in part by economic conditions, as reflected in the unemployment rate and the extent to which voters' felt confident about their prospects and those of business in general. As with Labour support in the Blair era, the party's successes and, ultimately, its failures under Gordon Brown, were driven primarily by reactions to economic conditions and by the shadow of what for many British voters had turned out to be the failed, if not disastrous, intervention in Iraq.

4 | 'I agree with Nick'

Campaigning for change in 2010

The timing of the 2010 British general election had a high degree of predictability. When Gordon Brown announced that he would not seek a new mandate in October 2007 following widespread speculation that there would be an early election call, this had two effects. First, it precipitated a rapid erosion of his personal popularity and an end to the public opinion honeymoon which he had enjoyed since taking residence in Number 10 in June 2007. These dynamics were discussed in Chapter 3. But the decision to postpone had a second effect – it informed everyone that the next general election would be delayed until spring 2009 at the earliest and quite likely even longer. In fact, by early 2009, some four years after the previous election, Labour was too far behind in the polls to win,[1] so from that point on it was clear that the next election would be put off until the last possible date – the spring of 2010. This meant that although the official 2010 campaign was a month long as usual, the unofficial 'long' campaign which preceded it lasted the best part of a year. From late spring 2009 knowledge that the election would take place a year later permitted the parties to start campaigning early without fear that their efforts would be wasted. As a result, the run-up to the official 'short' campaign involved an unusually long unofficial campaign and this helped to shape the outcome.

With this point in mind, the present chapter is divided into four sections. In the first section we describe the official or 'short' campaign which lasted from the date the election writs were issued on 6 April to polling day on 6 May. The analysis begins by placing the official campaign in context by describing events earlier in the year which preceded it. Public opinion dynamics during the official campaign are examined using the daily 'replicate' surveys conducted in the BES Rolling Campaign Panel Study (RCPS) described in Chapter 1.

In a second section we consider the Ground War – the campaign at the constituency level. We know from previous research that local constituency campaigns matter both for stimulating turnout and affecting levels of party support (Clarke *et al.*, 2004b, 2009b; Denver *et al.*, 2002; Fieldhouse and Cutts, 2008; Fisher and Denver, 2008; Pattie *et al.*, 1995; Seyd and Whiteley, 2002; Whiteley and Seyd, 1994). The aim is to delineate how much the local campaigns mattered in 2010, particularly in view of the fact that the result was much closer than those for three preceding general elections. One important innovation in the present analysis involves constituency electioneering during the long campaign. Changes in electoral law and the design of BES surveys enable us to investigate constituency campaigning prior to the official announcement of the election in April 2010. Earlier research on constituency-level electioneering has focused heavily on activities during the official campaign itself, but thanks to additional data gathered in the BES CMS surveys we can examine the preceding long campaign.

The third section looks at the 'Air War' – the campaign at the national level. Once again earlier research has documented that national-level events occurring during the official campaign can have an important influence on voting (Clarke *et al.*, 2004b, 2009b). Such events will be examined in relation to the 2010 campaign, but another important innovation in studying the Air War is to consider the impact of the media on public opinion. There has been considerable research on media effects in election campaigns (Iyengar, 1991; Ronis and Lipinski, 1985; Sanders and Gavin, 2004; Soroka, 2006; Soroka *et al.*, 2009). Here, we will study key media-related variables which may have influenced voters during the official campaign. The aim is to delineate the dynamic relationship between media-related variables and voting, controlling for a variety of other factors which affect electoral choice. In a final section, we discuss implications of principal findings for understanding electoral choice in contemporary Britain.

Towards the official campaign

In late 2009 a member of David Cameron's campaign team is reported to have said: 'On 4th January the election campaign begins' (Kavanagh and Cowley, 2010: 127). The predictability of the election date meant that the Conservatives were anxious to seize the initiative at the start of 2010 to steal a march on their rivals. The Conservative campaign was launched by a speech from David Cameron on 2 January 2010. This speech was designed to coincide with the release of part of the Conservative manifesto, together with the kick-off of a poster campaign in

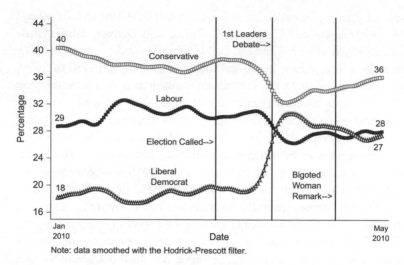

Figure 4.1 Trends in voting intentions, 1 January–5 May 2010.
Source: 163 polls, UK Polling Report: ukpollingreport.co.uk

key constituencies across the country. The aim was to create momen-
tum and put Gordon Brown's government on the back foot, knowing
that the prime minister had to go to the country within a matter of
months. The launch of Conservative campaign was given a boost on 6
January when two former Labour cabinet ministers, Geoff Hoon and
Patricia Hewitt, called for a secret ballot to resolve the issue of Gordon Brown's leadership. Although the challenge fizzled out rapidly,
his unpopularity in his party and the country as a whole was readily
apparent. The Hoon–Hewitt gambit was the last of a series of anti-
Brown plots – real and rumoured – that had dogged his premiership
since late 2007.

As Figure 4.1 illustrates, the Conservative lead over Labour was
pegged at nearly a dozen points in early January 2010, suggesting that
it was reasonable for David Cameron and his colleagues to expect
that they could win an overall majority. However, starting in early
February the Conservatives began to lose ground and Labour support
increased. The Conservative lead in the polls narrowed. This was partly
because they had difficulty articulating a coherent message. Starting
with Cameron's initial speech on 2 January, they could not resolve
the issue of whether to campaign positively or negatively, and factions
inside the party argued about this in strategy meetings. Kavanagh and
Cowley (2010: 128) report that the argument was the origin of a rather

curious Conservative poster. It showed a picture of David Cameron accompanied by a quote: 'We can't go on like this. I'll cut the deficit, not the NHS.' It is odd because the two parts of the slogan appear to be unrelated to each other and the first, negative, part sits uneasily with the second, positive, part. The poster came about because Andy Coulson, the party's director of communications and strategy and former employee of Rupert Murdoch's News International wanted attack messages, whereas Steve Hilton, Cameron's strategy advisor, wanted positive messages about Conservative values and policy initiatives. The result was an uneasy compromise between the two and it subsequently became newsworthy because of claims that the photo of Cameron had been retouched. The poster proved easy to spoof and a website was set up inviting visitors to design their own versions.[2]

In the meantime Labour launched an attack on Conservative promises with a weighty policy document called 'Conservative Tax and Spending Promises' which alleged that there was a £34 billion 'black hole' in the Tories' spending plans. Credibility was lent to this attack when the Conservatives' claim that they could save £400 million by ending Child Tax Credits for families on incomes over £50 000 was challenged by the Treasury and the independent Institute for Fiscal Studies. Similarly, Conservative charges that Labour had presided over a rise in violent crime were described as 'misleading' by the UK statistics authority. These criticisms worked to offset any traction the Conservatives might have gained by the early launch of their campaign.

A second element in Labour's modest recovery was the fact that the recession peaked by the start of 2010 with an announcement in January that unemployment had started to fall for the first time since May 2008. Economic growth was still anaemic with an increase in GDP of only 0.1 per cent in the fourth quarter of 2009, but a recovery appeared to be in sight. The possibility of an economic revival buttressed Labour's argument that Gordon Brown's wise policies had saved the country from a 1930s-style depression. The result was that the Conservative lead over Labour in the polls narrowed and the prospects for a hung Parliament grew as the election approached.

During this period Liberal Democrat support hovered at between 15 and 20 per cent with a modest but discernable increase occurring just before the official campaign started. The party was hoping to repeat the pattern of previous general elections, in which its support increased once the official campaign got under way. The media focus on the party in the context of an election campaign explains this pattern. The party receives the 'oxygen of publicity' during the official campaign and this commonly boosts their vote (Whiteley *et al.*, 2006). A day before the official election campaign began, a YouGov poll in the *Sun* gave the Conservatives 39%, Labour 29%, the Liberal Democrats 17% and other parties 10%.

Once the dissolution of Parliament was announced on 6 April the Conservatives landed the first effective blow by announcing endorsements by several senior business leaders. This was timed to coincide with the final pre-election Prime Ministers Question Time in the House of Commons on 7 April. These endorsements dominated the news agenda at the start of the campaign. When Parliament finally dissolved on 12 April Labour launched its manifesto, with the Conservative and Liberal Democrat launches following over the next two days.

Labour's manifesto had a distinctly 1940s retro look with a cover depicting a traditional family of the husband, wife and two children gazing across a stylized English landscape with the slogan 'A Future Fair for All' written over a rising sun. In the introduction Gordon Brown highlighted intensive global competition, climate change, an ageing society and Afghanistan as the 'major challenges of the next ten years' (Labour Party, 2010: 2). The statement 'Labour believes we must not put the recovery at risk by reckless cuts to public spending this year' (Labour Party, 2010: 3) was prominently displayed. Labour's manifesto began by emphasizing the importance of achieving economic recovery and stimulating growth before discussing education, health and crime in later sections. A key dividing line with the Conservatives was a pledge to 'secure the recovery by supporting the economy now, and more than halve the deficit by 2014 through economic growth, fair taxes and cuts to lower priority spending' (Labour Party, 2010: 1–3).

The Conservative manifesto was called: 'An Invitation to Join the Government of Britain' and, unlike Labour's, it avoided looking like a political pamphlet. The introduction set the tone:

'Today the challenges facing Britain are immense. Our economy is overwhelmed by debt, our social fabric is frayed and our political system has betrayed the people. But these problems can be overcome if we pull together and work together. If we remember that we are all in this together'. (Conservative Party, 2010: ii)

This was a traditional appeal to 'One Nation' Conservatism, echoing the views of Tory leaders in the Macmillan and earlier eras reaching back to Disraeli. A major difference with Labour was spelled out in the section on macroeconomic policy: 'We will safeguard Britain's credit rating with a credible plan to eliminate the bulk of the structural deficit over a Parliament' (Conservative Party, 2010: 7). The Conservative manifesto promised cuts in government departments and 'wasteful spending', but 'ring-fenced' the NHS by promising rising real-term expenditures each year. Unusually for the party, overseas aid also was exempted from cuts. Overall, the Conservative message was a gloomy one – austerity and sacrifice would be the order of the day with Mr Cameron in Number 10. Bright days would be ahead, but no time soon.

The Liberal Democrat manifesto made much of the theme of fairness in relation to taxation, job creation and education. Also, in a section described as 'Cleaning Up Politics,' the document emphasized the importance of dealing with the crisis in trust that the MPs' expenses scandal had created. To this end, voters would be given the right 'to sack MPs' (Liberal Democrats, 2010: 7). On the issue of the deficit, the manifesto declared:

'We must ensure the timing is right. If spending is cut too soon, it would undermine the much-needed recovery and cost jobs. We will base the timing of cuts on an objective assessment of economic conditions, not political dogma. Our working assumption is that the economy will be in a stable enough condition to bear cuts from the beginning of 2011–12'. (Liberal Democrats, 2010: 4)

Clearly, the party's policy on the deficit was much closer to Labour's than to the Conservatives, since if the cuts were delayed until the 2011–12 financial year, the deficit likely would not be substantially reduced during the next Parliament. In other respects the Liberal Democrat manifesto was more radical than the other two parties, particularly in relation to the banking crisis. It explicitly called for banks to be: 'split up in order to insulate retail banking from investment risks' (Liberal Democrats, 2010: 6). Neither the Conservatives nor Labour articulated such a clear-cut proposal for structural reform of Britain's much-criticized banks.

Figure 4.1 tracks voting intentions for the three major parties during the 30-day official campaign which began on 6 April. The figure indicates that when the campaign started, the Conservatives still had a reasonable expectation that they could gain an outright majority having 39 per cent of the vote in comparison with Labour's 30 per cent. At that point the Liberal Democrats were hovering around the 20 per cent mark.

The dynamics of the campaign were changed dramatically by the first party leader debate which took place on 15 April. This was the first leaders' debate in the history of British general elections and Liberal Democrat leader, Nick Clegg, emerged as a clear winner. His success was partly related to the 'oxygen of publicity' point made earlier. Also, his presence as an equal competitor in the debate invited voters disillusioned with 'politics as usual' to see the Liberal Democrats as a viable alternative to the two old parties. Clegg recognized his opening and seized it. More generally, he gave a strong performance – talking directly to the camera and making a point of mentioning the names of members of the audience who had asked questions. He came across as commanding and refreshing in contrast with Gordon Brown who looked tired and followed his usual habit of trying to demonstrate a high level of competence by quoting a flood of statistics. As the debate progressed, David Cameron appeared to be slightly unnerved by Clegg's strong showing and as a result underperformed. Adding to Clegg's emerging advantage, at various points in the debate his rivals endorsed his opinions by saying: 'I agree with Nick.' This seemingly encouraged many in the huge television audience to do so as well.

Perhaps because of their novelty, the debates attracted a very large audience. Approximately 60 per cent of the respondents in the BES Rolling Campaign Panel Survey said that they had seen part or all of the first debate. Fully 78 per cent of these people judged that Nick Clegg had delivered the best performance (Figure 4.2). In contrast, only 13 per cent thought that David Cameron performed best and only 9 per cent opted for Gordon Brown. When asked who had done worst in the debate, a majority (55 per cent) chose Brown, 42 per cent selected Cameron and merely 3 per cent designated Clegg. In the aftermath of the event, press and public were quick to agree that Clegg clearly had bested his rivals.

Trends in public reactions to the party leaders' performance during the 30-day official campaign are displayed in Figure 4.3. It is apparent that there was large variation in perceptions of which leader was doing the best job. Positive evaluations of Nick Clegg's performance grew

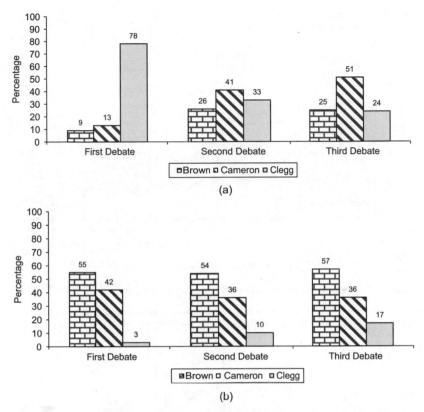

Figure 4.2 Public reactions to the nationally televised party leader debates: A. Who performed best? B. Who performed worst?
Source: 2010 BES Rolling Campaign Panel Survey.

rapidly following the first debate and they stayed high through to polling day. Although he did not generate surges in support in the remaining two debates, overall impressions of him remained quite positive. As for David Cameron, after faltering in the first debate his performance improved, especially in the third debate on 29 April. As result, public reactions to him at the end of the campaign were very similar to what they had been when it began. In contrast, Gordon Brown's ratings fell after each of the debates so that judgments about his performance were roughly halved over the campaign as a whole.

Additional insight into the performance of the leaders during the official campaign is provided in Figure 4.4 which displays trends in voters'

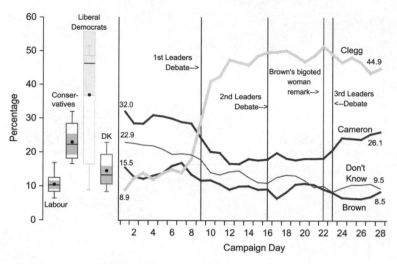

Figure 4.3 Public views of leader conducting best campaign, 7 April–5 May 2010.

Source: 2010 BES Rolling Campaign Panel Survey.

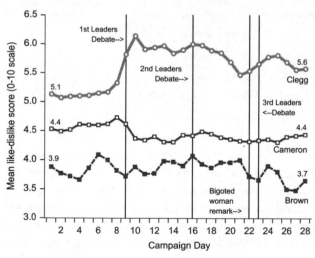

Figure 4.4 Trends in feelings about party leaders during election campaign, 7 April–5 May 2010.

Source: 2010 BES Rolling Campaign Panel Survey.

feelings about them using scores on a 0 (dislike) to 10 (like) scale. As discussed in Clarke *et al.* (2009b: ch. 5) leaders' affect scores constitute an excellent summary measure of what the public think about them – correlating very strongly with ratings for more specific attributes such as competence, trustworthiness and responsiveness. The data displayed in Figure 4.4 are similar to those shown in Figure 4.3 in that Clegg clearly emerged as most likeable. In contrast, Cameron's ratings were lukewarm throughout the campaign and Brown's were consistently quite dismal. As anticipated given public reactions to their debate performances, Clegg's rating climbed sharply after the first debate, and he finished at an impressive 5.6 points. In contrast, affect for Brown – low at 3.9 points to begin with – fluctuated modestly, before falling slightly at the end of the campaign to 3.7 points. Feelings about Cameron exhibit a similar dynamic, with his affect score ending at the same mediocre level (4.4 points) where it began.

In addition to failing to capitalize on the debates, Brown committed a widely publicized gaffe on the campaign trail when he failed to realize that a microphone he was wearing was still live after a 'meet the voters' walkabout in Rochdale. He was heard to describe Mrs Gillian Duffy, a 66-year-old pensioner and lifelong Labour supporter with whom he had just been talking, as a 'bigoted woman' because she expressed concerns about immigration rather than focusing on the economy as Mr Brown wanted. Brown also angrily castigated his staff, particularly Sue Nye, for allowing him to be exposed to Mrs Duffy. The 'bigoted woman' remark was made the day before the final debate, so it is difficult to untangle the effects of the two events, but the incident provoked a firestorm of adverse publicity that the struggling prime minister could ill afford. His apology to Mrs Duffy did nothing to alleviate the problem.

Overall, the portrayal of the official campaign in the media was dominated by the party leader debates, if only because they were a salient innovation in British electoral politics and so were a source of endless commentary. The audience for the first debate was just under 10 million viewers (Kavanagh and Cowley, 2010: 164) and it was the pre-eminent event on the campaign calendar. The two subsequent debates had smaller audiences but they also were major campaign events. We return to the topic of media effects below, but first we analyze the impact of the Ground War – the local constituency campaigns up and down the country.

Close to home: the Ground War

Constituency campaigning or the Ground War has been a subject of considerable research over past two decades (e.g. Clarke *et al.*, 2004b, 2009b; Denver *et al.*, 2002; Fieldhouse and Cutts, 2008; Seyd and Whiteley, 2002). Different methodological approaches have been employed, varying from aggregate analyses of campaign spending data to expert surveys of constituency agents, surveys of party activists who do the actual campaigning and surveys of voters who are the targets of all these efforts. The different methodologies converge in testifying that a well-organized local campaign can mobilize voters and help to win seats in marginal constituencies.

The data used for the individual-level analysis is the British Election Study's Rolling Campaign Panel Survey (RCPS), a large national, three-wave panel. As discussed in Chapter 1, the first wave had 16 816 respondents and it was conducted immediately prior to the announcement of the election campaign. The second wave took place during the campaign and consisted of re-surveying random subsamples of approximately 550 respondents every day. Finally, there was a post-election wave of 13 356 respondents that recorded vote decisions and reactions to the election outcome.

A question in the pre-campaign wave of the RCPS asked respondents if they had been contacted by any of the political parties in the previous six months. This makes it possible to monitor local campaigning before the official election campaign began. A similar question was asked in the post-election survey about party contacting during the 30-day official campaign. In the event, 39 per cent of the respondents reported being contacted before the official campaign began, and 47 per cent reported being contacted at some point during the campaign. Thus, there was a considerable amount of constituency campaigning going before the official campaign began and this reinforced the parties' electioneering efforts.

Figure 4.5 shows how many of those contacted were reached by the different political parties before and after the official campaign began. It is apparent that the Conservatives did the most campaigning, both in the long and short campaigns, with 25 per cent of the respondents reporting a Conservative contact before the official campaign began and 37 per cent reporting one in their post-election survey. Labour was in second place with 21 per cent reporting contact beforehand

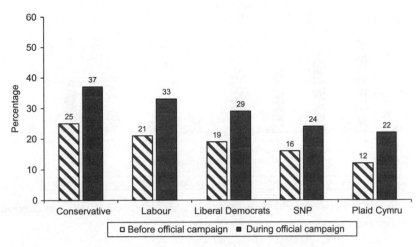

Figure 4.5 Party contacting before and during 2010 election campaign.
Source: 2010 BES Rolling Campaign Survey.

and 33 per cent afterwards. The Liberal Democrats trailed Labour
with reported contact rates of 19 per cent and 29 per cent, respectively. Contact rates by the nationalist parties in Scotland and Wales
were below the rates for the three major parties in Britain as a whole,
although there is evidence of considerable activity by the SNP in Scotland and Plaid Cymru in Wales before the official campaign kick-off.

Prior to the 2010 election, observers speculated that the contest
would witness an electronic revolution in campaigning. It was widely
believed that Barack Obama's victorious campaign in the 2008 American presidential election had been energized by technological innovations that emphasized using new social media resources such as
Facebook and Twitter to reach voters, particularly younger ones. Commentators contended that British parties would mimic the American
experience and marshal the new technology in their search for votes.
Although party strategists may well have been attracted by the idea,
evidence indicates that electronic campaigning was very limited in its
reach in 2010. Specifically, the 2010 RCPS post-election survey data
reveal that, altogether, only 10 per cent of the electorate were contacted
electronically by one or more of the parties. As Figure 4.6 illustrates,
the Conservatives reached the most people – 6 per cent, with Labour
and the Liberal Democrats each reaching 3 per cent. And, although

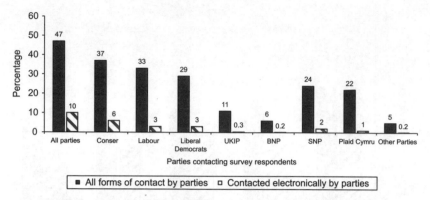

Figure 4.6 Electronic and total party contacting during 2010 general election campaign.
Source: 2010 BES Rolling Campaign Panel Survey.

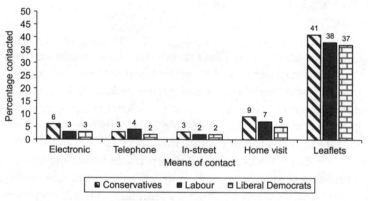

Figure 4.7 Alternative ways of direct voter contacting, 2010.
Source: 2010 BES Rolling Campaign Panel Survey.

one might surmise that minor parties would be attracted to the new electronic media because of its presumed cost-effectiveness, only 1 per cent or less of the RCPS respondents said that one of the smaller parties had contacted them this way. Although new social media may have facilitated communication about the election, the touted electronic revolution in party campaigning remained largely unrealized.

The vast majority of people contacted by parties in 2010 were reached in traditional ways. As Figure 4.7 shows, leaflets were the pre-eminent method of communicating directly with voters. Slightly over two-fifths of the RCPS post-election respondents reported receiving a Conservative leaflet, and only slightly fewer reported receiving one from Labour or the Liberal Democrats. Comparable SNP and Plaid Cymru figures (not shown) are 31 and 35 per cent in Scotland and Wales, respectively. In contrast, personal contacts, either on the doorstep or in the street, were much less frequent – only 12 per cent reported an in-person contact by the Conservatives and 9 and 7 per cent reported one by Labour or the Liberal Democrats. Again, the SNP and Plaid Cymru numbers are similar. Nor was telephone popular – no more that four RCPS respondents in 100 reported being contacted by phone by any of the parties. Although various means of contacting voters may have been effective, in 2010 the parties were united in their preference for a very old technology, the printing press, as the principal means of delivering their messages.

Thanks to changes in election law, in 2010 the Electoral Commission monitored spending by the local parties prior to beginning of the official campaign. This makes it possible for researchers to identify parties' longer-term spending. The inability to monitor pre-campaign spending in earlier studies implies that campaign effects indexed by spending data may have been underestimated since only part of the story was told. The Electoral Commission defined the long campaign as the period from 1 January 2010 to the date when the election was called (Electoral Commission, 2011). Spending after that date was classified as taking place during the official campaign. Given that we have individual-level survey data from RCPS and aggregate spending data from the Electoral Commission, the analytic strategy used here involves estimating multilevel models of turnout and party choice. Direct contact with voters is modelled at the individual level and campaign spending is modelled at the constituency level.

Britain's first-past-the-post system for Westminster elections encourages parties to concentrate campaigning in the marginal seats which are susceptible to changing hands. Figure 4.8 shows the relationship between constituency spending as a percentage of the maximum allowed by law and the marginality of seats in the previous (2005) general election. The spending data are the averages for the Conservatives, Labour and Liberal Democrats combining long and official campaign figures. Not surprisingly, the three major parties behaved strategically when investing their campaign funds, with marginal seats receiving the most money and safe seats the least. The overall correlation (r)

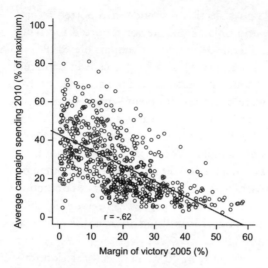

Figure 4.8 Constituency-level spending by the three major parties in 2010 by constituency marginality in 2005.
Source: Norris, 2010 British general election constituency results and Electoral Commission.

between campaign spending and marginality of seats in the preceding election was −0.61, strong evidence of a strategic approach to allocating campaign resources.[3] Again demonstrating their strategic bent, all three parties paid attention to their margins of victory in 2005 when deciding how much to spend defending seats in 2010, with the correlation between marginality of seats won by Labour in 2005 and Labour spending in 2010 being −0.55 (see Figure 4.9). Comparable figures for the Conservatives and Liberal Democrats are −0.43 and −0.51, respectively. These correlations indicate that all three parties were spending their local campaign money sensibly, focusing on marginal constituencies rather than locales where they were quite likely to win or lose regardless of local campaign efforts.

Modelling the Ground War

When analysing the influence of constituency campaigning in the 2010 general election we consider both turnout and party choice. To study the latter we utilize model specifications developed in earlier chapters and apply them to the context of the election campaign itself.

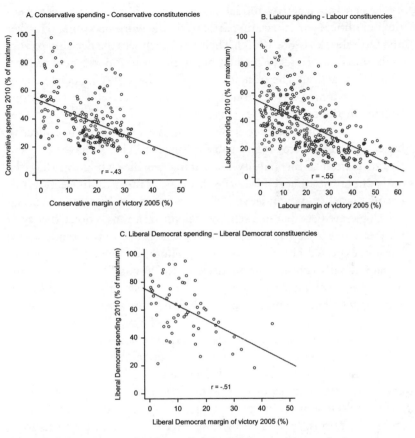

Figure 4.9 Constituency-level spending by the three major parties in seats won in 2005.
Source: Norris, 2010 British general election constituency results and Electoral Commission.

We are also interested in the relationship between turnout and campaigning since turnout in 2010, although higher than in 2001 and 2005, was only 65.1 per cent – low by post-Second World War standards.[4] We investigate the impact of campaigning on electoral participation with the assistance of multiple theoretical perspectives. In previous research we have examined a number of different accounts of turnout (see Clarke *et al.*, 2004b, 2009b; Whiteley and Seyd, 1994). These models include: general incentives, civic voluntarism, cognitive engagement, equity fairness and social capital. To begin, we briefly outline their features.

The general incentives model has its origins in rational choice theories of political participation, particularly the work on voting by Riker and Ordeshook (1968, 1973). Their approach sees the decision to vote as the outcome of a set of calculations of the costs and expected benefits of political action. The principal benefit is the utility associated with one party winning the election rather than another. This is a collective benefit, in the sense that it is available to all regardless of whether an individual contributes to it by voting. As is well known, collective benefits produce a free-rider problem, since individuals have an incentive to maximize their utility by reaping benefits while avoiding the costs of contributing (Olson, 1965). In the context of an election this means that electors will leave it to others to bear the costs of voting. This logic predicts that in a narrowly defined rational choice theory of turnout few people will go to the polls. The problem is actually worse because expected benefits must be discounted by the probability that an individual's vote will prove decisive (or 'pivotal') to the outcome. In a mass electorate, that probability is vanishingly small (Gelman et al., 1998). The product of that probability times benefits will almost certainly be less that the costs of going to the polls, even though the latter may be quite small. Rational voters stay home.

For this reason the general incentives model takes into account a wider range of incentives which influence voting. Most of these incentives have their origins in social-psychological theories of choice. They include selective or individual benefits, group benefits, system benefits and social norms. Individual benefits refer to the private returns from participating in politics which are not available to those who abstain. Group benefits refer to the returns which might accrue to groups that the individual cares about. System benefits involve people's perceptions that they have a duty to society as a whole which might encourage them to participate. Finally, social norms refer to group beliefs about the desirability of voting that individuals recognize and react to by going to the polls themselves.

In contrast to the general incentives model, the civic voluntarism model explains participation in terms of resources which individuals bring to the exercise of voting, together with the mobilizing activities of political parties and other groups. Resources in this model refer to an individual's occupational status and educational attainment, the time available for participating, and skills which assist electoral participation (Verba and Nie, 1972; Verba et al., 1995). High-resource persons are more likely to vote than low-resource ones because they have a greater stake in the system, as well as more of the kinds of skills which facilitate involvement.

The cognitive engagement model focuses on levels of political information and the degree of interest in politics which individuals bring to the task of participating. If people are politically knowledgeable and engaged, take an interest in an election and can make sense of the campaign and the wider political world, they are likely to vote. In contrast, if they have difficulty understanding politics, are disengaged and take little interest in the election, they are unlikely to go to the polls (Dalton, 2008; Nie *et al.*, 1996).

The equity-fairness model is based on the idea that individuals can be motivated to participate by a sense of relative deprivation (Runciman, 1966; Walker and Smith, 2002). Relative deprivation refers to the gap between people's expectations of what they should receive from government and society and what they actually do receive. A growing gap between expectations and reality will give rise to a sense of deprivation. Expectations arise from making comparisons with peers or reference groups and relative deprivation comes from a feeling that a person is losing out in comparison with others. Studies have shown that relative deprivation can motivate political protest (Gurr, 1970; Muller, 1979). Clearly, it could also motivate some people to vote against a political party which is held responsible for their perceived deprivation.

The social capital model is based on the idea that individuals who are well integrated into society and embedded in expansive social networks are more likely to trust each other and to be trustworthy. Norms of reciprocation engendered in voluntary organizations and informal networks make people willing to cooperate with others to solve collective action problems. People's willingness to trust others and cooperate with them makes it more likely that they will participate in politics and, by implication, vote in elections (Coleman, 1988; Putnam, 1993, 2000).

This brief sketch of major theories of turnout illustrates that a wide variety of factors has been hypothesized to influence electoral participation. No single theory appears to have a monopoly of explanatory power since predictor variables associated with different theories have statistically significant effects in analyses of voting turnout (Blais, 2000; Clarke *et al.*, 2004b). In addition, the theories are not mutually exclusive but overlap to a significant extent which explains why a composite model that includes variables from different theoretical approaches provides the strongest account of turnout (Clarke *et al.*, 2004b, 2009b). We consider measurement issues associated with these theories in the next section before analysing a composite model of turnout in the 2010 general election.

Measurement: Starting with the general incentives model, the measure of collective benefits is based on party utility differentials calculated for each voter. The logic is that if voters see a big difference between the utility of their preferred party winning an election and that of its rivals, this gives them an incentive to go to the polls. In contrast, if they see little difference between the parties in the utility produced by a win by any given party, they have little incentive to vote. Accordingly, a party differential measure is calculated for each respondent based on their replies to a set of 'like–dislike' questions for each of the parties.[5] This variable is computed for the three major parties, as well as for the SNP in Scotland and Plaid Cymru in Wales.

In the general incentives model the utility associated with each of the parties is discounted (weighted) by the probability of that party winning the election. Originally, this probability referred to the likelihood of an individual casting the vote which decided the outcome of an election (Riker and Ordeshook, 1968). However, as observed above, in practice this 'pivotality' probability is indistinguishable from zero so the measure clearly fails to provide an adequate account of the way that people reason in practice. If it did, no one would vote since costs would always exceed pivotality-discounted benefits. Accordingly, we weight differential utilities of various parties winning by a voter's sense political efficacy, measured on a 0–10 scale that indexes an individual's perception of being able to influence politics and public affairs.

Other variables in the general incentives model are designed to capture the different motivations people have to participate. Perceived costs of participating are captured by the indicator 'People are so busy that they do not have time to vote'. Respondents agreeing with this statement are likely to be conscious of the costs of electoral participation and therefore less likely to vote. In fact, there are relatively few people who agree with it (16 per cent), so the costs of voting generally are not perceived to be high. Individual benefits are captured by the statement 'I feel a sense of satisfaction when I vote' and many respondents agree with this. The statement taps the private or selective incentive for participating in contrast to the collective incentives

Table 4.1 *Binomial logit models of turnout in the 2010 election: the Ground War*

Predictor variables	β	β	β
Long campaign party mobilization	0.12***	0.07***	0.04*
Short campaign party mobilization	0.09***	xx	0.05***
Efficacy × collective benefits	xx	−0.00	−0.00
Costs	xx	−0.07***	−0.07***
Individual benefits	xx	0.10***	0.10***
Group benefits	xx	−0.06*	−0.06
System benefits	xx	0.24***	0.24***
Social norms	xx	0.07***	0.07***
Interest in the election	xx	0.21***	0.21***
Education	xx	0.05***	0.05***
Relative deprivation index	xx	−0.02	−0.02
Social capital index	xx	0.01	0.01
Age	xx	0.01***	0.01***
Gender	xx	0.06	0.06
Ethnicity	xx	0.44***	0.43***
Occupational status	xx	0.02**	0.02**
Country of residence:			
Scotland	xx	−0.11	−0.10
Wales	xx	−0.05	−0.05
McFadden R^2	0.01	0.08	0.08

xx – variable not included in model.
*** $p \leq 0.001$, ** $p \leq 0.01$, * $p \leq 0.05$, + $p \leq 0.10$; one-tailed test.

measured by the party differential scale. The group incentives indicator receives less support than the individual incentives measure, although approximately half of the respondents agree with it. The system benefit measure is the perception that a good citizen has a duty to vote. Finally, social norms are measured by perceptions of what family and friends think about voting.

Table 4.1 presents binomial logit estimates (Long and Freese, 2006) of the parameters in the turnout models. Effects of the campaign variables are considered first, and subsequently indicators of the different theoretical models added to the specifications. Note that there are two campaigning variables – one measures pre-election party contacting and the second measures party contacting during the official campaign.

The first variable indexes effects of campaigning before the election was called, and the second captures effects during official campaign. The dependent variable is self-reported vote turnout in the post-election wave of the BES RCPS survey. The first model suggests that campaign activity in both the long and short campaigns had statistically significant effects on turnout, although the goodness-of-fit statistic suggests that the explanatory power of the model is unimpressive. The second model estimates the impact of pre-election campaigning, controlling for various predictor variables in the competing theoretical models. The third model contains the campaign measures and all of the control variables.

The main point to make about the third model in Table 4.1 is that the long campaign continues to exert a modest effect on turnout once the short campaign variable is included in the specification. In other words, people are mobilized to vote principally by the official campaign but effects of the long campaign are still felt on polling day. It also can be seen that only some of the indicators from the theoretical models made a contribution to explaining turnout. The weighted collective benefits measure from the general incentives model has a negligible impact on turnout. In contrast, turnout was affected by perceived costs, individual benefits, system benefits and social norms in predicable ways. Although the relative deprivation measure and the social capital index were not significant, the two predictors in the cognitive engagement model – interest in the election and educational attainment – both positively influenced turnout. Social class, a predictor in the civic voluntarism model, also had a positive impact. Finally, we note that multilevel models (e.g. Raudenbush and Bryk, 2002) of turnout were estimated which included parties' campaign spending at the constituency level as additional predictors. None of these second-level variables has significant effects on individual-level turnout, so these results are not reported in Table 4.1.

Table 4.2 reports the relationship between party choice and campaigning in 2010. Predictor variables include partisanship, party leader images, party performance evaluations on most important issues, economic evaluations and issue–party proximities. These proximities are measured by perceived distances between voters and parties on 11-point tax versus spending trade-off scales. The first analysis reported in the table is a binomial logit model which pits Labour voting versus voting for any other party. The second analysis is a multinomial logit

Table 4.2 *Logit models of party choice in the 2010 election: the Ground War*

Individual-level effects	Binomial logit models		Multinomial logit model	
	Labour v. others	Conservative v. Labour	Liberal Democrats v. Labour	Other parties v. Labour
Party best most important issue:				
Labour	0.36***	−0.73***	−0.56***	−1.07***
Conservatives	−0.54***	0.93***	0.21	−0.00
Liberal Democrats	−0.65***	−0.03	0.89***	−0.14
Other party	−0.12	0.15	−0.24	0.76***
Party leader image:				
Brown	0.23***	−0.40***	−0.26***	−0.31***
Cameron	−0.12***	0.46***	0.06***	0.12***
Clegg	−0.04***	−0.06	0.21***	0.02
Party identification:				
Labour	1.23***	−1.33***	−1.06***	−1.51***
Conservative	−1.03***	1.63***	0.30	0.28
Liberal Democrat	−0.58***	−0.07	1.14***	−0.28
Other party	−0.23*	0.19	0.19	1.22***
Economic evaluations	0.03***	−0.05***	−0.02	−0.06***
Tax–spend issue–party proximities:				
Labour	−0.01***	0.02***	0.01***	0.02***
Conservative	−0.00	−0.02***	0.00	−0.00
Liberal Democrat	−0.00	0.00	−0.01	0.00
MPs' expenses scandal	−0.15*	0.18	0.23**	0.18
Campaign contact:				
Labour	0.57***	−0.50***	−0.63***	−0.44***
Conservative	−0.04	0.45***	−0.03	−0.02
Liberal Democrat	−0.48***	0.16	0.90***	0.38**
Other party	−0.00	−0.13	−0.02	0.23**
Gender	−0.18***	0.05	0.21***	0.39***
Age	0.01***	0.01***	−0.01*	0.02***
Ethnicity	0.29***	0.15	−0.03	0.01
Occupational status	−0.01***	0.02	0.05***	0.02
Country of residence:				
Scotland	0.20	−0.86***	−0.49***	0.31
Wales	0.06	−0.58**	−0.25	−0.03

(cont.)

Table 4.2 (cont.)

Aggregate-level effects	Binomial logit models		Multinomial logit model	
	Labour v. others	Conservative v. Labour	Liberal Democrats v. Labour	Other parties v. Labour
Labour spending	0.01***	−0.02***	−0.02***	−0.02***
Conservative spending	−0.01***	0.01***	0.01***	0.01**
Liberal Democrat spending	−0.01***	0.01**	0.01***	0.00
Other party spending	−0.01	0.01	0.00	0.03***
Aggregate level R²	0.26	0.22	0.37	0.21

*** $p \leq 0.001$, ** $p \leq 0.01$, * $p \leq 0.05$, + $p \leq 0.10$; one-tailed test.

model which focuses on Conservative, Liberal Democrat and other party voting, with Labour voting treated as the reference category.

We employ the same approach used in the turnout analyses, so that the control variables were measured before the campaign started, campaign variables were measured in the second wave of the survey and voting was measured in the post-election wave. This enables us to study the impact of the campaign on party choice, controlling for pre-campaign effects. These are multilevel models with the party campaign spending variables included at the aggregate (i.e. constituency) level in the analysis.

In the model of Labour voting, all of the control variables are statistically significant with the correct signs, apart from the Conservative and Liberal Democrat tax–spend spatial variables and the other party best on most important issue measure (see Table 4.2). Thus, partisanship, leader images and Conservative, Labour and Liberal Democrat performance on important issues all behaved as expected, with the Labour variables increasing the probability of a Labour vote and rival party measures reducing it. It is noteworthy that only two of the campaign variables were significant in this model, with Labour campaigning increasing the Labour vote, and Liberal Democrat campaigning reducing it. Conservative and other party campaigning did not influence Labour voting. However, this does not mean that the Conservative campaign had no influence on the Labour vote, since at the aggregate level Conservative spending had a highly significant negative effect. We mentioned earlier that spending captures the capital investment aspects of campaigning, while the individual-level campaign variables measure the 'boots-on-the-ground' aspects. It appears that the former paid off for the Conservatives, but not the latter. With respect to Labour, present findings resemble those from previous studies and show that both aspects of campaigning helped to bolster Labour's vote share (Clarke *et al.*, 2009b: 215–21).

Results for the multinomial logit models displayed in Table 4.2 have a similar interpretation as those for the Labour model. Positive feelings about Gordon Brown, positive economic evaluations and Labour partisanship all reduced the probability of voting Conservative, whereas positive feelings about David Cameron, Conservative partisanship and pessimism about the economy all increased the likelihood of casting a Tory vote. The Labour and Conservative tax–spend, issue–party proximities also behaved in predictable ways – being close to Labour enhanced the likelihood of voting Labour and being close to the Conservatives diminished it. Again, being close to the Conservatives raised the probability of a Conservative vote and being close to Labour lessened that probability. Also noteworthy is that the probability of voting Conservative does not appear to be influenced by attitudes towards Nick Clegg, Liberal Democrat partisanship, perceptions that the Liberal Democrats were best at handling the most important issue or proximity to the Liberal Democrats on the tax–spend trade-off. The implication is that attitudes towards the Liberal Democrats and their leader had little direct influence on the competition for votes between Labour and the Conservatives.

Regarding campaign contacting measures, Labour campaigning reduced the likelihood of a Conservative vote whereas Conservative campaigning increased it and Liberal Democrat or other party campaigning had no effect. This last point has to be modified in light of the aggregate-level analysis. It is clear that Labour spending reduced the Conservative vote and Conservative spending increased it. Intriguingly, Liberal Democrat spending helped to boost the Conservatives in the contest between Labour and the Tories. In other words, Liberal Democrat campaign efforts worked to weaken the incumbent party at the expense of its principal rival.

Regarding Liberal Democrat voting, perceiving the party as best on most important issue, having a positive image of Nick Clegg and

Liberal Democrat partisanship all behaved as expected, raising the probability of voting for the party. However, the equivalent Conservative variables were not significant, with the exception of feelings about David Cameron. Positive feelings about him made voters more likely to opt for the Liberal Democrats at the expense of Labour. Regarding spatial variables, a voter's proximity to Labour reduced the likelihood of opting for the Liberal Democrats, but proximity to the Conservatives or the Liberal Democrats was not influential. Once again, at the aggregate level Conservative spending appears to have boosted Liberal Democrat voting at the expense of Labour. These results suggest that the Liberal Democrats and Conservatives were helped by each others' campaign efforts.

Finally, the analysis of 'other party' voting showed that attitudes towards the Conservatives and Liberal Democrats had few significant effects. Exceptions were feelings about David Cameron which helped the other parties at the expense of Labour as did Conservative campaign spending. However, evaluations of Conservative and Liberal Democrat performance on the most important issue, partisanship and issue–party proximities all were insignificant. Labour campaigning reduced the probability of supporting one of the minor parties and Liberal Democrat campaigning had the opposite effect.

The overall picture depicted by the analysis of the Ground War is that the campaign variables significantly affected turnout and party choice in the 2010 general election. With respect to turnout, these effects operated only at the individual level, but with regard to party choice, individual- and aggregate-level campaign measures were both influential. In the next section we consider the 'Air War' and ask how this might have influenced turnout and party choice in 2010.

Modelling the Air War

We model the Air War using the 'daily replicate' RCPS surveys conducted throughout the official campaign. In this analysis, the aggregate variables are measured over time rather than across constituencies and we focus on the leadership debates which, as the earlier discussion indicates, dominated the campaign. The dependent variables are the same as in the Ground War models, namely turnout and party choice recorded after the election took place. The predictor variables are all measured prior to the official campaign, except in the case of the campaign measures which are recorded at various times during the campaign.

The strategy adopted in the Air War analysis is the same as for the Ground War. We specify comprehensive models of turnout and party choice using predictor variables discussed earlier. We then augment these variables with additional measures of campaign activity. In this way, we can estimate the independent impact of the campaign variables.

Campaign measures: In the case of the Air War, the influence of the national media is studied by including newspaper readership in the set of campaign measures. As is well known, although television and radio in Britain are statutorily regulated to provide balanced coverage of election campaigns, the print media are free to be as partisan as they wish. Typically, Britain's major newspapers exhibit partisan biases. They endorse specific political parties during election campaigns and their coverage tends to be aligned with these endorsements. The Conservatives had a large advantage in endorsements in 2010 with a raft of newspapers such as the *Daily Telegraph* and the *Daily Mail* strongly supporting them. Labour was endorsed by only one national newspaper, the *Daily Mirror*, with the *Independent* and the *Guardian* supporting the Liberal Democrats. Accordingly, three dummy variables were created which identified if respondents were regular readers of a newspaper which endorsed the Conservatives, Labour or the Liberal Democrats.[6]

Another important feature of the Air War is public perceptions of the effectiveness of parties' campaigns. Perceptions of how leaders performed, for example, in the debates are already captured by the leader image measures in the party choice models, but additional survey questions were asked about which parties were perceived to have run the best and worst campaigns. Net scores on these measures for each respondent are included in the party choice models.[7] Our conjecture is that a perception that a party ran an effective campaign should have a positive impact on willingness to vote for that party.

The third variable associated with the national campaign captures evaluations of party political broadcasts that occurred during the campaign. These broadcasts are allocated to political parties in proportion to their vote shares in the previous election, and earlier research suggests that they are an influential aspect of the Air War (Clarke *et al.*,

2004b, 2009b). Respondents were asked to evaluate the broadcasts along a five-point scale from 'very favourable' to 'very unfavourable', and these measures were included in the models. The hypothesis is simple: a favourable impression of a party's broadcasts should have a positive impact on voting for that party and an unfavourable impression should have a negative impact.

The three campaign variables mentioned up to this point all are associated with the Air War, but clearly it is important to control for the impact of the Ground War in the models. We do this by including the direct contact measure for the parties examined earlier in the Ground War analyses. This approach makes it possible to compare Air War and Ground War effects in the same model. Overall, there are four campaigning variables in the Air War models and in the next section we examine their effects on turnout and party choice.

Campaigning, turnout and party choice

Binomial logit estimates for the Air War turnout model appear in Table 4.3. The model includes the same set of control variables used in the turnout model discussed earlier (see Table 4.1), along with the campaign measures. One version of the turnout model contains the campaign variables together with the demographic controls. The second version incorporates the additional predictor variables specified in the composite turnout model discussed earlier.

Parameter estimates in Table 4.3 indicate that some campaign variables stimulated turnout and others suppressed it. The strongest effects are associated with the Ground War measures, that is, personal contact between voters and party activists. Such contact consistently stimulates turnout, thereby suggesting the power of face-to-face interaction when it comes to influencing voters. Perhaps the least effective influence on turnout relates to newspaper readership. Readership of a Labour newspaper appeared to have a weak effect in the first model, but this disappeared in the second model when controls were incorporated. Equally, although reading a newspaper supporting the Liberal Democrats was significant in the second model, it was not significant in the first, thereby suggesting that this effect is not robust.

Evaluations of the parties' campaigns influenced turnout, but in this case positive evaluations of the Conservative and Liberal Democrat campaigns stimulated turnout, whereas positive evaluations of

Table 4.3 *Models of turnout in 2010: the Air War*

Predictor variables	β	β
Political efficacy × collective benefits	xx	0.00
Costs	xx	−0.04
Individual benefits	xx	0.08**
Group benefits	xx	−0.10***
System benefits	xx	0.25***
Social norms	xx	0.06**
Interest in the election	xx	0.16***
Relative deprivation index	xx	−0.01
Social capital index	xx	−0.00
Newspaper Readership:		
Labour newspaper	0.18*	0.12
Conservative newspaper	0.02	−0.07
Liberal Democrat Newspaper	−0.12	−0.36***
Evaluations of parties' campaigns:		
Labour campaign	−0.30***	−0.30***
Conservative campaign	0.49***	0.46***
Liberal Democrat campaign	1.09***	1.09***
Other parties' campaigns	−0.21***	−0.14**
Evaluations of parties' political broadcasts:		
Labour broadcasts	0.20***	0.17***
Conservative broadcasts	−0.03	−0.05
Liberal Democrat broadcasts	0.17	0.18***
Other parties' broadcasts	0.10***	0.10***
Direct party contact:		
Labour	1.15***	1.13***
Conservatives	1.06***	1.02***
Liberal Democrats	0.63***	0.64***
Other parties	0.38***	0.32***
Age	0.02***	0.02***
Gender	0.13**	0.09
Ethnicity	0.26***	0.30***
Occupational status	0.04	0.01
Country of residence:		
Scotland	0.14	0.07
Wales	−0.01	−0.01
McFadden R^2	0.21	0.24

xx – variable not included in model.
*** $p \leq 0.001$, ** $p \leq 0.01$, * $p \leq 0.05$, + $p \leq 0.10$; one-tailed test.

the Labour and other party campaigns inhibited it. There were actually very few respondents who thought that Labour ran an effective campaign, and the number of respondents evaluating other parties' campaigns positively also was limited. Further analysis showed these two types of respondents tended to be less attentive to politics than voters in general. Their inattentiveness is consistent with their failure to participate in the election.

Finally, the party political broadcast measures for Labour and Other parties both had positive effects on turnout in the first model. They were joined by evaluations of Liberal Democrat party political broadcasts as positive predictors of turnout in the second model. These results are consistent with the idea that these broadcasts can have a positive impact on mobilizing voters to go to the polls. However, the Conservative party political broadcasts appeared to have little effect on mobilizing voters which may reflect the ambivalent nature of the party's campaign messages referred to earlier.

A multilevel version of the turnout model was estimated with the three different leader debate dummy variables included at the aggregate level. These dummy variables were created to capture the effect of each of the three debates, scoring zero prior to the debate and one thereafter. This specification ensures that they captured the permanent impact of the three debates on turnout in the campaign. In the event, they had no significant effect on individual turnout. Although the debates may have dominated the thirty-day campaign, these results suggest that they had little discernible impact in terms of motivating people to go to the polls.

Turning next to the influence of campaigning on party choice, the estimates for the model of Labour voting appear in Table 4.4. The reference category is voting for any of the other parties. Again there are two versions of the model, one containing the campaign variables and sociodemographic controls and the second incorporating predictors of party choice discussed earlier. Parameter estimates for the first model indicate that all of the campaign variables influenced Labour voting with the exception of direct contact by other parties. Equally, all of the signs were consistent with expectations such that Labour broadcasts, direct contact between Labour campaign workers and voters and positive evaluations of the Labour campaign stimulated voters to support the party, whereas positive evaluations of other parties' campaigns reduced the propensity to cast a Labour ballot.

Table 4.4 *Binomial logit model of Labour voting in 2010: the Air War*

Predictor variables	β	β
Party best most important issue:		
Labour	xx	0.21***
Conservatives	xx	−0.57***
Liberal Democrats	xx	−0.77***
Other party	xx	−0.16
Party leader image:		
Brown	xx	0.18***
Cameron	xx	−0.09***
Clegg	xx	−0.02
Party identification:		
Labour	xx	1.36***
Conservative	xx	−1.14***
Liberal Democrat	xx	−0.48***
Other party	xx	−0.20
Economic evaluations	xx	0.03**
Tax–spend issue–party proximities:		
Labour	xx	−0.02***
Conservative	xx	−0.00
Liberal Democrat	xx	0.00
MPs' expenses scandal	xx	−0.20**
Newspaper readership:		
Labour newspaper	0.57***	−0.01
Conservative newspaper	−0.15**	0.07
Liberal Democrat newspaper	0.32***	0.17
Evaluations of parties' campaigns:		
Labour campaign	0.86***	0.10
Conservative campaign	−0.49***	−0.02
Liberal Democrat campaign	−0.17**	−0.23**
Other parties' campaigns	−0.22***	−0.20**
Evaluations of parties' political broadcasts:		
Labour broadcasts	1.02***	0.43***
Conservative broadcasts	−0.31***	−0.06
Liberal Democrat broadcasts	−0.36***	−0.24***
Other parties' broadcasts	−0.21*	−0.14

(cont.)

Table 4.4 (cont.)

Predictor variables	β	β
Direct party contact:		
Labour	0.94***	0.78***
Conservatives	−0.28***	−0.11
Liberal Democrats	−0.63***	−0.61***
Other parties	−0.02	−0.00
Age	0.01***	0.01**
Gender	0.01	−0.08**
Ethnicity	0.13	0.24**
Occupational status	−0.00	−0.01
Country of residence:		
Scotland	0.38***	0.25**
Wales	−0.07	−0.06
McFadden R^2	0.23	0.41

xx – variable not included in model.
*** $p \leq 0.001$, ** $p \leq 0.01$, * $p \leq 0.05$, + $p \leq 0.10$; one-tailed test.
Note: voting for any party but Labour is the reference category.

However, not all of these effects were robust as the second model demonstrates. The effects of the campaign variables in the second model in Table 4.4 are more mixed than those of the first model. It appears that the effects of newspaper readership are negligible once various control variables are incorporated. There is the noteworthy finding that although positive evaluations of the Labour campaign and the party's broadcasts boosted the Labour vote, comparable Conservative variables had no effect. A similar point can be made about the Ground War indicators which index the influence of contact by party activists. Direct contact by Labour activists boosted the probability of a Labour vote while contact by the Liberal Democrats reduced that probability. Contact by Conservative activists did not affect Labour support.

These findings suggest that the real competition in the 2010 campaign was between Labour and the Liberal Democrats, once the standard predictors of party choice were taken into account. This reinforces the point made earlier in the discussion of the Ground War. Positive evaluations of the Liberal Democrat campaign, apart from newspaper readership, reduced the Labour vote. In contrast, none of the equivalent Conservative campaign variables influenced Labour support. Thus, it appears that the key rivalry – as far as campaigning was concerned – was between the Liberal Democrats and Labour.

The control variables in the second model in Table 4.4 all behaved as expected. Party best on most important issue, partisanship, feelings about party leaders and economic evaluations all influenced Labour voting in expected directions. However, the tax–spend issue-proximity variables for the Conservatives and Liberal Democrats were not statistically significant. Although the perceived distance of Labour from a voter's preferred tax–spend position affected the probability that they would vote Labour, comparable measures for distances between voters and other parties proved nonsignificant. As in 2001 and 2005, spatial variables tend to play secondary roles in explaining electoral choice (see Clarke *et al.*, 2009b).

Table 4.5 contains parameter estimates for the models of voting for the Conservatives, Liberal Democrats and other parties. The first column contains parameter estimates for Conservative voting, and shows that issue perceptions, leadership evaluations and partisanship were influential predictors of Tory support. Positive evaluations of the economy, Gordon Brown and Labour partisanship reduced the probability of voting Conservative. Similarly, Conservative partisanship and positive evaluations of David Cameron enhanced the likelihood of casting a Tory ballot. More generally, parameter estimates for Conservative voting indicate that there was a real contest between Labour and the Conservatives when the two parties are compared directly. In contrast, the Liberal Democrat variables were less influential, except for feelings about Nick Clegg which reduced the probability of opting for the Conservatives. Finally, although a large number of Conservative MPs had been implicated in the scandal, negative reactions to the MPs' expenses revelations enhanced the likelihood of voting Labour rather than Conservative.

Regarding the campaigning variables, newspaper readership was influential in the Conservative model. Reading a Conservative newspaper boosted the probability of a Tory vote, whereas reading a Liberal Democrat newspaper reduced it. Positive evaluations of the Conservative campaign enhanced the likelihood of Conservative voting at the expense of Labour, and positive evaluations of the Labour

Table 4.5 *Multinomial logit model of voting in the 2010 election: the Air War*

Predictor variables	Conservative β	Liberal Democrat β	Other parties β
Party best most important issue:			
Labour	−0.36*	−0.23**	−0.89***
Conservatives	0.83***	0.16	−0.01
Liberal Democrats	0.14	0.97***	−0.05
Other party	0.06	−0.17	0.68***
Party leader image:			
Brown	−0.31***	−0.18***	−0.23***
Cameron	0.34***	0.03*	0.10***
Clegg	−0.05**	0.12***	−0.02
Party identification:			
Labour	−1.44***	−1.21***	−1.48***
Conservative	1.62***	0.47**	0.46*
Liberal Democrat	−0.16	0.98***	−0.33
Other party	0.01	0.07	1.17***
Economic evaluations	−0.04*	−0.01	−0.04*
Tax–spend issue–party proximities:			
Labour	0.02***	0.01**	0.02***
Conservatives	−0.01**	−0.00	−0.00
Liberal Democrats	−0.00	−0.01	−0.00
MPs' expenses scandal	0.23*	0.25**	0.37***
Newspaper readership:			
Labour	−0.08	−0.12	−0.26
Conservative	0.28**	−0.26**	−0.18
Liberal Democrat	−0.55**	−0.24	0.34
Evaluations of parties' campaigns:			
Labour campaign	−0.50***	−0.28**	−0.13
Conservative campaign	0.49***	−0.00	0.19
Liberal Democrat campaign	−0.15	0.74***	0.12
Other parties' campaigns	0.15	0.01	0.70***
Evaluations of parties' political broadcasts:			
Labour broadcasts	−0.96***	−0.93***	−0.92***
Conservative broadcasts	0.71***	−0.02	−0.02
Liberal Democrat broadcasts	−0.01	0.65***	−0.01
Other parties' broadcasts	−0.00	0.21	1.02***

Table 4.5 (cont.)

Predictor variables	Conservative β	Liberal Democrat β	Other parties β
Direct party contact:			
Labour	−0.91***	−1.13***	−0.77***
Conservatives	0.59***	0.01	0.02
Liberal Democrats	0.22	1.20***	0.34**
Other parties	−0.05	−0.04	0.35***
Age	0.01**	−0.00	0.02***
Gender	−0.08	0.08	0.26***
Ethnicity	0.25	0.02	0.13
Occupational status	0.02	0.04**	0.02
Country of residence:			
Scotland	−0.90***	−0.70***	0.39**
Wales	−0.39	−0.08	0.56**
McFadden R^2		0.52	

*** $p \leq 0.001$, ** $p \leq 0.01$, * $p \leq 0.05$, + $p \leq 0.10$; one-tailed test.
Note: Labour voting is the reference category.

campaign measures predictably reduced that likelihood. Liberal Democrat or 'other party' campaign variables did not influence the probability of support the Conservatives.

The second column of Table 4.5 compares Liberal Democrat and Labour voting, and it can be seen that, not surprisingly, the Conservative campaign hardly influenced this contest. With the exception of Conservative partisanship which boosted the Liberal Democrat vote at the expense of Labour, the contest was very much between Labour and the Liberal Democrats. With respect to party best on most important issue, partisanship and leader images, positive scores for the Liberal Democrats boosted the Liberal Democrat vote at the expense of Labour and negative evaluations had the opposite effect. Negative reaction to the MPs' expenses scandal also helped to propel a Liberal Democrat rather than a Labour vote choice. Proximity to the Liberal Democrats on the tax–spend trade-off also was not influential.

Finally, the third column of Table 4.5 shows parameter estimates for 'other party' voting. Predictably, evaluating one of the other parties as best on an issue judged most important, identifying with one of these parties and having positive feelings about the leader all enhance the likelihood of voting for one of the minor parties. Campaign variables were also at work, with evaluations of minor parties' political broadcasts, direct contacts by these parties, and more general evaluations of their campaigns have the expected positive effects on the likelihood of voting for one of them. Reactions to the expenses scandal also were influential; other factors aside, reacting negatively to the scandal increased the probability of supporting a minor party.

A multilevel version of the multinomial model was estimated with the three leadership debate measures incorporated at the aggregate level. These variables were not influential, so the results differ from those of the Ground War in Table 4.2 where aggregate campaign spending variables influenced the vote directly. However, it would be premature to conclude that the debates had no influence on voting in 2010. These debates focused on the party leaders and put them squarely in the spotlight of national publicity. It is possible that the debates had an indirect impact which worked by affecting the images of the party leaders. We know from a wealth of previous research (e.g. Clarke *et al.*, 2004b, 2009b) that leader images play very important roles in explaining the vote, so this is a lively possibility. To assess it we need to step back in the 'funnel of causality' and examine the impact of the debates on party leader images. This is our next task.

The campaign and leader images

The effects of the debates on feelings about the party leaders are investigated using a multilevel regression model (see Table 4.6). Pre-campaign measures of feelings about the leaders are included as control variables in each of the models. The dependent variables in this analysis are the 0–10 affect scores for each of the party leaders measured during the campaign wave of the RCPS, so the specification captures the dynamics of these feelings as the campaign evolved. There are no effects associated with the outcome of the election itself since the dependent variables were measured before polling day. Each model incorporates the campaign measures discussed in the earlier analyses.

Table 4.6 *Multilevel regression models of the impact of campaign events on feelings about party leaders*

	Gordon Brown	David Cameron	Nick Clegg
Aggregate-level model			
First debate	−0.01	−0.14**	0.73***
Second debate	0.06	0.02	−0.15*
Third debate	−0.20***	0.02	−0.13*
'Bigoted woman' incident	0.02	−0.10	−0.11
R^2	0.35	0.31	0.84
Individual-level model			
Pre-campaign feelings about leader	0.81***	0.77***	0.59***
Newspaper readership:			
Labour	0.12**	−0.21***	−0.10*
Conservative	−0.08**	0.19***	−0.23***
Liberal Democrat	0.17***	−0.19***	0.10
Evaluations of parties' campaigns:			
Labour	0.32***	−0.20***	−0.10**
Conservative	−0.16***	0.39***	−0.20***
Liberal Democrat	−0.02	−0.09**	0.62***
Other parties	−0.04	−0.05	−0.29***
Evaluations of parties' political broadcasts:			
Labour	0.22***	−0.09***	0.01
Conservative	−0.04*	0.28***	−0.11***
Liberal Democrat	−0.06**	−0.05**	0.61***
Other parties	−0.02	−0.01	0.04*
Direct party contact:			
Labour	0.12***	−0.04	0.05
Conservatives	−0.02	0.12***	−0.17***
Liberal Democrats	0.00	−0.11***	0.08*
Age	−0.00	0.01***	−0.01***
Gender	−0.06**	−0.03	−0.16***
Ethnicity	−0.13*	0.09**	0.10**
Occupational status	−0.01	0.00	0.01
Country of residence:			
Scotland	0.14**	−0.17***	−0.08
Wales	0.03	−0.09*	−0.04
R^2	0.79	0.76	0.41

*** $p \leq 0.001$, ** $p \leq 0.01$, * $p \leq 0.05$, + $p \leq 0.10$; one-tailed test.

It is noteworthy that the newspaper readership measures influenced party leader images in a way which they did not in the earlier voting models. In Gordon Brown's case, reading the *Daily Mirror*, the *Guardian* and the *Independent*, all had a positive impact and reading newspapers endorsing the Conservatives had the predicted negative effect. The *Guardian* had endorsed Labour in many previous elections despite the fact that it supported the Liberal Democrats in 2010 so this effect is not surprising. In addition to the effect of newspapers, positive evaluations of Labour's campaign and party broadcasts increased positive feelings about Brown, whereas positive evaluations of the Conservative campaign and Conservative broadcasts had negative effects. In addition, direct contact by Labour appeared to have a positive impact on feelings about their party leader, although contact by the other parties had no effect.

Cameron and Clegg's models show similar patterns to those just described. The newspaper readership variables all have the expected effects and, with one exception, all are statistically significant. Similarly, with few exceptions, evaluations of the party campaigns and the party political broadcasts are influential. Clearly, the campaign effects are more extensive than they were in the voting models and they have a variety of expected effects on the leaders' images. These results demonstrate that campaign effects had significant indirect influences on voting, operating via party leader images which are major predictors of electoral choice.

Turning next to aggregate effects, again there are interesting findings. First, it appears that Gordon Brown was not permanently weakened by the first debate – recall that he was already quite unpopular, although his popularity was further undermined at the time of the third debate. A control variable for the 'bigoted woman' incident is included in the specification since this occurred just before the third debate and could have inflated the effects. However, it appears not to have had an independent influence on Brown's popularity. As for David Cameron, parameter estimates confirm that he was harmed by his lacklustre performance in the first debate, in contrast to Nick Clegg who enjoyed a large boost as a result of his widely praised performance. However, Clegg's image was eroded by each of the two subsequent debates, although the parameter estimates for the three debates (+0.73, −0.15 and −0.13, respectively) indicate that a sizable portion of the effect of the first debate carried through until polling day. Clearly, the debates did have an influence on voting, but their effects were largely indirect, as they worked to shape voters' images of Messrs Brown, Cameron and Clegg.

Conclusion: campaigning and electoral choice in 2010

The Air War and the Ground War were both influential in the 2010 British general election campaign. When all of the important baseline influences are incorporated into models of turnout and party choice, significant campaign effects remain. These effects operated on the voters via direct contact between them and party activists, through the influence of party political broadcasts and, more generally, by voters' evaluations of the effectiveness of the parties' campaigns. But they also worked indirectly by shaping public perceptions of the party leaders. Neither newspaper readership nor the leadership debates appeared to influence voting directly, but both had important indirect influences by helping to mould the leaders' images. Leader images are a key transmission mechanism linking campaigns with voting, something which is not surprising in the modern era when national campaigns personalize politics around the leaders. The advent of nationally televised debates provides the leaders and their strategists with an important new venue for producing consequential campaign effects.

The evidence presented in this chapter also indicates that direct contact by party activists is very important for influencing the vote. The key problem is that party activism is dying out as fewer and fewer people join and become involved in political party organizations. This is a problem for most mature democracies, not just for Britain (Whiteley, 2012). In the long run, the demise of party activism is likely to weaken local election campaigns, if only because direct contact with activists appears to be such an important factor. Whether new forms of party contacting via electronic social media such as texting, Facebook and Twitter will take up the slack remains to be seen. To date, they have not done so.

In 2010, British parties, large and small, continued to rely on familiar low-tech ways of conveying their messages. The one major campaign innovation, the nationally televised party leader debates, was hardly 'leading edge'. By contemporary standards, television is an ancient communications technology and leader debates were pioneered over a half century earlier in the fabled Kennedy–Nixon encounters in the 1960 US presidential election. At long last, leader debates have come to British general election campaigns and their potential to influence the dynamics of public support for parties and their leaders is apparent.

5 | *Making political choices*
2010

Understanding party choice is a central concern for students of voting and elections. In previous chapters of this book and in earlier studies (Clarke *et al.*, 2004b; 2009b) we have estimated various models of voting with the aim of determining which one provides the best account of the electoral choices people make. These statistical comparisons favour a composite model since no single theoretical account captures all of the factors which influence party choice. However, it bears emphasis that the valence model exhibits the strongest explanatory power. The valence politics model proved itself in the 2001 and 2005 general elections in Britain as the best single model for explaining why people vote as they do (Clarke *et al.*, 2004b, 2009b). The valence model also consistently performs very well in analyses of voting in national elections in Canada and the United States (Clarke *et al.*, 2009a; Clarke *et al.*, 2012) and there is evidence to suggest that it works well in other mature and emerging democracies (Clarke and Whitten, 2013; Ho *et al.*, 2013; Lewis-Beck *et al.*, 2012). In all these cases, statistical analyses indicate that the valence model dominates rival models of voting behaviour, although it does not formally encompass them in the sense of completely accounting for competitors' contributions to explaining why individuals vote as they do (Charemza and Deadman, 1997). As a result, a composite specification generally provides marginally greater explanatory purchase than a pure valence model.

One important question that remains largely unanswered is the extent to which competing models provide a stable explanation of party choice over time. For example, if key predictor variables in the valence politics model are more important in one election rather than another, then explanations of voting for parties are incomplete and additional theory is needed to account for the instability of the effects. In contrast, if various models are very stable when applied to different elections in various countries at different points in time then little in the way of extra theorizing is needed. On the face of it we might

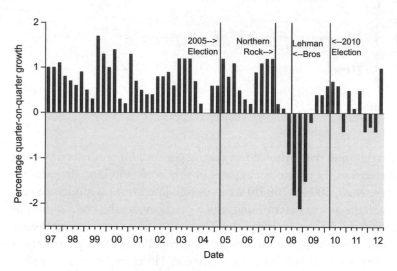

Figure 5.1 Growth in UK GDP, second quarter 1997–third quarter 2012.
Source: Office of National Statistics.

expect the model to perform differently in different contexts, since the
settings in which elections take place can differ markedly. As an obvious example, the 2005 British general election took place in a period
of prosperity in which the economy had been growing, sometimes
quite strongly, for more than a decade (see Figure 5.1). In sharp contrast, the 2010 general election was held in the midst of a protracted
financial crisis that produced the deepest economic downturn since the
1970s and the most serious recession since the Great Depression of
the 1930s. Given these widely different contexts, we might expect the
components of the various models would play different roles depending on the changed circumstances. Accordingly, one of the goals of this
chapter is to investigate the stability of models over time.

The chapter begins with a brief review of the three key rival models of party choice which contribute to the composite model. This
discussion is followed by a section in which this composite model is
estimated using the 2010 BES rolling campaign internet panel (RCPS)
data. This updates the discussion in Chapter 2 and expands the analyses in Chapter 4 where the focus was on campaign effects. In the
third section we introduce a strategy for investigating the temporal
stability of effects in the composite model. The aim is to examine the
extent to which the effects of various predictor variables change over

time and, if so, whether such changes occur in response to predictable contextual influences. This analysis is performed using data from the 2004–10 BES monthly Continuous Monitoring Surveys. These data, gathered each month over a six-year period, enable us to determine how the effects of predictor variables in the voting models changed as the economic environment in Britain went from boom to bust.

Rival models revisited

The composite model advanced in this and other studies is based on three rival theoretical accounts of party choice. These are the valence, spatial and sociological models. Based on pathbreaking work by Stokes (1963; see also Stokes, 1992), the valence model maintains that voters choose the party which they perceive will deliver the best outcome on issues they care about and about which there is a broad consensus about what the goals of public policy should be (Clarke *et al.*, 2004b, 2009b; Clarke *et al.*, 2009a). In contrast, inspired by Downs's (1957) classic study, the spatial model proposes that voters choose the party with which they are in closest agreement concerning positional issues which divide the electorate (see e.g. Adams *et al.*, 2005; Merrill and Grofman, 1999). Examples of prominent position issues in contemporary British politics include the optimal balance between taxation and spending on public services, the extent to which attention should focus on crime prevention versus the rights of the accused and the desirability of Britain's continued membership in the European Union. Finally, the sociological model contends that party choice reflects voters' sociodemographic characteristics. In the British case, analysts long were united in designating social class as the dominant politically relevant social cleavage (e.g. Butler and Stokes, 1969). Although the erosion of the correlation between class and voting was observed as early as the mid-1970s (Sarlvik and Crewe, 1983), prominent political sociologists continued to insist on the centrality of the class cleavage for understanding voting behaviour and the outcome of British elections (e.g. Heath *et al.*, 1985, 1991).

The classic valence issue is the economy both because it is very salient for most people and because there is an overwhelming consensus that prosperity is preferred to poverty – growth is preferred to stagnation, employment to joblessness and sound money to rising prices. The vast majority of voters will support a party which can deliver 'good times'

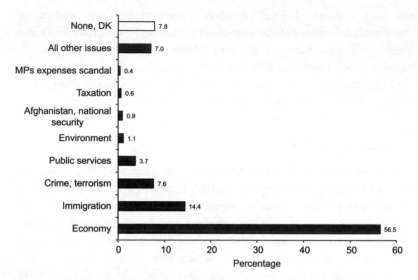

Figure 5.2 Most important issue at the beginning of 2010 election campaign. *Source:* 2010 RCPS pre-campaign survey.

and oppose one which appears unable to do so. However, the valence model is not just about the economy, since the ability to provide a panoply of public services is also an important factor in most people's evaluations of party performance. If a party can deliver low crime rates, high-quality education, effective health care and efficient transport, this will contribute to its electoral success.

As noted, the valence politics model contends that the issues such as the economy, about which there is a broad consensus about the desired ends of public policy, typically dominate the issue agenda in national elections. This was certainly true in 2010. As Figure 5.2 illustrates, on the eve of the campaign kick-off, nearly three respondents in five (56.5 per cent) in the pre-campaign wave of the BES RCPS survey designated the economy generally or some aspect of it such as unemployment as the most important issue. The next most widely cited issue, immigration, was mentioned by less than one vote in six (14.4 per cent). In the British context, where there is widespread agreement that immigration should be curtailed, immigration too is a valence issue. The third most widely cited issues, crime and terrorism, mentioned by 7.6 per cent, are also valence issues. The dominance of these issues in the minds of voters in 2010 means that their judgments about the party best able to handle them very largely involve evaluations of party performance on valence issues.

In the 2010 RCPS pre-campaign survey, only one respondent in five (20 per cent) judged that Labour could do the best job on these issues. Slightly over one in four (26 per cent) favoured the Conservatives, less than one in ten (9 per cent) chose the Liberal Democrats and another 9 per cent opted for one of the minor parties. Most striking, more than one person in three (36 per cent) said that no party could handle important issues, or that they 'didn't know' which party could do the best job. As the campaign began, valence issues dominated as they normally do in British general elections, but none of the parties had the confidence of electorate regarding its ability to address them. The vast majority of voters did not believe that Labour could do the job, but none of the opposition parties had taken its place.

The valence politics model also explicitly maintains that voters are endowed with agency, but not omniscience. In a sense, voters are 'smart enough to know that they are not smart enough' to make decisions according to the strictures of rational choice theories of political decision making. Rather, consonant with research in experimental economics and political psychology (e.g. Gigerenzer, 2008; Gigerenzer *et al.*, 2011; Lupia and McCubbins, 1998; Lupia *et al.*, 2000; Sniderman *et al.*, 1991) voters rely heavily on cues provided by party leader images and partisan labels. Leader images and partisan attachments constitute easily accessible, cost-effective heuristics for voters confronted with a need to make consequential decisions in a political world where it is frequently difficult to discern the optimal course of action.

Leader images are amalgams of traits such as trustworthiness, competence and perceived responsiveness to voters' interests. Previous research (Stewart and Clarke, 1998; Clarke *et al.*, 2009b) shows that these traits can be effectively indexed by a summary leader affect scale which measures voters' feelings of 'like' and 'dislike' about competing leaders. Leader images are an important heuristic which voters use to judge the ability of parties to deliver desired policy outcomes. People do not need to know about the intricacies of fiscal and monetary policies a party is likely to pursue if they rely on judgments about that party's leader. If a leader appears to be a 'safe pair of hands' who can do the job, then it is reasonable to trust the leader to handle economic and sundry other problems. Such evaluations are particularly useful when contemplating voting for parties which lack a track record in office. In such cases judgments about party competence in managing the economy necessarily are very uncertain. Evaluations of their leaders provide a concrete, readily available, alternative. If people respond favourably to a party's leader, they will feel comfortable in supporting that party without engaging in the difficult task of trying to discern what the party would try to do, or how it would perform, in office.

The third component of the valence politics model is partisanship which can conceptualized as a summary 'running tally' of the performance of parties and their leaders. This interpretation of partisanship, based on pioneering work by Fiorina (1981), differs from the original social-psychological notion of party identification developed at the University of Michigan in the 1950s (Campbell *et al.*, 1954; Campbell *et al.*, 1960; Miller and Shanks, 1996; see also Green *et al.*, 2002). According to the Michigan social psychologists and their intellectual heirs, partisanship is a durable psychological trait typically acquired in childhood or adolescence as a result of primary-group socialization by family, friends and neighbours (Jennings and Niemi, 1974). Except in times of major socioeconomic and political upheavals, partisan attachments are highly inertial. The normal trajectory is for partisanship to strengthen in intensity over the life-cycle as a result of behavioural reinforcement processes – party identifiers become more strongly attached to their party as a result of voting for it in successive elections.

Although the dynamics (or lack thereof) of aggregate- and individual-level partisanship have been subjects of extended debate, abundant evidence now supports the proposition that partisanship is potentially mutable and subject to change according to economic and political circumstances (e.g. Clarke *et al.*, 2004b; Clarke and McCutcheon, 2009; Neundorf *et al.*, 2011). There are many durable partisans in the British electorate, but there are also many others whose partisan attachments are flexible and may shift in response to the perceived performance of political parties and their leaders. If an incumbent party fails to deliver policies voters demand, attachments to that party will weaken and some people will abandon it for one of its rivals. Equally, if a party is successful in delivering on important policies, its cohort of partisans will increase. In the world of valence politics, partisan change is an ongoing, politically consequential possibility for a sizable segment of the electorate.

The valence model can be compared with its main rival, the spatial model of party competition, which originates in theoretical work by

Duncan Black (1958) and Anthony Downs (1957). As mentioned ear-lier, the trade-off between taxation and public spending is a quintessen-tial example of a spatial issue. Some voters prefer low taxes even if this means cuts in public services, whereas others prefer higher taxes to gen-erate the revenues needed for generous funding of such services. Spatial theory predicts that individuals with these competing preferences will support parties which come closest to promising the objectives they prefer. According to spatial theory, the calculus of voting is based on people's perceptions of their proximity to competing parties on such divisive issues. Consonant with the strictures of neoclassical microeco-nomic theory, voters' preferences (their 'ideal points') are exogenously determined and parties are rational actors which manoeuvre strategi-cally in a possibly multidimensional issue space to maximize electoral support.

As observed above, statistical analyses have documented that the valence model consistently dominates its spatial rival in analyses of party choice in Britain and elsewhere. This is because voters find valence considerations more reliable and easier to use than attempts to make accurate spatial calculations. Valence factors are easier to use because they require much less information processing; a voter only has to judge if a party or a leader has delivered, or is (un)likely to deliver on policies that matter. According to the spatial model voters must know their own policy preferences regarding various position issues and also the positions of competing parties on those issues. In addition, in some versions of spatial theory, voters are required to discount party promises since parties have an incentive to dissemble about what their positions are and to inflate claims about policy-delivery capacity (see e.g. Adams *et al.*, 2005). Since the valence politics model only requires voters to focus on demonstrated performance and make use of readily available leader image and partisan cues, it is not surprising that it dominates spatial models in empirical analyses of voting behaviour.

Although the valence model is statistically superior to its rivals, spatial considerations remain relevant since there are issues over which the electorate is divided and parties advocate very different policy objectives. In this regard, the past is not always a good guide to the future and voters may be influenced by what parties say they will do on these contentious issues, should they gain power. In addition, voters' proximities to parties on spatial issues can reflect basic values central to voters' belief systems (Sanders *et al.*, 2011a). Given these considerations, it is not surprising that spatial calculations help to explain electoral choice.

The valence and spatial models both dominate the sociological model, which is the third type of model we consider. As observed above, sociological accounts of voting behaviour in Britain traditionally have accorded pride of place to social class. In the canonical study in this genre, Butler and Stokes (1969) explained party choice in terms of a simple causal chain in which class location drives partisanship which, in turn, largely determines voting in successive general elections. For Butler and Stokes, the Michigan version of partisanship was the central psychological variable linking social locations with political behaviour. In their model, middle-class voters largely identify with and vote for the Conservatives and working-class voters largely identify with and vote for Labour. In the dominant two-party system of the 1960s, Butler and Stokes felt no need to explain support for other parties such as the Liberals. The Liberals and other minor parties were vestiges of a pre-industrial age and their support, already much diminished, was destined to fade away as post-Second World War Britain completed its transition to modernity.

Subsequent work has shown that at least since the British election studies began in the mid-1960s, social class and other measures of socioeconomic status have played a considerably smaller role in explaining voting behaviour in Britain than advocates of the sociological model would allow (Clarke *et al.*, 2004b). Currently, these effects are very modest. Nevertheless, since these variables do contribute to explaining party choice, we include them in our composite model.

Party choice in 2010

Table 5.1 summarizes the performance of valence, spatial and sociological models of voting in the 2010 general election. Panel A of the table shows the results of binomial logit analyses that pit Labour voting against voting for any of the opposition parties, and panel B shows the results of multinomial logit models of Conservative, Liberal Democrat and 'other party' voting, with Labour voting treated as the reference category. The valence model has three components: party judged best on most important issue, party leader images and partisanship. The spatial model contains variables measuring perceived issue–party proximities for the tax–spend and prevent crime versus

Table 5.1 *Performance of rival models of party choice in the 2010 election*

Model	McFadden R^2	McKelvey R^2	Per cent correct	AIC[†]
A. *Labour v. all other parties – binomial logit model*				
1. Sociodemographics	0.06	0.10	71.5	12 643.28
2. Spatial	0.18	0.36	75.3	10 955.00
3a. Most important issue	0.35	0.49	84.3	8741.05
3b. Party identification	0.38	0.53	85.0	8273.72
3c. Party leaders	0.40	0.59	83.4	8102.55
4. Valence politics[‡]	0.52	0.67	87.7	6563.25
5. Composite	0.55	0.71	88.8	6103.65
B. *Opposition parties with Labour as reference category – multinomial logit model*				
1. Sociodemographics	0.07	–	37.8	27 543.57
2. Spatial	0.21	–	55.7	23 111.95
3a. Most important issue	0.34	–	65.9	19 514.85
3b. Party identification	0.36	–	69.5	18 752.52
3c. Party leaders	0.39	–	68.9	17 978.44
4. Valence politics[‡]	0.51	–	75.9	14 494.36
5. Composite	0.55	–	78.3	13 393.90

[†] Akaike Information Criterion; smaller values indicate better model performance.
[‡] valence politics model includes party best on most important issue, party leader images and party identification.
– not defined for multinomial logit model.

protect rights of accused persons scales. Since proposals in the Liberal Democrat's manifesto became issues during the 2010 campaign, reactions to these proposals are included in the spatial model as well. The sociodemographic model includes several variables: age, education, gender income, private- versus public-sector employment, social class, trade union membership and region/country.

As expected given previous research, the valence model outperforms it spatial and sociological competitors as measured by several criteria. For example, for the analysis of Labour versus voting for any other parties (Table 5.1, Panel A), the McFadden R^2 for the valence model is 0.52, whereas the McFadden R^2's for the spatial and sociological models are 0.18 and 0.06. The equivalent McKelvey R^2's are 0.67, 0.36 and

0.10, respectively. In terms of ability to classify voters correctly, the valence model is again ranks first, correctly classifying 87.7 per cent as compared to 75.3 per cent for the spatial model and 71.5 per cent for the sociological model. The valence model also is superior when assessed in terms of the AIC model selection criterion[1] (Burnham and Anderson, 2002). Its AIC value is considerably smaller (better) than those for its spatial and sociological rivals. All of these findings are replicated in the analysis of voting for various opposition parties with Labour as the reference category (Table 5.1, Panel B).

This is not to say that the valence model renders its rivals irrelevant. Rather, and replicating findings from earlier research, Panels A and B of Table 5.1 show that a composite model that contains the predictor variables from the valence, spatial and sociological models performs better than the pure valence model. The composite model has larger McFadden and McKelvey R^2's, a higher percentage of correctly classified voters and a smaller AIC than the valence model. However, these differences are small – the statistical power of the valence politics model for explaining voting in 2010 is almost as great as the conceptually and operationally more complex composite model.

Parameter estimates for the composite party choice model are presented in Table 5.2. This model is designed to replicate the features of the 2005 party choice model discussed in Chapter 5 of *Performance Politics and the British Voter* (Clarke *et al.*, 2009b). The 2005 and 2010 models are not exactly the same, principally because context-specific factors vary across time. Thus, the 2010 model takes into account the MPs' expenses scandal which rocked Parliament in 2009 but which was not on the political agenda in 2005. Similarly, the 2005 model incorporates public attitudes towards the Iraq War, whereas the 2010 model incorporates attitudes to the Afghanistan War in which British troops were engaged when the election took place.

The 2010 model also includes two context-specific variables measuring public reactions to policy proposals in the Liberal Democrats' manifesto. After Nick Clegg's very strong showing in the first leaders' debate and his party's subsequent surge in the polls, the Conservatives and Labour counter-attacked by criticizing Liberal Democrat policies. Public opinion about six of these policy proposals was measured in the post-election wave of the BES RCPS. The data show that, although large majorities of voters agreed with two of the proposals (exempting the first £10 000 of earnings from income tax and charging a

Table 5.2 *Composite model of party choice in the 2010 election*

	Panel A		Panel B
	Labour	Conservative	Liberal Democrat
Predictor variables	β	β	β
Leader images:			
Brown	0.29***	−0.35***	−0.26***
Cameron	−0.13***	0.51***	0.06***
Clegg	−0.15***	−0.06**	0.28***
Partisanship:			
Labour	1.24***	−1.47***	−1.13***
Conservative	−1.32***	1.43***	0.25
Liberal Democrat	−0.92***	0.26	1.06***
Other party	−0.73***	−0.06	−0.16
Party best most important issue:			
Labour	0.64***	−1.01***	−0.59***
Conservative	−0.97***	0.93***	0.14
Liberal Democrat	−0.73***	0.03	0.75***
Other party	−0.36**	0.05	−0.28*
Issue–party proximities:			
Labour	0.11***	−0.15***	−0.10***
Conservative	−0.04***	0.10***	0.03**
Liberal Democrat	−0.04**	0.00	0.07***
Policies:			
Economic	−0.15***	−0.17**	0.28***
Political	−0.15***	−0.16***	0.30***
Economic evaluations	0.08**	−0.10*	−0.07*
Economic emotions	−0.03	−0.02	0.06
Afghanistan War	0.05*	−0.02	−0.06*
MPs expenses scandal	−0.04	0.03	0.02
Tactical voting	−1.04***	0.63***	1.35***
Age:			
18–25	0.29	−0.31	−0.09
26–35	0.29*	−0.32	−0.08
36–45	0.43***	−0.63***	−0.28
46–55	0.18	−0.43**	−0.04
56–65	0.08	−0.26	−0.07
Education	−0.10***	0.02	0.15***
Gender	−0.15*	−0.15	0.17*
Income	−0.02*	0.05***	0.01

(*cont.*)

Table 5.2 (cont.)

	Panel A		Panel B
	Labour	Conservative	Liberal Democrat
Predictor variables	β	β	β
Private/public sector	−0.12*	0.19*	0.07
Social class	−0.03	−0.03	0.12
Union Membership	0.19*	−0.38***	−0.20*
Region:			
South East	−0.57***	0.67***	0.53***
South West	−0.78***	0.41	0.91***
Midlands	0.10	0.11	−0.20
North	0.35***	−0.45**	−0.25*
Scotland	0.13	−0.73***	−0.50***
Wales	0.00	−0.50*	−0.06
McFadden R^2	55	0.55	
McKelvey R^2	0.71	†	
Per cent correctly classified	88.8	78.3	
Log likelihood	−3011.82	−6536.95	
AIC	6103.65	13393.90	
N	11389	11389	

Note: Labour analysis is a binomial logit (Labour v. all other party voting); Conservative and Liberal Democrat analysis is a multinomial logit with Labour as the reference category. Other party voting is included in the multinomial logit analysis but coefficients are not displayed in table.

*** $p \leq 0.001$; ** $p \leq 0.01$; * $p \leq 0.05$, one-tailed tests for all variables except age, gender and region.

† Not defined for multinomial logit model.

'mansion tax' on properties worth over £2 million), there was considerable division regarding the other four (see Figure 5.3). Clearly, Liberal Democrat policy proposals were acting as position, not valence, issues and attitudes towards them can be treated as contextually relevant components of a spatial model of electoral choice for voting in 2010. Finally, we include a measure of private- versus public-sector employment to capture reactions of people in these two occupational groups to Conservative proposals to downsize the public sector as a means of reducing Britain's rising debt burden.

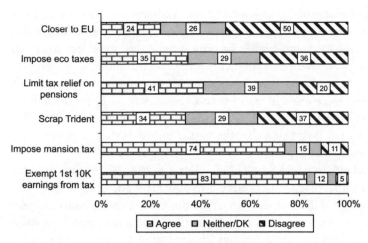

Figure 5.3 Attitudes towards Liberal Democrat policy proposals.
Source: Post-election wave, 2010 RCPS survey.

Table 5.2, Panel A presents the composite model of Labour versus other party voting. Partisanship, leader images and party best at handling issues deemed most important are highly significant predictors. If a respondent perceives that the Conservatives, Liberal Democrats or a minor party are best at handling a most important issue this reduces the probability of voting Labour. In addition, images of Gordon Brown, David Cameron and Nick Clegg all have significant effects on the probability of casting a Labour ballot. As expected, a positive image of Brown enhances the probability of voting Labour, whereas positive images of Cameron and Clegg diminish it. In addition, economic evaluations, but not emotional reactions to the economy, have significant positive effects on voting for the party. Partisanship operates as expected as well, with Labour partisanship enhancing the likelihood of a Labour vote and identification with any of the other parties reducing it.

Spatial variables are relevant too. Support for Labour is strongest among voters who perceive that they are close to Labour on the tax–spend and crime-rights trade-offs. As also anticipated, greater distances from the Conservatives or the Liberal Democrats on these issues increase the probability of casting a Labour ballot. Reactions to Liberal Democrat policy proposals are at work too, with favourable opinions of the proposals reducing the likelihood of voting Labour. In addition, favourable perceptions of the Afghanistan War boosted the probability of supporting the party. As for sociodemographics, men, the well-educated and higher income individuals were less likely to vote Labour, as were private-sector workers and middle-class people. Trade union members, middle-aged people and residents of the North of England were more likely to vote Labour, whereas people residing in the South East or South West were less likely to do so. Finally, controlling for everything else, the model indicates that tactical voting hurt Labour in 2010.

Coefficients in Panel B of Table 5.2 are multinomial logit estimates of factors affecting Conservative and Liberal Democrat voting with Labour as the reference category.[2] In the Conservative analysis, perceptions that the party was best at handling the most important issue helped it, as did positive feelings about David Cameron, Conservative partisanship and proximity to the party on tax–spend and crime–rights spatial issues. Persons favouring Liberal Democrat policy proposals also were less likely to vote Conservative. Similarly, positive feelings about Gordon Brown and Nick Clegg, Labour partisanship and proximity to Labour on issues considered important by the voters reduced Conservative support as did positive evaluations of the economy. Sociodemographics were relevant; the Conservatives were less likely to receive support from trade union members, persons in the 46–55 and 56–65 age brackets, and those living in the North and Scotland. Residents of the South East and private-sector workers were more likely to vote Conservative. Finally, tactical voting helped the Conservatives vis à vis Labour.

The Liberal Democrat analysis in Table 5.2 yields rather similar results to those for the Conservatives. Perceptions that Labour was best at handling the most important issue reduced Liberal Democrat support, as did positive evaluations of the economy. Positive feelings about Gordon Brown decreased Liberal Democrat support whereas positive feelings about Nick Clegg increased it. In addition, a positive image of David Cameron had a positive impact on voting Liberal Democrat (rather than Labour). Regarding partisanship, identifying with the Liberal Democrats predictably raised the probability of a Liberal Democrat vote, whereas identifying with Labour reduced it. Spatial variables were relevant with proximity to the Liberal Democrats and the Conservatives on the tax–spend and crime–rights trade-offs increasing the likelihood of voting Liberal Democrat and proximity to

Labour reducing it. And, predictably, those favouring Liberal Democrat policy proposals also were more likely to vote for the party. Some sociodemographics were not influential, but middle-class individuals, men and well-educated persons all were more likely to vote Liberal Democrat as were people living in the South East or South West. Those living in the North or Scotland were less likely to do so. Tactical voting was at work too – like the Conservatives, the Liberal Democrats benefited as the expense of Labour.

Since the coefficients in Table 5.2 were produced by logit analyses which have a nonlinear functional form, it is difficult to discern the magnitude of effects associated with various predictor variables (e.g. Long and Freese, 2006). To provide intuition about the size of these effects, we construct scenarios in which significant predictors are varied from their minimum to their maximum values while holding all other predictors constant at their means (in the case of continuous variables) or at zero (in the case of dummy variables). The results, presented in Figures 5.4, 5.5 and 5.6, confirm the substantive significance of variables in the valence politics model. In the Labour, Conservative and Liberal Democrat analyses, party leader images have the largest effects. Varying Gordon Brown's image from its lowest to its highest value in the Labour model increases the probability of voting Labour by $\Delta p = 0.49$ points (Figure 5.4). The comparable increases in the Conservative and Liberal Democrat models are fully 0.81 points for David Cameron in the former, and 0.46 for Nick Clegg in the latter (Figures 5.5 and 5.6).

Other variables in the valence model are powerful as well. For example, in the Labour model, shifting from being a Conservative identifier to being a Labour identifier raises the probability of voting Labour 0.43 $(0.23 + 0.20)$ points. Similar increases can be seen in the Conservative model where a shift from Labour to Conservative partisanship raises the probability of a Tory vote by 0.46 $(0.29 + 0.17)$ points (Figure 5.5). In the Liberal Democrat model, moving from being a Labour identifier to being a Liberal Democrat identifier enhances the likelihood of voting Lib Democrat by 0.26 $(0.19 + 0.07)$ points (Figure 5.6). Judgments about party performance also matter. For example, in the Labour analysis, changing from believing the Conservatives perform best to believing Labour performs best raises the probability of voting for the latter party by 0.27 $(0.12 + 0.15)$ points. Similar increases are evident in the Conservative and Liberal Democrat analyses as well.

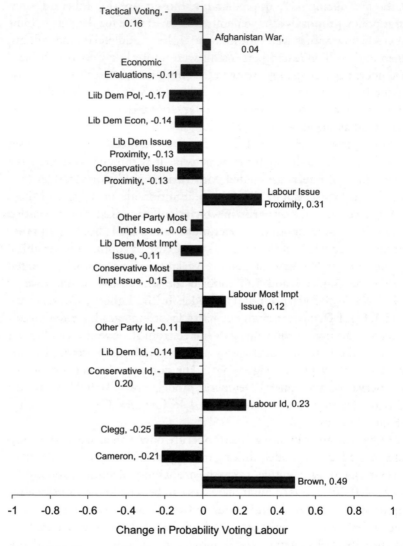

Figure 5.4 Effects of significant predictors on probability of voting Labour, 2010.

The numbers displayed in Figures 5.4, 5.5 and 5.6 also testify that spatial variables have sizable effects. In the Labour model, changes in proximities to the party can enhance the likelihood of a Labour vote by $\Delta p = 0.31$ points, with the comparable increases in the Conservative and Liberal Democrat models being 0.30 and 0.17 points respectively.

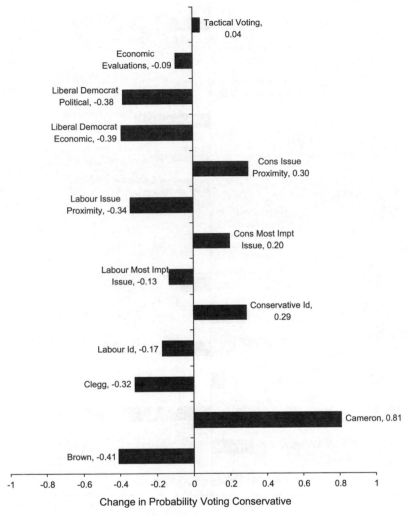

Figure 5.5 Effects of significant predictors on probability of voting Conservative, 2010.

Positions on Liberal Democrat policies debated during the 2010 campaign mattered as well. The effects were particularly noticeable in the Liberal Democrat and Conservative analyses. In the former case, moving from very negative to very positive positions on these issues raises the likelihood of voting Liberal Democrat by 0.39 and 0.28 points. Comparable decreases in the likelihood of voting Conservative are

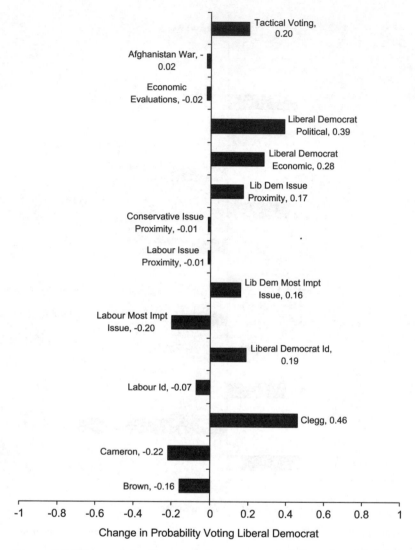

Figure 5.6 Effects of significant predictors on probability of voting Liberal Democrat, 2010.

0.38 and 0.39 points. Effects of these variables on the probability of voting Labour were smaller – 0.17 and 0.14 points, respectively.

Finally, tactical voting had nontrivial effects. If a voter was thinking tactically, this was sufficient to raise the probability of voting Liberal Democrat by $\Delta p = 0.20$ points and to reduce the probability of voting Labour by 0.16 points. Conservative voting, in contrast, was not strongly affected by tactical considerations in 2010. The change in the likelihood of opting for the Conservatives prompted by tactical calculations is only 0.04 points.

Overall, the results of the analysis of party support in the 2010 election resemble those for earlier British elections (Clarke, 2004b, 2009b). However, these results do not tell us if the strength of various predictors has changed systematically over time. In the next section, we incorporate contextual variables into the analysis of party support and estimate how predictor variables in a composite party choice model behave in response to systematic changes in these variables over time.

Context and party choice

The effects of varying contexts on electoral choice can be investigated using a multilevel model specification and data gathered in the BES Continuous Monitoring Survey (CMS). Recall that the CMS consists of successive cross-sectional surveys of approximately 1000 cases conducted on a monthly basis beginning April 2004. Through August 2012 the cumulative CMS database contains nearly 120 000 cases[3] and the series encompasses a lengthy period of economic prosperity followed by the financial crisis and subsequent recession. Thus, there is ample variation in the economic context within which the monthly surveys were gathered. The strategy adopted here is to estimate a multi-level party choice model using the monthly CMS surveys and examine if key coefficients change in predictable ways over time. This is done by incorporating aggregate-level time series measures into the individual-level model.

There are trends in British politics which provide guidance as to what might emerge from a dynamic multilevel model of this type. Considering partisanship, weakening partisan attachments long has been a feature of British electoral politics (e.g. Sarlvik and Crewe, 1983). Data from successive election studies show that partisanship weakened more or less continuously since it was first measured in the British Election Study of 1964 through to the early years of this century (Clarke *et al.*, 2004b; 2009b). This trend suggests that partisanship may also have declined in importance as a determinant of electoral choice. This will be evident in the individual-level voting model if the coefficients for the partisanship variables decrease in magnitude over time. Partisanship still continues to be a significant predictor of voting, but a reduction in the magnitude of these coefficients would suggest that it is somewhat less important now than in the past.

Despite the decline in partisanship being well documented, the mechanism which explains this is not well understood. The debate which occurred in the 1970s and 1980s about partisan dealignment concerned the extent to which it was a product of changes in occupational structure of British society or due to other factors (Crewe, 1986; Heath *et al.*, 1985, 1987; Sarlvik and Crewe, 1983). Regarding occupational structure, the argument is that as middle-class professional occupations grow in number and working-class occupations decline, the traditional Michigan model of partisanship predicts a decline in Labour support concomitant with a growth in Conservative support. This seemed plausible during the years of Conservative electoral hegemony that followed Mrs Thatcher's first election victory in May 1979.

However, the Michigan model of partisanship also implies that working-class support for Labour will continue relatively unchanged within that shrinking occupational group, so that class loyalties to the party would persist. A similar point can be made about middle-class support for the Conservatives. In this view Labour would retain its support amongst the working class, subject perhaps to some slow generational changes, but nonetheless lose ground overall because its class base is shrinking in size. Similarly, the Conservatives would retain their support among the middle class but gain ground because that class is growing in size. The implication is that class effects measured by the impact of occupational status on voting behaviour should remain strong and largely unchanged over time.

The alternative view, consistent with a dynamic version of partisanship, is that changes in the occupational structure tend to play a minor role in explaining changes in partisanship. If partisan support varies over time in line with the running-tally interpretation, then people in the working class will be quite capable of deserting Labour and middle-class persons will abandon the Conservatives if these parties are unsuccessful in delivering policy outcomes that their supporters care about. Equally, partisan support for Labour should increase both within the middle class and the working class if the party succeeds in delivering on key valence issues, something that New Labour did by presiding a growing economy during a decade-long expansion between

1997 and 2007. This suggests that there is a valence explanation of partisan dealignment, namely that in the long run neither major party has been seen to deliver on the issues which matter most for many voters.

However, this valence interpretation does not necessarily imply a uniform decline in partisanship. At a time of severe economic recession the incumbent party is likely to lose support, but an opposition party will gain it if the voters believe it has a credible alternative economic strategy and is competent to accomplish it. On the other hand, if voters do not believe that any of the major parties can deliver the prosperity and quality of public services that they expect, then all these parties will lose in the long run. This analysis implies that significant changes should occur in the coefficients for the partisanship variables in the party choice models over time, and these should reflect the parties' perceived success or failure in delivering preferred policy outcomes.

The decline of partisanship has implications for the other variables in the valence model, namely, leadership images and party performance judgments. If partisanship is weakening, then leader images and party performance evaluations on valence issues might well grow in importance. Regarding leadership, there is a long-standing debate about the increasing 'presidentialization' of British politics. The argument is that incumbent prime ministers are becoming more and more important in exercising power over parliament and the executive, and their role in election campaigns has become increasingly significant. This idea was introduced by Richard Crossman (1963) in his introduction to a new edition of Walter Bagehot's classic study *The English Constitution*, and it has been subject to considerable debate ever since (e.g. Clarke *et al.*, 1998, 2000; King, 2002). Analyses presented in Chapter 4 documented how the leaders' debates dominated the 2010 election campaign. More generally, it is evident that prime ministers such as Margaret Thatcher and Tony Blair commanded the political stage during their lengthy tenures in office, and that coverage of prime ministers and leaders of opposition parties has been vastly expanded by the growth of television and 24/7 electronic journalism. All of these factors suggest that leadership effects on voting may well have strengthened over time. If the conjecture is true then we might expect to see coefficients for the leadership variables in party choice models become larger over time.

Regarding valence issues, if voters are now less likely to use partisan cues then they may be more willing to use valence issue cues, ensuring that the latter grow more important. If the running-tally interpretation of partisanship is correct, a weakening of partisanship constitutes a weakening of the effects of 'historical' valence issues on contemporary party choice. As contemporary valence issues grow in importance and historical ones decline, electoral choice is likely to become more volatile as the role of inertia in voters' decisions weakens. In most instances inertia or past history should play an important role in a voter's overall party evaluations, but if there is an abrupt change in the economic climate such as that signalled by the run on the Northern Rock bank in 2007, history becomes a less reliable guide to performance. Accordingly, we should expect the role of contemporary evaluations of party performance to increase in strength after the economic crisis began in late 2007.

Modelling context and party choice

There is a set of questions in the BES Continuous Monitoring Survey asking respondents how likely it is that they would *ever* vote for various political parties, where a score of zero means that they are 'very unlikely' to vote for a particular party and a score of ten means that they are 'very likely' to do so. These measures can be used to model party choice over time in the absence of a reported vote variable such as the one used in the party choice models discussed above. Over the eight-year period covered by the CMS data, the mean scores for the parties on these scales were 4.6 for the Conservatives, 4.7 for Labour and 4.1 for the Liberal Democrats. Although these summary numbers are quite similar, the scores for each party display considerable variation over time. As Figure 5.7 shows, Labour had a comfortable lead at the time of the 2005 election. However, the party's score subsequently eroded and Labour had fallen behind its rivals by the time of the 2010 election. It is also noteworthy that the Liberal Democrats were in second place in May 2005, indicating that many more people were willing to consider voting for the party than actually did so in that election. However, the attractiveness of the Liberal Democrats was far from immutable. Soon after the 2010 election their score on the 'likely to vote for' measure dropped precipitously after they entered into Coalition government with the Conservatives and executed U-turns on university tuitions and other policy commitments.

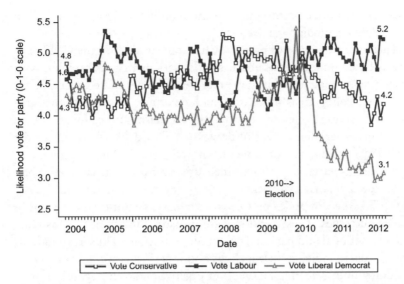

Figure 5.7 Likelihood of ever voting for one of the major parties, April 2004–August 2012.
Source: April 2004–August 2012 monthly CMS.

These 'likely to vote' scores are not the same as actually voting for a party, but they have the advantage of capturing uncertainties surrounding a vote choice when an election is not actually taking place. The standard CMS measure of vote intentions uses the following question: 'If there were a General Election tomorrow, which party would you vote for?' This question has the disadvantage of not providing a measure of uncertainty, since respondents have to opt for one party when answering. In contrast, the likelihood of voting questions have the advantage of distinguishing people who are strong supporters or opponents of a party from individuals who are lukewarm and might be persuaded to change their vote.

The composite party choice model estimated using these CMS data is not exactly the same as the model in Table 5.2 although there are strong similarities. Both models include the party best on most important issue variables, leader images (affect), economic evaluations, partisanship and standard demographic characteristics. Differences relate to policy performance measures and spatial variables. The most important difference concerns the former; there are much more extensive measures of policy performance in the monthly CMS surveys than in the election campaign survey.

There are two types of policy evaluation variables in the CMS. The first is based on questions about the delivery of various policies, with respondents being asked if they perceive outcomes to be getting better or worse. Policy areas monitored include crime, education, immigration, the National Health Service, anti-terrorism and railways. These questions cover major areas of domestic policy delivery outside of the economy. A principal components analysis reveals that a single latent factor drives variation in these measures and this is used to measure policy performance evaluations in these several non-economic areas.[4] A second aspect of policy performance concerns emotional reactions to policy outcomes. These reactions are measured the same way as reactions to national and personal economic conditions. Thus, respondents were asked to indicate their feelings about performance in various policy domains by selecting among four positive and four negative words. The overall measure was constructed by computing the number of positive descriptors minus the number of negative ones.[5]

Regarding spatial variables, the CMS lacks the issue-proximity scales contained in the campaign study. As an alternative, we construct proxy spatial variables using data on respondents' views about two salient and divisive issues in recent British politics. The first is the issue of continuing British membership in the European Union. In the pooled April 2004–August 2012 CMS data 49.8 per cent of the respondents approved UK membership and 50.2 per cent disapproved, so the country was split down the middle, making EU membership an ideal spatial issue. The second issue concerns public attitudes towards the Iraq War. In this case opinions were hardly equally divided, with 49 per cent of the pooled respondents disapproving of Britain's involvement in the war and 21 per cent approving. Iraq was nonetheless a divisive issue and attitudes towards the conflict varied considerably over time (Clarke *et al.*, 2009b, ch. 4).

Ideally, we would use the CMS data to model contextual effects across the entire April 2004–August 2012 period. However, the change in government in May 2010 poses a problem for multilevel analysis. This is because, although there are 71 second-level observations for the period prior to May 2010, there are only 27 for the period since then (June 2010–August 2010). Analyses of the statistical properties of these models indicate that one should have a minimum of

50 second-level cases (here months) to have confidence in the standard errors of parameter estimates[6] (Hox, 1998; Maas and Hox, 2005). Accordingly, we confine our attention to the period before the 2010 election.

Table 5.3 contains coefficient estimates in models of the likelihoods of voting for Labour, the Conservatives and the Liberal Democrats using the pooled April 2004–April 2010 CMS data. With such a large number of cases it is not difficult for individual predictors to achieve statistical significance. However, we note that the models exhibit excellent fits with the data, particularly in the Labour and Conservative cases. Virtually all coefficients for party best on most important issue, feelings about party leaders and partisanship are statistically significant with the correct signs, indicating that these variables play important roles in explaining the likelihood of voting for these parties. In addition, positive economic evaluations and positive emotional reactions to the economy helped Labour, as did positive evaluations of policy performance in non-economic areas. Equally, if Labour was judged as best for managing the economy this gave the party a large advantage and reduced support for the Conservatives. Conservative and Liberal Democrat support was also eroded by positive judgments about economic conditions.

As for partisanship, Table 5.3 shows that partisan attachments had highly significant effects on the likelihood of voting for various parties. For example, Labour partisanship increased the likelihood of voting for that party by nearly 3 points on the 11-point scale. Liberal Democrat partisanship had an equally sized impact on the tendency to vote for that party, and Conservative partisanship raised the likelihood of casting a Tory ballot by 3.5 points. To a lesser extent, attachment to a rival party reduced the likelihood of voting for a given party, with one exception. The exception occurs in the Liberal Democrat model where Labour partisanship had a modest positive influence (0.24 points) on the likelihood of supporting Liberal Democrats. In the Conservative model both Labour and Liberal Democrat partisanship worked to reduce the likelihood of a Tory vote.

In addition to these effects associated with predictor variables in the valence model, there is evidence that position issues were influential. Disapproval of UK membership in the European Union, a proxy spatial measure, hurt Labour and the Liberal Democrats and helped the Conservatives, who garnered support from Eurosceptics in the

Table 5.3 *Individual-level effects in pooled party choice models, April 2004–April 2010 CMS surveys*

Individual-level effects	Labour	Conservatives	Liberal Democrats
Party best most important issue:			
Labour	0.02	−0.30***	−0.48***
Conservatives	−0.18***	1.08***	−0.38***
Liberal Democrats	−0.40***	−0.38***	1.01***
Other party	−0.11*	−0.00	−0.34***
Leader images:			
Labour	0.41***	−0.04***	−0.07***
Conservative	−0.08***	0.50***	−0.05***
Liberal Democrat	−0.01*	−0.06***	0.64***
Economic evaluations	0.13***	−0.11*	−0.14***
Emotional reactions to economy	0.07***	0.03**	0.01
Labour best on economy	1.27***	−0.66***	0.10*
Partisanship:			
Labour	2.86***	−0.41***	0.24***
Conservative	−0.94***	3.52***	−0.53***
Liberal Democrat	0.05	−0.32***	3.01***
Other party	0.002	0.01	0.21*
Reactions to policy outcomes:			
Cognitive	0.08***	0.03	0.02
Affective	−0.001	−0.00	0.01
EU membership	−0.13***	0.07***	−0.22***
Iraq War	−0.10***	0.09***	−0.12***
Gender	0.08***	0.12***	−0.01
Age	−0.01***	−0.004***	−0.01***
Ethnicity	0.09***	0.04	0.24***
Social class	0.04***	0.10***	0.07***
Region/country:			
North	−0.04	−0.12***	−0.05
Midlands	−0.003	0.02	−0.09**
South East	−0.13***	0.01	−0.05
South West	−0.19***	−0.02	0.11***
Wales	−0.06	−0.29***	−0.17***
Scotland	−0.24***	−0.47***	−0.43***

Level 1 N = 87,360
Level 2 N = 71
*** $p < 0.001$; ** $p < 0.01$; * $p < 0.05$; one-tailed test.

electorate. Approval of the Iraq War helped the Conservatives and reduced support for both Labour and the Liberal Democrats. In the latter case, this is easy to understand since, unlike Labour and the Conservatives, the Liberal Democrats openly opposed the war. And, unlike the party leadership, many in Labour's 'heartlands' were opposed as well.

One interesting difference between the models in Table 5.2 and Table 5.3 concerns regional differences in voting. We observed in Table 5.2 that Labour did better in the North, Midlands, Wales and Scotland in 2010. But when it comes to the likelihood of ever voting for the party, the situation is different. Labour had negative scores in the South East and South West which is not surprising given that these regions are traditional bastions of support for the Conservatives and Liberal Democrats, respectively. But Labour vote intentions were also lower in Scotland, reflecting the challenge presented by the SNP. Although Labour has considerable support in Scotland, there is a polarization of opinion, with many people refusing even to consider voting Labour. Regional effects extend to the other major parties, with Table 5.3 indicating that willingness to consider voting Conservative or Liberal Democrat is lower in both Scotland and Wales.

The next step involves examining trends in the coefficients for predictor variables between April 2004 and April 2010. To this end, we include a second-level linear trend in the multilevel model of the likelihood of voting for the three parties. The trend variable starts with a value of one in April 2004 and increases by one unit each month until April 2010. This enables us to detect the impact of time on the effects of individual-level predictor variables. To illustrate how this works, Table 5.3 shows that if a respondent thought that Labour was the best party for handling their most important issue, this increased the likelihood of voting Labour by 1.3 points on the 11-point scale. The trend analysis indicates that this positive effect fell by -0.003 points each month from April 2004 to April 2010 since there is a statistically significant cross-level interaction effect for the individual-coefficient for the 'Labour best on the economy' variable and the time trend. The total decrease in the size of the effect across the entire time period would be 0.22 points (-0.003×73 months). Generally, if significant trend coefficients have the same signs as comparable coefficients in Table 5.3, the effects become stronger over time, but if the signs are inconsistent they weaken.

A large majority (41) of the 60 trend coefficients are not statistically significant. This includes 9 of 12 of the cross-level interactions involving perceptions of party best on most important issue. However, these interactions indicate that effect on likelihood of casting a Labour vote of perceiving one of the minor 'other' parties best on most important issues strengthened over time. There is also evidence that the impact of perceptions of the Liberal Democrats as best on most important issues on the likelihood of Conservative voting strengthened over time. In addition, it appears that the effect of this variable on the likelihood of ever voting Liberal Democrat weakened.

In the case of the leader image interaction coefficients, the effects of feelings about the party leaders did not change over time in the Labour model. However, the impact of feelings about Labour leaders on the likelihood of voting Conservative increased, as did feelings about Conservative leaders. The latter effect implies that the arrival of David Cameron as Conservative leader in December 2005 increased the strength of the Conservative challenge to Labour – people were increasingly willing to consider voting for his party after Cameron became its leader. In contrast, the significant negative trend of feelings about Labour leaders in the Conservative model suggests that the arrival of Gordon Brown as Labour leader and prime minister in late June 2007 worked to erode the cohort of potential Conservative voters. At the same time, the combination of a significant positive Labour leader coefficient in the Liberal Democrat analysis in Table 5.3 and a significant positive trend coefficient in the comparable analysis in Table 5.4 indicates that the arrival of Brown may actually have enhanced the likelihood that voters would consider voting Liberal Democrat.

The economic measures in the Labour model are all statistically significant and negative, which means that their effects weakened over time. We observed in Table 5.3 that economic evaluations, emotional reactions to the economy and perceptions that Labour is the best party on the economy had positive impacts on the likelihood of supporting Labour. However, the results of the trend analysis indicate that economic effects on propensities to support the party decreased as time went by. This is a puzzle given the arrival of the recession which on the face of it might be expected to strengthen the impact of economic considerations when thinking about whether to support an incumbent party. We return to this issue below.

Table 5.4 *Macroeconomic mood coefficients in party choice models,
April 2004–April 2010*

	Party		
	Labour	Conservatives	Liberal Democrats
	β	β	β
Intercept	−0.020	−0.014	0.017
Party best most important issue:			
Labour	−0.014*	−0.008	−0.008
Conservatives	0.007	0.005	−0.013
Liberal Democrats	−0.009	0.015	0.031***
Other party	0.019*	−0.004	−0.007
Leader images:			
Labour leaders	−0.002	0.003**	−0.007***
Conservative leaders	0.001	−0.007***	0.002
Liberal Democrat leaders	−0.000	−0.002	−0.002
Economic evaluations	0.002	−0.004	−0.007*
Emotional reactions to economy	0.006***	0.001	0.004**
Labour best on economy	0.029***	0.003	0.022*
Partisanship:			
Labour	0.001	0.001	0.012
Conservative	−0.002	0.069***	−0.013
Liberal Democrat	0.009	−0.013	−0.020
Other party	−0.002	0.003	−0.023*
Reactions to policy outcomes:			
Cognitive evaluations	0.001	0.002	−0.001
Affective reactions	−0.001*	−0.000	−0.001**
Attitudes towards EU membership	0.006**	0.001	0.001
Attitudes towards Iraq War	−0.012***	0.003	0.003
Social class	0.001	0.002	0.001

*** p < 0.001; ** p < 0.01; * p < 0.05; two-tailed test.
Note: Cross-level interactions with trends are controlled in the analysis.

As for non-economic policy reactions, the trend analysis indicates that although the effects of emotional reactions did not vary over time, the impact of cognitive evaluations on the likelihood of voting Labour became stronger. As noted above, these evaluations tap public attitudes to public service delivery in salient areas including the NHS, crime, education and transport. It appears that Labour was increasingly judged on its ability to deliver these services. We also note that the comparable Liberal Democrat interaction effect is significant and positive, thereby suggesting that positive judgments in non-economic policy domains were working to increase people's willingness to consider supporting the party.

We conjectured earlier that the impact of partisanship might decline over time, even though it remains an important predictor of voting. However, the trend analysis provides very little support this hypothesis, since there were no significant trends in the effects of partisanship in the Labour model. In the Liberal Democrat trend analysis, the Liberal Democrat partisanship coefficient is positive, thereby indicating that the effect strengthened over time. The 'other party' partisanship coefficient is also significant and positive. Given that the comparable coefficient in Table 5.3 is positive, this result suggests that the impact of minor party partisanship on the likelihood of voting Liberal Democrat was positive at the outset and strengthened over the period. The only indication of weakening partisan effects is found in the Conservative analysis, where the Conservative interaction coefficient is negative and significant. The magnitude of this coefficient (-0.018) indicates that over the entire April 2004–April 2010 period, the impact of Conservative partisanship on the likelihood of voting for the party decreased by about 1.3 points (-0.018×73 months). This decrease notwithstanding, the effect of Conservative partisanship remained a sizable 2.3 (3.5–1.3) points at the end of the period.

Regarding spatial variables, Table 5.3 indicates that approval of European Union membership helped Labour. The trend effect associated with that coefficient suggests that the impact of this variable strengthened over time. The Iraq War variable had a significant individual-level effect in the Labour model, with the negative sign indicating that people who approved the war were less likely to entertain the idea of casting a Labour ballot. However, the positive interaction effect for this coefficient suggests the effect weakened over time.[7]

One final aspect of the trend analysis relates to our earlier discussion of partisan dealignment and class politics. There is mild evidence that the impact of social class on likelihood of voting Conservative may have weakened over time (-0.0004, $p < 0.10$). If the Michigan interpretation of partisanship is correct the size of class effects should remain unchanged, albeit within the context of a shrinking working class.

To summarize, although there were significant changes in the impact of some predictor variables in the party choice models over the 2004–10 period, many of the predictors exhibited stable effects and the overall picture is complex. There is some evidence of dynamism in the effects of partisanship, but this is far from uniform for all parties. A few leader image effects also exhibit dynamism, with the strengthening effect of Conservative leader images on the likelihood of voting Conservative being particularly noteworthy. Non-economic performance judgments on valence issues also strengthened in importance for the governing party, but there is the puzzle that the economy appeared to become less significant. The linear trend variable employed in these analyses suggests that there are some secular changes taking place in the strength of predictor variables party choice model, but a simple trend counter does not explain why these changes might be occurring. Manifestly, the major contextual change in the 2004–10 period was the financial crisis and serious recession which followed. We next investigate how this change affected the likelihood of voting for various parties.

The political economy of recession

As illustrated above in Figure 5.1, the sometimes vigorous growth, which had characterized the British economy since New Labour came to power in 1997, evaporated after the Northern Rock crisis in autumn 2007. Economic activity slowed markedly and by the second quarter of 2008, the recession had arrived. Over the next four quarters, the economy contracted, before beginning to grow very slowly in the runup to the 2010 election. Thereafter, the economy continued to sputter, registering negative growth for the last quarter of 2010 and falling back into recession at the end of 2011.

Mounting joblessness accompanied the downturn in economic activity, with unemployment moving sharply upwards in the latter part of 2008. Two months before the 2010 election unemployment stood at 8.0 per cent and again, the situation did not improve afterwards. Indeed, jobless figures remained stubbornly high, reaching fully 8.4 per cent in November 2011 before declining modestly in summer 2012. Traditionally unemployment is one of the last economic indicators to be affected by the onset of a recession and it is usually the slowest to recover (Reinhart and Rogoff, 2009). Five years after Northern Rock hard times continued.

The British public were well aware of their misery. Indeed, the CMS monthly survey data indicate that retrospective and prospective evaluations of the national economy quickly crashed shortly after the Northern Rock crisis, reaching a nadir around the time of the failure of Lehman Brothers in September 2008 and then rebounding in the months before the 2010 election (see Figure 5.8, Panel A). Emotional reactions to national economic conditions followed the same trajectory. Soon after the election and the installation of the new Conservative–Liberal Democrat Coalition Government, public pessimism about the economy returned, with pervasive negativity characterizing the entire period since the Coalition took power. People's reactions to their personal financial situation were similarly bleak – Figure 5.8 Panel B shows that reactions to personal economic circumstances exhibited exactly the same dismal dynamic as did reactions to the national economy.

A dynamic factor analysis (Drukker and Gates, 2011) is used to summarize these monthly aggregate CMS data on evaluations of and emotional reactions to national and personal economic conditions. This analysis yields a single factor, scores for which are displayed in Figure 5.9. Not surprisingly, these factor scores adhere to the same trajectory as the individual series of which they are composed and, as the 95 per cent confidence bands indicate, there is little uncertainty in the estimated monthly scores. Changing macrolevel orientations such as those summarized by this dynamic factor are akin to the macro 'policy moods' measured by Stimson and his colleagues (Carmines and Stimson, 1989; Erikson *et al.*, 2002). The macroeconomic mood variable in Figure 5.9 reflects collective judgments about, and emotional reactions to, changing economic conditions. The measure shown in Figure 5.9 indexes Britain's macroeconomic mood over the 2004–12 period and it summarizes the subjective economic context in which party support decisions were made.

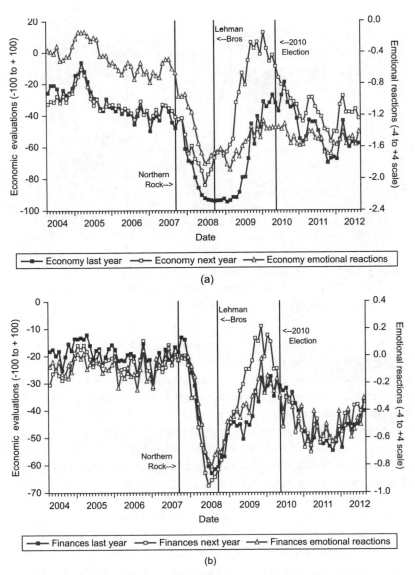

Figure 5.8 Economic conditions – evaluations and emotional reactions, April 2004–August 2012: A. The national economy B. Personal financial situation. *Source:* April 2004–August 2012 monthly CMS.

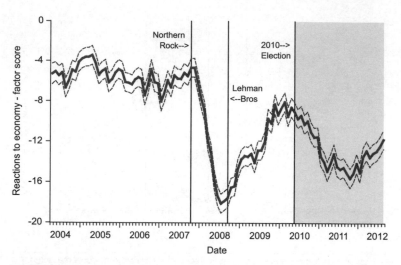

Figure 5.9 Britain's economic mood, April 2004–August 2012.
Note: dashed lines are 95 per cent confidence bands.
Source: April 2004–August 2012 monthly CMS.

Effects of the changing macroeconomic mood on the likelihood of voting for various parties are summarized in Table 5.4. As in the previous multilevel analysis of contextual effects, we confine attention to the April 2004–April 2010 period when Labour was in power. The present analysis includes cross-level interactions between the macroeconomic mood variable at the second (monthly aggregate) level and predictors of party choice and the first (individual) level. The macroeconomic series is lagged one period to strengthen our ability to infer a flow of influence from the economic context to voters' party support decisions.

Similar to the linear trend analyses discussed earlier, a large majority (43 of 60) of the macro-mood interaction effects depicted in Table 5.4 are statistically insignificant, thereby indicating that the influence of associated individual-level predictor variables did not vary in tandem with changes in the electorates' economic mood. Moreover, most of the interaction effects are quite modest, thereby suggesting that their substantive impact is minimal. That said, significant interactions associated with reactions to the economy are theoretically interesting. Specifically, mood interactions for the impact of emotional reactions to the economy and perceptions of Labour as best on the economy are positive, thereby indicating that an upward move in the macro-mood strengthens the effects of these variables on the likelihood of voting Labour (individual-level effects are positive too). The implication is that when the macroeconomic policy mood is positive, economic variables play a more important role in explaining the likelihood of voting for Labour, and when it turns negative cognitive and emotional reactions become less important.

To reiterate an earlier point we would expect the economy to become more salient for voters when the recession arrived in 2008, making the coefficients in the Labour model stronger rather than weaker. However, one clue why this pattern does not obtain can be found in the Conservative model in Table 5.4. The cross-level interaction between the impact of emotional reactions to the economy at the individual level and the macroeconomic mood variable is statistically insignificant, indicating that as the economy deteriorated the Conservatives were no more likely to benefit from negative economic news than they had been were the economy was in better shape. This means that when the economy turned sour after 2007, the impact of economic conditions on the likelihood of voting Conservative did not strengthen. A possible implication is that the Conservatives did not articulate an attractive economic strategy. However well justified as a remedy for Britain's difficulties, the Conservative austerity programme did not have sufficient appeal to alter the structure of the calculus of party support. If the Conservatives had adopted a more appealing set of economic policies, they might have benefited more strongly from the growing pessimism and discontent with Mr Brown and his government. Promising hard times is a hard sell.

These relationships between macroeconomic and microeconomic evaluations in the models also speak to the topic of partisan dealignment. The reward–punishment model of how economic performance affects party support has a long history, extending back to V.O. Key (1968) and earlier. The conjecture is very simple – incumbents lose and oppositions gain when the economy goes into recession. However, we see that these reactions did not become a more important influence on the likelihood of voting for the major opposition party as the macroeconomic mood darkened in reaction to hard times. By extension, there may be implications for the party system more generally. In this regard, the suggestion was made earlier that long-run partisan dealignment may reflect an overall failure of the major parties

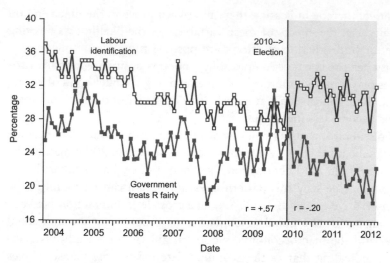

Figure 5.10 Labour partisanship and perceptions of fair treatment by government, April 2004–August 2012.
Source: April 2004–August 2012, CMS Surveys.

to deliver a consistent flow of policy outcomes consonant with the expectations that voters have developed about economic performance.

Figure 5.10 is relevant to this point. It depicts the macro-level relationship over the April 2004–August 2012 period between the percentage of respondents who are Labour partisans and the percentage who agree with the statement 'The Government treats people like me fairly.' The latter is a relatively simple indicator of the extent to which individuals think that the government is delivering on the things that they care about. It is apparent that the two series track each other fairly closely until the 2010 general election producing a correlation (r) of +0.57, and it is noteworthy that there is a parallel decline in both series over this period. After the election the correlation between Labour partisanship and perceptions of fair treatment by government, changes to −0.20. Thus, Labour partisanship is closely related to perceptions of satisfactory policy delivery when Labour is in power, but much more weakly related to delivery in the opposite direction when it is in opposition.

This implies that governments may be more strongly punished in the sense of losing partisan supporters than oppositions are rewarded by gaining them. This pattern is quite consistent with a running-tally interpretation of partisanship and also with a long-term decline in partisan support for both major parties. One party loses partisans when it is in power, and this can happen even during a period of relative prosperity which occurred from 2004 up to 2008. But when the same party is in opposition during a period of quite severe recession, it gains only weakly from the failure of its incumbent rival. If this process is repeated over time it will produce a loss of partisans for both major parties. This manifestly is not a definitive test of the determinants of nearly fifty years of partisan dealignment, but it suggests that policy concerns are at the heart of this process.

Yet another interesting effect in Table 5.4 is that the coefficient for the interaction between the impact of David Cameron's image on the likelihood of voting Conservative carries a negative sign (-0.007, $p < 0.001$). This indicates that as macroeconomic mood becomes more pessimistic, Cameron's image strengthens as a driver of Conservative support. The equivalent interaction coefficient for the impact of the Labour leader's image on Conservative support is positive, indicating that when the macroeconomic policy mood worsens, the effect of that image weakens. In the context of the public negativism about the economy which prevailed in the run-up to the 2010 general election, these results imply that public feelings about a possible alternative prime minister, David Cameron, were becoming increasingly important relative to those about the current incumbent, Gordon Brown. In contrast, the positive interaction coefficient for Brown's image in the Liberal Democrat analysis (see Table 5.4) indicates that the darkening economic mood was enhancing a 'Brown effect' in the calculus of likely Liberal Democrat voting. More generally, the analysis suggests that leader image effects, although consistently strong, are conditioned by the context within which voters are considering which party or parties might merit their support.

Conclusion: political choices in context

This chapter has documented the dominance of the valence politics model for explaining electoral choice in 2010. As in analyses of voting in earlier British elections, positional issues are of secondary importance and social class and other sociodemographic characteristics make only modest contributions to understanding how voters cast their ballots. The chapter also has established that some of the coefficients in a composite party choice model that includes valence, spatial and sociodemographic variables changed over time. One reason for this was the significant change in the macroeconomic context, with Britain moving rapidly from prosperity to recession soon after the Northern Rock crisis in the autumn of 2007. The crisis and subsequent recession were reflected in the electorate's rapidly darkening macroeconomic mood.

Notwithstanding these dramatic changes in economic context, the valence model continues to provide the strongest explanation of party choice in 2010. And, similar to previous elections, spatial and sociological variables make lesser, but significant, contributions. The end result is that a composite model incorporating valence, spatial and sociodemographic variables consistently does the best job in explaining party support. There is clearly a difference between modelling the vote just after an election, when the relevant dependent variable is the survey respondent's actual vote, and in inter-election periods when survey questions about future voting intentions necessarily are more hypothetical. But these differences should not be exaggerated – the explanatory power of variables relevant for understanding party choice is very similar in both cases.

The overall success of our composite model of party choice does not mean that it works in exactly the same way in all contexts. It is apparent that there is systematic variation in the effects of various predictor variables as a result of the context within which party support decisions are made. Effects of some key valence variables, including party performance evaluations on important issues, leader images and partisan attachments, showed evidence of over-time variation. There was also evidence of temporal mutability in the influence of economic evaluations and emotional reactions to economic conditions, as well as variables tapping position issues such as attitudes towards the Iraq War and Britain's membership in the EU. Most of these effects were modest, testifying to the ongoing strength of valence politics variables in the skein of forces affecting party support.

This concludes our analysis of factors affecting party choice in 2010 and the six years preceding that election. Much of the discussion up to this point in the book has focused on New Labour and how it fared in office between 1997 and 2010. In the next chapter we shift the focus to the Conservative–Liberal Democrat Coalition Government which came to power in May 2010 to see how it has performed – in terms of both policy and politics – in the context of the worst recession since the 1930s.

6 | *Bearish Britain*

The Coalition in power

The 2010 general election resulted in a hung parliament and a Conservative–Liberal Democrat Coalition government. Had the numbers added up differently it is likely that the Liberal Democrats would have made a deal with Labour rather than the Conservatives, but that was not to be. After five days of intense negotiations, the first formal coalition government in Britain since the Second World War was announced on 11 May 2010. The Conservative–Liberal Democrat duo was an unlikely match, composed of two parties with historically different ideologies, policy goals and bases of support.

The agreement between the Coalition parties provided a roadmap for their partnership and it constructed a narrative which argued that Britain needed a strong, stable and prudent government to deal with what had become a protracted economic crisis. This was a popular message at the time. The June 2010 BES Continuous Monitoring Survey revealed that 41 per cent of respondents stated that the Conservatives were the best party for handling the economy, and a further 11 per cent said that the Liberal Democrats could do the best job. In sharp contrast, only 23 per cent replied that Labour was best on the economy. Labour was clearly paying a heavy price for being in power during the financial meltdown and subsequent recession. The political-economic context thus did much to validate the terms of the Coalition Agreement and the new government it produced.

The aim of this chapter is to examine the formation of the Coalition in May 2010 and to study factors affecting public support for the Conservative and Liberal Democrat parties and their opposition rivals since the Coalition came to power. Most basically, it is no exaggeration to say that the success or otherwise of the Conservative–Liberal Democrat government is being determined by how it manages the central issue of the economy. The Coalition started with a mandate to address the debt crisis and associated economic recession and it prosecuted the task with vigour. Immediately after the general election there was a great deal of support for the proposed austerity programme, with widespread agreement among elites and public alike about what should be done. However, as analyses presented below show, public attitudes have subsequently evolved with increasingly sharp disagreements emerging over the Coalition's austerity policy.

The chapter begins with a discussion of the negotiations over the Coalition Agreement which took place after the 2010 general election. We discuss the Agreement itself, paying particular attention to economic policy. We then examine the evolution of the economy both in relation to objective measures such as inflation and unemployment, but also the 'subjective economy' which involves people's perceptions of national and personal economic conditions. This analysis considers inter-relationships between the objective and subjective economies, focusing on the influence of expectations about the future course of the economy on objective conditions. The chapter concludes with an examination of the impact of the subjective economy on support for the Coalition parties and their opposition rivals. This discussion considers broader attitudes to the financial crisis and the government's handling of the recession during the mid-term period in 2012.

We first consider the negotiations which led up to the creation of the Coalition Agreement in May 2010, looking closely at what emerged from the bargaining between the Conservatives and Liberal Democrats following the general election.

The Coalition Agreement

When the results of the election were announced and it was clear that no party had an overall majority, the process of bargaining between the three major parties began. In the event, the Liberal Democrats were the only party which had given some thought to the exercise of coalition formation prior to the election. Nick Clegg had set up a committee to consider this possibility in 2009 (Kavanagh and Cowley, 2010: 205). This gave the Liberal Democrats a head start in the process and the other parties had to scramble to put together proposals for a possible coalition at the last minute. There were fitful negotiations between the Liberal Democrats and Labour during the five days it took to form the new government, but the serious negotiations were with the Conservatives who were the most likely partners from the beginning. This was true for a number of reasons.

First, electoral arithmetic strongly influenced the process, with a Liberal Democrat–Conservative Coalition constituting a majority of 80 in the House of Commons while a Liberal Democrat–Labour coalition would have been a minority government. As such, the latter would have needed the support of a diverse group of minor parties such as the Greens, Plaid Cymru and Northern Irish MPs to obtain a bare majority. As Kavanagh and Cowley (2010: 225) have observed, such a 'rainbow' coalition might have been able to muster enough votes to defeat a motion of no confidence in the House of Commons, but it would not have had enough cohesiveness to govern effectively.

The second obstacle to forging a Labour–Liberal Democrat coalition was Gordon Brown. As discussed in earlier chapters, Brown was an unpopular prime minister who had lost his legitimacy as a result of his party's electoral defeat. Nevertheless, he wanted to stay in office. The Liberal Democrats would have immediately been accused of propping up a discredited administration if they had formed a coalition with the Labour and Brown had remained in Number 10. Some people held him personally responsible for his party's defeat. In fact, although Brown undoubtedly contributed to that defeat, there was no obvious alternative in Labour's ranks who could have avoided it (Worcester *et al.*, 2011: 89). Then again, if Brown had agreed to step down as party leader as part of the bargaining process, the country would have had to wait for the emergence of a new Labour leader to restart the negotiations. At a time when the economic crisis was in full swing the prospects of no government in Whitehall for an extended period could well have magnified uncertainty over the ailing economy and perhaps even precipitated a run on the pound. This lent considerable urgency to the whole exercise. Experience shows that coalition negotiations in continental European countries can go on for months, but the tradition of a rapid change of government in Britain together with the ongoing economic crisis created an imperative to make a quick decision.

The third factor pushing the Liberal Democrats towards the Conservatives was the announcement by Nick Clegg that David Cameron would be given the first refusal to agree a coalition because the Conservatives had won more votes and seats than Labour. This meant that negotiations with the Conservatives would have to break down for a deal with Labour to be possible. Initially, the option of supporting a minority Conservative government with a so-called 'confidence and supply' agreement remained open. This would have involved the

Liberal Democrats backing such a government on votes of no confidence and budgetary matters, but not necessarily in relation to
other policies. However, this option was unattractive to the Liberal
Democrats for one major reason. They were anxious to be part of
the government because this would enable them to rebut the repeated
accusation that a vote for the party was wasted because it could never
achieve power. This perception had cost the Liberal Democrats support in previous elections (Whiteley *et al.*, 2006).

The Coalition Agreement was a comprehensive document rather
similar to a party election manifesto, setting out 31 different policy
headings including banking reforms, national security, foreign affairs
and the NHS (see The Coalition Programme for Government, 2010).
There was a section on universities and further education, reflecting
the controversy over student fees arising from commitments made
by the Liberal Democrats before the election. Key priorities were set
out in a foreword, co-authored by David Cameron and Nick Clegg. It
stated that:

'We are agreed that the first duty of government is to safeguard our national
security and support our troops in Afghanistan and elsewhere – and we
will fulfil that duty. We are also agreed that the most urgent task facing
this coalition is to tackle our record debts, because without sound finances,
none of our ambitions will be deliverable'. (The Coalition Programme for
Government, 2010: 7)

In Chapter 4 we examined the manifestos published by the three
major parties and observed that the Conservatives and Liberal
Democrats were at the opposite ends of the spectrum on the issue
of budget cuts. The Conservatives wanted big reductions implemented
over a relatively short period of time, whereas the Liberal Democrats
wanted smaller cuts phased in over a longer period. In this regard, it
was noteworthy that the Coalition Agreement stated that:

'We will significantly accelerate the reduction in the structural deficit over the
course of a Parliament, with the main burden of deficit reduction borne by
reducing spending rather than increasing taxes'. (The Coalition Programme
for Government, 2010: 15)

Clearly, Conservative priorities had prevailed in the negotiations
on this key aspect of the agreement. However, the Liberal Democrats
did well in getting many of their policy priorities written into the

agreement. A content analysis of the document compared with the party manifestos showed that it was closer to the Liberal Democrats than to the Conservatives on the left–right ideological dimension that historically has done much to structure policy debate in British politics (Quinn *et al.*, 2011). Thus, both parties secured some of their policy priorities in the agreement, even if the core issue of budget cuts favoured the Conservatives. With this agreement as a backdrop, we next examine the economic austerity plans as they evolved over time.

Economic and fiscal performance since 2010

One of the earliest changes made by the Coalition Government was to establish a new Office of Budgetary Responsibility charged with publishing data on government spending, monitoring fiscal targets and providing short- and medium-term economic forecasts. Setting up the OBR was a response to the criticism that the Treasury had been repeatedly over-optimistic in its forecasts of growth and spending under the previous government. As is well known, Chancellors of the Exchequer have an incentive to massage the figures to make them look more favourable than they are, and this tendency had gradually weakened the credibility of Treasury forecasts (Office for Budgetary Responsibility, 2012). The OBR was the organizational aspect of a plan to gain credibility in financial markets by specifying substantial cuts while at the same time having them monitored by an arms-length agency.

Initially, the Coalition Agreement specified cuts of £6 billion to nonfrontline services in the financial year 2010–11, while at the same time announcing an emergency budget aimed at further reducing the deficit. This budget planned spending cuts of £32 billion per year by 2014–15 and a spending review was announced later in the year to work out the details. In addition, an £11 billion reduction in welfare spending and a two-year freeze in public-sector pay were announced. On the taxation side, the budget sought to raise an additional £8 billion in revenue by increasing the value-added tax from 17.5 to 20 per cent and by increasing the standard and higher rates of Insurance Premium Tax to 6 per cent and 28 per cent respectively from January 2011 (HM Treasury, 2010). Other measures included a bank levy forecast to raise £1.2 billion in 2011–12 and £2.3 billion in 2012–13, and an increase in the capital gains tax for the highest earners (Office for Budgetary Responsibility, 2012).

The emergency budget report summarized the plans in the following terms:

'The budget and the plans the Government inherited represent a total consolidation of £113 billion per year by 2014–15 and £128 billion per year by 2015–16, of which £99 billion per year comes from spending reductions and £29 billion per year from net tax increases. By 2015–16 77 per cent of the total consolidation will be delivered through spending reductions'. (HM Treasury, 2010: 2)

Drawing on forecasts from the newly established Office of Budget Responsibility the Coalition Government claimed that public-sector borrowing would decline to 1.1 per cent of gross domestic product by 2015–16, the structural deficit would be eliminated by 2014–15 and a surplus of 0.8 per cent of GDP would emerge by 2015–16. Finally, the new Government argued that public-sector net debt would peak at 70 per cent of GDP in 2013–14 before declining to 67 per cent of GDP in 2015–16 (HM Treasury, 2010: 2). This was a very ambitious plan which aimed to deal with the deficit within the lifetime of a parliament.

It bears emphasis that the economics of the plan were pre-Keynesian in the sense that it prioritized a balanced budget over all else, arguing that this was an essential precondition for economic recovery. Governments in the late 1920s and early 1930s had taken the same approach and Keynes famously had strongly disagreed with them. His key contribution to macroeconomic policy-making was to stress the importance of supporting consumption spending during a recession (Keynes, 1936, 245–54; Skidelsky, 2009, 174–8). Keynes argued that there was no automatic mechanism for increasing spending in this situation so that full employment would eventually be reached. In contrast, the pre-Keynesian or classical analysis held that a reduction of interest rates would achieve this by discouraging savings and stimulating consumption, while at the same time promoting investment as entrepreneurs could borrow at very cheap rates. In classical theory, the interest rate, or the price of borrowing, was the mechanism that brought savings and investment into equilibrium.

For Keynes no such mechanism existed, since in his view even if interest rates were reduced to zero this would not necessarily stimulate investment if entrepreneurs were uncertain of demand for their products. Similarly, savers would not necessarily be persuaded to spend more and run down their savings even if they were getting no returns on them at all, again because of uncertainty about the future. Keynes argued that individuals hold money, in part, for speculative reasons and this could override any desire to save money when interest rates are high and spend it when they are low. For example, if there was a widespread expectation that interest rates would rise in the future, this would encourage individuals to hold their money in liquid form because a rise in rates would produce a fall in the price of bonds.[1] If this happened they could get the same return for a smaller investment, and so they would wait to see what happened. Anticipation of falling bond prices in the future would encourage them to hold their money rather than invest it.

According to Keynes, the absence of government intervention would prompt a spiral of falling consumption leading to rising unemployment and negative growth. In contrast, government cuts in taxation and, above all, increased public expenditure would fill the gap in consumption and eventually restore the economy to full employment. If government took the opposite tack of rapidly cutting public expenditure, it would merely make the situation worse. From a Keynesian perspective this analysis implies that the Coalition's austerity policy is likely to fail, since it needs to focus much more on boosting confidence in the economy and less on cuts in public expenditure. In Keynes's analysis consumer and investor expectations about the future – that is, the subjective economy – play a key role in influencing outcomes. 'Animal spirits' matter. The classical mechanism of low interest rates fails to work because fiscal policy is too tight and confidence is too low. Under such a regime, the economy is unlikely to recover, and a dismal suboptimal equilibrium becomes entrenched.

Figure 6.1 displays trends in unemployment and inflation between April 2004 and August 2012. As observed in earlier chapters, the collapse of the Northern Rock bank in September 2007 signalled the start of the economic crisis and both inflation and unemployment rapidly increased in 2008. If we examine the performance of the economy after the Coalition Government came to power after the 2010 general election two features stand out. First, inflation rapidly increased in late 2010 and did not start to decline until the beginning of 2012. Second, unemployment started to rise again as the double-dip recession arrived

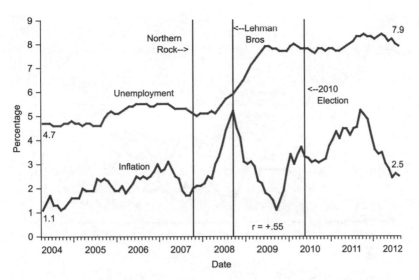

Figure 6.1 Trends in inflation and unemployment, April 2004–August 2012.
Source: Office of National Statistics.

in 2011 and 2012, with joblessness only beginning to decline towards the end of this period. In terms of two traditional yardsticks for measuring a government's economic performance – unemployment and inflation – the Coalition's record up to the mid-term was, to use David Cameron's term, 'disappointing'.

Turning to indicators of public evaluations of party effectiveness on the economy, Figure 6.2 displays CMS survey data that track public perceptions that the Coalition Government was handling the economic crisis well and perceptions that Labour would have handled the crisis well if it were in power. The figure shows that the reputation of the Coalition Government for managing the economy 'very' or 'fairly' well declined almost continuously after the general election, falling from 47 per cent in June 2010 to 21 per cent in August 2012. Indeed, the linear correlation (r) with time is fully −0.93. Equally, a large majority of the public did not believe that Labour would improve the situation much if they were in power. The percentage claiming Labour would manage the economy well actually declines over time from an initially meagre 24 per cent in June 2010 to 20 per cent in August 2012 (r = −0.75). Similar patterns showing a loss of confidence in the Coalition Government on the economy are evident in responses to a

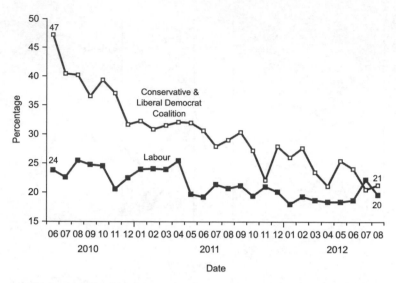

Figure 6.2 Trends in perceptions of party competence to handle the economic crisis, June 2010–August 2012.
Source: June 2010–August 2012 CMS surveys.

question in the CMS which asked respondents to choose which party they thought was best at handling it. In June 2010 some 41 per cent chose the Conservatives and only 23 per cent chose Labour. But by August 2012, the comparable numbers were 28 per cent and 27 per cent respectively. During this period there was also a big increase in the number of respondents who thought that no party was best, or who said that they did not know which party was best. Combined, these groups increased from 25 per cent in June 2010 to 39 per cent in August 2012. Overall, these data testify that as the mid-term of the 2010 Parliament approached, neither the Coalition Government nor the Labour opposition were widely seen as effective managers of the economy.

There has been much discussion about the causes of and remedies for the financial crisis and recession (Krugman, 2012; Reinhart and Rogoff, 2009; Tett, 2009). As discussed above, Keynes would have argued that if people are pessimistic about the future this will have the effect of undermining economic recovery. In earlier chapters we saw that economic optimism crashed after the run on the Northern Rock bank in September 2007, although it partly recovered in the run-up

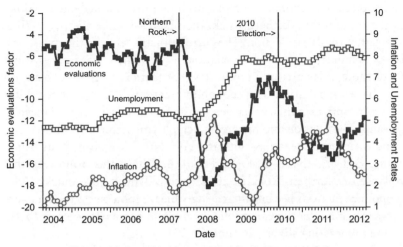

Note: correlations (r) between economic evaluations and inflation
and unemployment are -0.76 and -0.68, respectively.

Figure 6.3 Subjective economic evaluations, inflation and unemployment, April 2004–August 2012.
Source: April 2004–August 2012 CMS surveys and Office of National Statistics.

to and immediately after the 2010 general election. It is important to consider public evaluations of national and personal economic conditions if the impact of the economy on party support is to be understood.

With this in mind, we employed an aggregate subjective economic evaluation index, the macroeconomic mood variable, introduced in Chapter 5. Recall that this variable was constructed by performing a dynamic factor analysis of six subjective economic indicators in the Continuous Monitoring Survey.[2] The indicators are personal retrospective and prospective economic evaluations, national retrospective and prospective economic evaluations and personal and national emotional reactions to the economy.[3] The analysis yielded a single factor and a set of factor scores for each month of the CMS from April 2004 to August 2012. These monthly scores provide a summary measure of the dynamics of public's economic mood over this period.

Figure 6.3 shows the dynamics of the economic mood variable in conjunction with movements in inflation and unemployment over the April 2004–August 2012 period. It can be seen that inflation and the economic mood reflect each other very closely with inflation fluctuating and subjective economic reactions declining precipitously at the time of the collapse of Northern Rock, then increasing, before decreasing again after the 2010 election. The correlation (r) between the two series is −0.76 indicating that the association between them was quite strong. Predictably, this correlation indicates that there is a negative relationship between inflation and economic reactions – concomitant with increasing prices public reactions to the economy became increasing gloomy. The relationship between unemployment and economic reactions is similarly negative, with the correlation between them being strong and negative, −0.68. As Figure 6.3 illustrates, following the collapse of Northern Rock in 2007 unemployment rose quickly and economic reactions became increasingly bleak. Joblessness then moved upward again after the Coalition Government came to power in 2010, before moderating slightly in summer 2012.

The dynamics depicted in Figure 6.3 are interesting but they do not say anything about causal relationships between the objective economy and subjective reactions to it. Unemployment and inflation could be driving the public mood about the economy, or it could be the other way round. A third possibility is that the series influence each other. Accordingly, before we can understand the political implications of Britain's economic travails, it will be useful to examine relationships between the objective and subjective economies in greater depth. This is the topic of the next section.

The objective and subjective economies

Relationships between objective measures of economic performance and public reactions to economic performance have been a topic of interest to researchers for many years and it has recently become quite controversial in the voting literature. Early aggregate analyses of the political economy of party support employed objective measures to model the effects of economic conditions on voting intentions (e.g. Fair, 1978; Goodhart and Bhansali, 1970). Unfortunately, this approach failed to find consistent and robust effects across time and space (Dorussen and Taylor, 2007; Lewis-Beck and Paldam, 2000). Some of this research even turned up nonfindings, such as Alesina and Rosenthal's (1995) analysis which showed that fluctuations in the US economy only weakly influenced the electorate's perceptions of the competence of presidential administrations as economic managers.

Similarly, in a comparative analysis of economic voting in 17 countries over the postwar years, Paldam (1991) found little evidence to suggest that the electorate used objective economic data to evaluate the performance of governing political parties.

One of the reasons for these findings was a failure to take into account the context in which voters made judgments about the economy. As Powell and Whitten (1993) have argued, in political systems where responsibility for managing the economy is obscure, for example, in countries where multi-party coalition governments predominate, economic voting should be weak. In contrast, in settings where the responsibility for managing the economy is very clear, as in countries with traditions of single-party government, economic voting should be stronger. Powell and Whitten's analysis supported their conjecture (see also Hellwig, 2001; van der Brug *et al.*, 2007).

It was also apparent from the early literature that subjective measures of the economy had much stronger statistical relationships with voting behaviour than objective measures such as unemployment and inflation rates (Lewis-Beck, 1988). This finding has encouraged some researchers to concentrate exclusively on subjective variables in their analyses of electoral support (e.g. Duch and Stevenson, 2008). However, in their recent comparative study of 15 European countries van der Brug *et al.* (2007) argued that subjective economic evaluations are consequences, not causes, of party support. Accordingly, analysts should concentrate exclusively on objective economic measures when studying the political economy of electoral choice or party support between elections.

Research by Sanders and Gavin (2004) supports the idea that objective and subjective measures of the economy are rather different from each other. They showed that once the media coverage of economic news is taken into account, objective measures of the economy such as unemployment, inflation and interest rates do not influence subjective economic expectations in an aggregate time series model. The implication is that the subjective economy is driven by media reporting of economic news rather than by economic reality itself.

Most research on economic voting by political scientists has neglected to examine the effects of the subjective economy on the objective economy, since the assumption is commonly made that the latter drives the former. However, an important feature of the literature on macroeconomics has concerned the effects of changing aspects of the subjective economy, especially expectations, on growth and employment. In this regard, subjective economic evaluations in the form of expectations about the future long have played a key role in macroeconomic analyses. Indeed, in Keynes original work and in much subsequent research, expectations are seen as crucial for understanding what it likely to happen to the economy (Keynes, 1936; see also Buiter, 1990).

If the relationship between the objective and subjective economies is to be understood, it is important that there should be adequate variation in both kinds of variables if effects are to be identified. For example, if the objective economy is growing slowly but steadily with only minor changes occurring in inflation and unemployment, then the relationship between these measures and voters' subjective evaluations can be difficult to discern. It is possible to detect relationships of interest only when there is significant short- and medium-term temporal variation in both the objective and subjective economies. For this reason CMS survey data collected both before and after the economic crisis began are particularly useful – as discussed above, objective and subjective economic variables both have varied substantially. With this in mind, we examine interactions between subjective and objective economic variables over the period from April 2004 – the starting point of the Continuous Monitoring Survey – to August 2012. This interval provides 101 aggregate-level monthly observations.

A large number of models have been developed in macroeconomics for explaining the behaviour of the objective economy and the task of specifying and testing these models is a discipline in its own right (see Fair, 2004). When first introduced in the mid-twentieth century, these models were quite elaborate, involving the specification and estimation of large numbers of simultaneous equations (Greene, 2003: 587). However, these models proved inadequate to the task of capturing economic dynamics and accurately forecasting quantities of interest, in part because they had to make possibly unrealistic assumptions about the values of some parameters in order to estimate others.

At the beginning of the 1980s a critique of the traditional approach authored by Sims (1980) introduced the Vector Autoregressive (VAR) strategy for economic modelling. Echoing Captain Renault in the movie *Casablanca*, Sims enjoined fellow economists to 'round up the usual suspects' – namely, a set of theoretically interesting variables – but Sims cautioned that they should not to try to develop a structural model of their interrelationships (e.g. Enders, 2009). Rather, by specifying dynamic relationships among theoretically interesting variables as a series of autoregressive 'reduced-form' equations, analysts could develop VAR models that would enable them to investigate dynamic interrelationships among the variables without imposing unrealistic parameter constraints needed to achieve identification. The VAR approach has attracted wide attention and it is well suited for studying relationships between aspects of the objective and subjective economies.

In the present context, we employ VAR methods to examine relationships among three variables: unemployment, inflation and expectations about the future of the national economy.[4] Expectations play an important role in many macroeconomic models, but typically they are inferred from an extrapolation of past behaviour rather than being measured independently (Murray, 2012: 9). Although modelling expectations 'by assumption' is a common approach, recent research in behavioural economics demonstrates that it is likely to be misleading (Cartwright, 2011). Here, we employ data from the CMS surveys to measure economic expectations directly as part of an analysis of dynamic interrelationships among expectations, inflation and unemployment.

We should be wary of drawing strong conclusions about relationships between the objective and subjective economies displayed in Figure 6.3 since series which are mean nonstationary – that is, ones that trend upwards or downwards over time – can yield highly significant relationships in regression analyses even if they are causally unrelated to each other.[5] This is the well-known phenomenon of 'spurious regression' which poses threats to inference in time series analysis (see Granger and Newbold, 1974). With this in mind we first analyze each of the three variables of interest to determine if they are mean nonstationary.[6] Dickey-Fuller (ADF) tests (Enders, 2009) for the presence of stochastic trends in each of the three variables show that the three series are nonstationary in their original level form and, thus, need to be transformed if the spurious regressions threat to inference is to be avoided. ADF test statistics indicate that once the series are first differenced – that is, expressed as changes from time t-1 to time t – they become stationary variables.[7] Accordingly, we model the three variables in differenced form.

VAR modelling lends itself to a type of causal inference introduced by Clive Granger (1969) and described in the literature as 'Granger-causality' testing. This is defined as follows: '[C]ausality in the sense defined by Granger (1969) and Sims (1980) is inferred when lagged values of a variable, say x_t, have explanatory power in a regression of a variable y_t on lagged values of y_t and $x_t \ldots$ ' (Greene, 2003: 592). Thus, if lagged values of x_t contribute to explaining variation in y_t over and above variation explained by lagged values of y_t, then we can say that x_t 'Granger-causes' y_t. If, in addition, x_t is not affected by lagged values of y_t, we say that x_t is strongly exogenous to y_t (Charemza and Deadman, 1997).

Employing the VAR modelling strategy to investigate relationships among inflation, unemployment and economic expectations involves estimating three different equations, one for each of these variables. The dependent variable in each equation is the contemporaneous (time t) measure of that variable. Each equation then contains the dependent variable lagged once, twice, and three times as a predictor on the right-hand side of that equation. In addition, each equation contains the other two variables in the system, both lagged once, twice and three times. Following the definition of Granger causality, we investigate if any of the other variables in the system contribute to explaining variation in a dependent variable, while controlling for the past behaviour of that dependent variable. The lags in the system allow for delayed impacts which might take up to three months to be realized as well as more temporally proximate effects.

The VAR methodology can be extended to study long-term relationships between sets of variables by including cointegrating vectors in the model (Enders, 2009). Cointegration among a set of variables must be demonstrated empirically rather than assumed. Here, we employ cointegration tests developed by Johansen (1991) to determine if there are one or more cointegrating relationships among inflation rates, unemployment rates and national economic expectations. With three variables, there might be zero, one or two such relationships (Johansen, 1991). If cointegrating relationships are detected, error correction components can be added to the equations of the VAR model to capture long-run relationships among the variables in the system (Enders, 2009).

Finally, three exogenous variables are included in the VAR to capture important shocks to the system. One is a dummy (0–1) variable scored one for each month after the run on the Northern Rock bank in September 2007, and zero for each month before that event. A second dummy variable is scored 1 for each month starting with the month (May 2010) when the Coalition Government came into office and zero beforehand. A third dummy variable is scored one for the first month (July 2007) when Gordon Brown replaced Tony Blair as leader of the Labour Party and prime minister and zero for other months. The aim of including these dummy variables in the VAR model is to control for discontinuities in any of the series caused by the Northern Rock shock, the change of government following the 2010 general election, and the change in prime ministers in the last Labour government.[8]

We begin the analysis of this VAR system by determining if there are one or more cointegrating relationships in the data. The results of the Johansen tests indicate that there is one such relationship. Johansen's trace test rejects the null hypothesis of no cointegrating vectors in favour of the alternative of one or more vectors ($\chi^2 = 42.868$, p < 0.001) (data not shown in tabular form). However, the trace test fails to reject the null hypothesis that there is at most one such vector ($\chi^2 = 11.893$, p = 0.162). The same message of one cointegrating vector is conveyed by Johansen's maximum eigenvalue test.[9] Given these results, we include one error correction term in each of the three equations of the VAR system for inflation, unemployment and national economic expectations.

We next estimate the resulting three-equation VAR system. Table 6.1 depicts the results of Granger-causality tests of the three variables – inflation, unemployment and economic expectations – in this system. These are obtained by testing if the removal of the lagged values of a predictor variable from one of the three VAR equations significantly reduces the explanatory power of that equation. If it does, this suggests that the predictor variable had a significant impact on variation in a dependent variable. Focusing on national economic expectations, there is evidence that these expectations Granger-cause inflation (p = 0.050), but not unemployment (p = 0.438) (see Table 6.1). This result suggests that the subjective economy 'Granger causes' price movements in the objective economy. Equally, there is evidence that the objective economy Granger causes national economic expectations. Both unemployment and inflation have significant effects on expectations (p = 0.046 and p = 0.024, respectively), net of controls for lagged values of the latter variable. Finally, the analyses also suggest that inflation Granger-causes unemployment (p = 0.069), but not vice versa (p = 0.309).

Table 6.1 *Granger causality tests for cointegrating VAR model of relationships involving national economic expectations, inflation rate and unemployment rate*

Dependent variable	Excluded predictor	χ^2	df	p
National economic expectations	Inflation rate	7.984	3	0.046*
	Unemployment rate	9.412	3	0.024*
	Inflation and unemployment	19.026	6	0.004**
Inflation rate	National economic expectations	7.809	3	0.050*
	Unemployment rate	3.590		0.309
	Expectations and unemployment	12.760	6	0.047*
Unemployment rate	National economic expectations	2.713	3	0.438
	Inflation rate	11.394	3	0.070+
	Expectations and inflation	11.394	6	0.077+

(N = 101)

Note: ** $p \leq 0.01$; * $p \leq 0.05$; + $p \leq 0.10$.

The strength of these relationships can be illustrated by using the VAR results to perform 'forecast variance decomposition' analyses (Enders, 2009). Figure 6.4 illustrates the results of this exercise with the VAR system projected several periods into the future. The analysis shows that after six months, nearly 40 per cent of the variance in economic expectations could be accounted for by autonomous innovations in inflation and unemployment. For their part, expectations could account for slightly less than one-fifth (18 per cent) of innovations in inflation and 7 per cent of innovations in unemployment. Like the Granger-causality analyses reported above, these results indicate that there is an intertemporal 'tennis match' among the objective and subjective economies.

Viewed generally, these findings are consistent with the argument by Sanders and Gavin (2004) that the subjective and objective economies are rather different from each other. In particular, the subjective economy is not simply an epiphenomenal reflection of the objective economy. Consistent with Keynes's arguments, although there is statistical evidence that inflation and unemployment rates affect expectations about the national economy, there is also evidence suggesting that

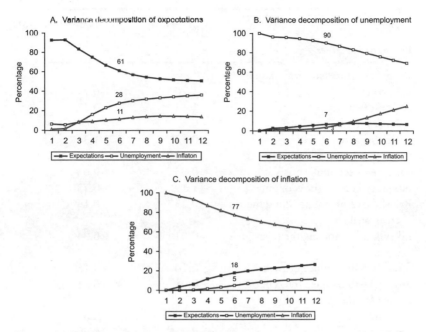

Figure 6.4 Variance decomposition of national economic expectations, inflation rates and unemployment rates.

expectations directly affect inflation rates and indirectly affect unemployment. We know from Chapter 5 that voters' judgments about parties' ability to handle the economy had a strong influence on voting behaviour in 2010. This, in turn, suggests that an economic strategy which largely ignores how people react to the conditions that strategy is seen to produce may generate substantial political risks for the Coalition Government. In the next section we use recent CMS data to analyze subjective economic and other determinants of support for the Coalition and its opposition rivals.

The subjective economy and party support in an era of austerity

To evaluate the influence of subjective economic evaluations and other theoretically interesting predictor variables on party support in the present era of austerity, we use pooled CMS survey data from January

Table 6.2 *Multinomial logit model of Coalition parties vote intentions, pooled January–August 2012 CMS surveys*

Predictor variables	Conservatives β	Liberal Democrats β
Party best most important issue:		
Labour	−1.20**	−0.71*
Conservatives	1.15**	0.23
Liberal Democrats	−0.47	2.07**
Other party	−0.53*	−1.34**
Subjective economic evaluations	0.30**	0.38**
Salience of economic crisis	0.03	−0.08
No party best on the economy	−1.19**	−0.73**
British government handling the crisis well	0.29**	0.16
Likelihood of solving the crisis in a year	0.01	0.04
Strategy will produce growth	0.20	0.15
Strategy will damage the economy	−0.08	0.31
Party identification:		
Conservative	1.76**	−0.01
Labour	−0.78**	−0.60+
Liberal Democrat	−0.15	2.98**
Other party	−0.35	0.64+
Party leader image:		
Miliband	−0.19**	−0.21**
Cameron	0.48**	−0.11*
Clegg	0.01	0.59**
Unemployed	−0.54*	0.60
Income	−0.01	−0.20*
Income squared	0.001	0.01*
Education	0.05	0.13*
Occupational status	−0.04	−0.06
Gender – male	0.09	0.19
Age	−0.04	0.07*
Age squared	0.00	−0.00
Ethnicity – white British	0.52**	0.12
Scotland	−0.62**	−0.60*
Wales	−0.41*	−0.09
McFadden R^2	0.68	

** $p \leq 0.01$; * $p \leq 0.05$; + $p \leq 0.10$.

Note: reference category is all other options, i.e. Labour and minor party vote intentions, declared intention to not vote and 'don't know'; N = 8563.

2012 to August 2012. The dependent variables measure support for various parties, with model parameters being estimated using multinomial logit techniques.

Table 6.2 displays the effects of several predictor variables on voting intentions for the Conservatives and the Liberal Democrats, with other alternatives (voting intentions for other parties, nonvoting and 'don't know's') treated as the reference category. Parameter estimates indicate that support for the Coalition parties was bolstered by positive economic evaluations and diminished by judgments that no party is competent to deal with the economy. The coefficients also testify that, with one exception, other indicators of public reactions to the recession are not significant drivers of Coalition vote intentions once subjective economic evaluations have been taken into account. The likelihood of solving the crisis over the next year and perceptions that the Coalition's austerity strategy will help or hurt the economy do not have direct effects on vote intentions.

A telling difference between the Conservative and Liberal Democrats is that the former party's prospects were enhanced by public perceptions that the Coalition Government is handling the crisis well (see Table 6.2). However, this was not the case for the latter party – Liberal Democrat support was not influenced by these perceptions. This finding implies that the Conservatives are likely to be credited for an economic revival if their current strategy proves to be successful, but their Liberal Democrat partners will not be so fortunate. The fact that the Conservatives are the dominant party and their austerity strategy was adopted by the Coalition against initial opposition by the Liberal Democrats is consistent with the idea that the public sees the strategy primarily as a Conservative policy. However, this is not all bad news for the Liberal Democrats since it also implies that they are less likely to be blamed if the perception that the Government is doing a bad job in managing the crisis continues to grow as the 2015 general election approaches.

Regarding other predictors, as expected, perceptions that Labour or other opposition parties are best at handling the most important issue designated by respondents undermines support for the Coalition parties. Equally, perceptions that either the Conservatives or the Liberal Democrats are best at handling such an issue boost support for these parties. However, the belief that the Conservatives are best on a most important issue does not affect Liberal Democrat support, and perceptions that the Liberal Democrats are best do not influence Conservative support. This suggests that the Coalition has effectively insulated its partner parties regarding vote intention decisions based on voters' perceptions of important issues.

A similar point can be made about partisanship: Conservative and Labour partisanship has influenced Conservative vote intentions in the expected directions, but Liberal Democrat partisanship has no effect. Equally, Labour and Liberal Democrat partisanship has affected Liberal Democrat vote intentions but these vote intentions have been unaffected by Conservative partisanship. The one exception to this pattern relates to party leader images. Positive feelings about Ed Miliband have reduced both Conservative and Liberal Democrat support, and positive feelings about David Cameron have strengthened Conservative support and weakened Liberal Democrat support. However, the pattern does not apply to Nick Clegg. A positive image of Clegg has enhanced Liberal Democrat vote intentions, but has no influence on the likelihood of casting a Conservative ballot. The implication is that David Cameron has had the ability to affect Liberal Democrat support, whereas Nick Clegg has lacked a similar capacity to affect Conservative support.

One final distinction in support for the Coalition partners in 2012 was that demographics had different effects on Conservative and Liberal Democrat vote intentions. Income, education and age affect Liberal Democrat, but not Conservative, vote intentions. In contrast, unemployment, ethnicity and residence in Wales have influenced Conservative but not Liberal Democrat vote intentions. Support for both parties has been negatively associated with residence in Scotland.

Table 6.3 estimates the effects of reactions to the recession and other predictor variables on support for Labour and minor opposition parties, with support for the Coalition partners as the reference category. The intriguing finding is that Labour voting intentions have not been affected by any of the economic variables including subjective economic evaluations, apart from perceptions that no party is best on the economy. In the latter case respondents who believed that no party could do the job were less likely to say that they would vote Labour just as in Table 6.2 they were less likely to say that they would vote Conservative or Liberal Democrat. Above, we observed that Labour has not recovered its reputation for economic competence following the 2010 election, and the findings in Table 6.3 reflect this. In the mid-term

Table 6.3 *Multinomial logit model of opposition parties vote intentions,
pooled January–August 2012 CMS surveys*

Predictor variables	Labour β	Minor opposition parties β
Party best most important issue:		
Labour	1.70**	0.22
Conservatives	−0.78**	−1.14**
Liberal Democrats	−1.63**	−1.80**
Other party	0.41	1.66**
Subjective economic evaluations	0.14	−0.14+
Salience of economic crisis	0.001	−0.01
Perception that no party is best on the economy	−1.08**	0.06
British government handling the crisis well	−0.06	−0.18*
Likelihood of solving the crisis in a year	−0.03	0.04
Strategy will produce growth	0.05	0.32*
Strategy will damage economy	0.25	0.37*
Party identification:		
Conservative	−1.25**	−0.71**
Labour	1.99**	−0.55**
Liberal Democrat	−0.54*	−0.49*
Other party	0.26	1.92**
Party leader image:		
Miliband	0.41**	−0.04
Cameron	−0.24**	−0.15**
Clegg	−0.13**	−0.10**
Unemployed	−0.34	−0.14
Income	−0.04	0.06
Income squared	0.002	−0.004
Education	0.04	0.05
Occupational status	0.03	−0.02
Gender – male	0.06	0.66**
Age	0.06*	0.07**
Age squared	−0.001*	−0.001**
Ethnicity – white British	−0.25	0.19
Scotland	−0.18	0.64**
Wales	0.71**	0.44+
McFadden R^2	0.56	

** $p \leq 0.01$; * $p \leq 0.05$; + $p \leq 0.10$.

Note: reference category is Conservative and Liberal Democrat vote intentions;
N = 8563.

of the Coalition Government, Labour was failing to receive electoral benefits from the 'double-dip' recession because a sizable number of voters thought that the party was at least partially responsible for the economic crisis that precipitated it.[10]

In other respects the likelihood of expressing a Labour vote intention was enhanced in anticipated ways by several predictor variables. These include Labour partisanship, a favourable image of Ed Miliband and perceptions that Labour was best at handling a respondent's most important issue. As also expected, Conservative and Liberal Democrat partisanship, positive evaluations of the leaders of these parties, and perceptions that the Conservatives or Liberal Democrats were best at handling the most important issue all reduced the likelihood of expressing a Labour vote intention. Finally, the quadratic effects for age (i.e. age and age squared) suggest that, circa 2012, Labour vote intenders tended to be middle-aged rather than members of younger or older age cohorts in the electorate. The party was also faring better in Wales than in England or Scotland. Clearly, the single most important problem facing Labour in the mid-term of the Coalition Government was its failure to attract voters discontented with the economic performance of the Conservatives and Liberal Democrats, despite the fact that there were a growing number of such people.

Support for 'Minor Opposition' parties in Table 6.3 refers to support for the nationalists in Scotland and Wales, and also UKIP, the Greens and the BNP. If we compare the determinants of vote intentions for one these parties with the drivers of support for the Coalition partners, we see that judgments that the Conservatives or the Liberal Democrats were best on the most important issue have had the predictable effect of lowering support for the minor parties. In contrast, judgments that Labour was best at handling the most important issue appear to have no effect on voting for these parties. Support for the minor parties was also bolstered by economic pessimism and by judgments that the Coalition was doing a bad job managing the economy. These findings suggest that various minor opposition parties have been recipients of economic discontent which in the past would have gone to Labour as the major opposition party and likely alternative government.

Regarding other predictor variables in the minor parties vote model, partisan attachments boosted support for these parties and identifications with one of their rivals reduced that support. As for leader images, positive images of David Cameron and Nick Clegg weakened support for the minor parties, whereas a positive image of Ed Miliband

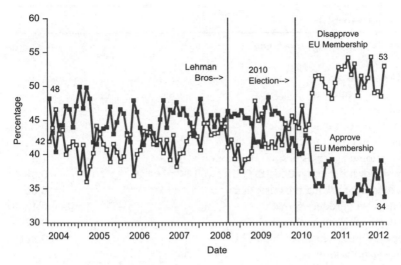

Figure 6.5 Attitudes towards British membership in the European Union, April 2004–August 2012.
Source: April 2004 – August 2012 CMS surveys.

had no effect. Finally, perceptions that one of the minor parties was best at handling a respondent's most important issue helped to raise support for them, whereas perceptions that the Conservatives or Liberal Democrats were best weakened it. Once again, perceptions that Labour was best had no effect on minor party support.

Viewed generally, the results in Table 6.3 suggest that at the midterm of the Coalition Government, minor parties have been beneficiaries of the continuing economic distress and the political discontent it has engendered. We can investigate this possibility in greater depth by studying support one of the minor parties, UKIP, a serious rival to the Conservatives in parts of southern England and East Anglia. In recent years, competition between UKIP and the Conservatives has grown stronger as both parties seek to profit from growing Euroscepticism in the electorate. In this regard, Figure 6.5 documents that public approval of British membership in the EU has fallen from 48 per cent in April 2004 to 34 per cent in August 2012, whereas disapproval has climbed from 42 to 53 per cent. The percentage disapproving EU membership has exceeded the percentage approving it in every month since March 2010 – shortly before the 2010 general election. Thus, the period since the Conservatives have been in office has provided

Table 6.4 *Binomial logit model of UKIP versus Conservative vote intentions, pooled January–August 2012 CMS surveys*

Predictor variables	β
Party best most important issue:	
Labour	0.58
Conservatives	−1.35**
Liberal Democrat	†
UKIP	1.44**
Subjective economic evaluations	−0.35*
Salience of economic crisis	−0.06
Perception no party is best on the economy	1.33**
British government handling the crisis well	−0.38**
Likelihood of solving the crisis in a year	0.06
Strategy will produce growth	0.11
Strategy will damage economy	0.63*
Approval British membership in EU	−0.88**
Party identification:	
Conservative	−1.86**
Labour	1.59**
Liberal Democrat	0.46
UKIP	1.03**
Party leader image:	
Miliband	−0.01
Cameron	−0.46**
Clegg	−0.10+
Unemployed	0.63
Income	0.21
Income squared	−0.01*
Education	−0.14
Occupational status	−0.02
Gender – male	0.09
Age	0.01
Age squared	0.00
Ethnicity – white British	−0.58+
Scotland	−0.11
Wales	0.56
McFadden R^2	0.75

** $p \leq 0.01$; * $p \leq 0.05$; + $p \leq 0.10$.

† No respondents in this sub-sample of Conservative and UKIP voters selected the Liberal Democrats as the party best able to handle what they designated as the most important issue.

Note: UKIP vote intentions are scored 1 and Conservative vote intentions are scored 0; N = 3112.

a favourable public opinion context for UKIP's brand of Eurosceptic politics. The interesting question is whether longstanding competition between the parties on the issue of Europe now extends to rivalry in relation to management of the economy.

Table 6.4 presents the results of a binomial logistic regression of UKIP voting intentions over the January–August 2012 period with Conservative voting intentions as the reference category. The model specification is the same as those in Tables 6.2 and 6.3 with the addition of an extra predictor – attitudes towards Britain's membership in the European Union. Not surprisingly, the large negative coefficient for this variable demonstrates that Euroscepticism is a predictable driver of UKIP support even when the only alternative is a Conservative vote intention. However, the rivalry between the two parties now extends to recession-related attitudes and management of the economy. Specifically, positive economic evaluations work to reduce UKIP vote intentions vis à vis the Conservatives as do judgments that the Coalition is doing a good job in managing the crisis. In contrast, judgments that that no party can manage the economy effectively and that the austerity strategy will damage economic recovery stimulate UKIP voting intentions at the expense of the Conservatives.

The relationship between judgments about Labour performance and UKIP support is very different from the comparable relationship for the Conservatives and UKIP. Perceptions that Labour is best at handling a respondent's most important issue are not a significant predictor of an intention to vote for UKIP, but perceptions that the Conservatives are best at handling a most important issue is a significant negative predictor of UKIP support. In addition, Conservative partisanship reduces UKIP voting intentions, whereas Labour partisanship increases them. Finally, feelings about Ed Miliband do not play a role in influencing the UKIP vote. This is in sharp contrast to feelings about David Cameron and, to a lesser extent, Nick Clegg. People who harbour disaffection with Cameron and Clegg are significantly more likely to vote UKIP than are those who are positively disposed towards them.

Conclusion: party support in an age of austerity

Analyses presented in this chapter testify that the subjective economy together with related measures of attitudes towards the recession and the financial crisis have played an important role in influencing voting intentions in recent years. The effects have been direct, but also indirect, operating via subjective economic evaluations. When the relationship between the subjective and objective economies is investigated, it appears that variations in inflation and unemployment affect the dynamics of expectations about the economy in predictable ways, but that those expectations, in turn, affect inflation and indirectly, unemployment. This latter finding is consistent with Keynes's insights about the importance of 'animal spirits' – expectations and uncertainty – on key macroeconomic outcomes, and it highlights the damage that a major economic crisis can have on governing parties' re-election chances.

Such is the magnitude of the political damage produced by the crisis that Labour failed to throw off the blame for it by the mid-term of the Coalition Government some two years after Labour's erstwhile leader, Gordon Brown, was evicted from Downing Street. The evidence presented here suggests that minor parties, particularly UKIP, have profited from growing disillusionment with the Coalition's austerity strategy. Labour's record during the years when Gordon Brown was in Number 10 grappling with the deepening global economic crisis has left a lingering legacy of mistrust and tarnished Labour's brand for managerial competence. This finding carries the implication that if the economy does improve before the general election of 2015, Labour is likely to lose ground. If the party is having difficulty regaining economic credibility when times are hard, it is unlikely to regain it when times get better.

That said, relationships between the objective and subjective economies suggest that prospects for a major economic recovery are hindered while the subjective economy remains seriously depressed. The macroeconomic mood is significantly more pessimistic in the mid-term of the Coalition Government than it was immediately after the general election. Moreover, the mood was much darker at the time of the election than it had been in the boom years before 2007. Events at the time of writing suggest that the Coalition is acutely aware of this problem and plans to reign in its austerity strategy as much as possible without spooking financial markets continuing to insist on structural reforms to the macroeconomy.

A harbinger of this change of course is the fact that the Coalition accepted the recommendations of Lord Heseltine's report 'No Stone Unturned in Pursuit of Growth' (Heseltine, 2012) when it was published in October 2012. This report called for a radical reappraisal of the last thirty years of laissez-faire thinking in relation to economic management. Lord Heseltine writes:

'We are experiencing the worst economic crisis of modern times. As a consequence many of the old certainties have come under intense scrutiny. There is a hunger for ideas that could contribute to the restoration of growth. There is no shortage of proposals. But what strikes me – and encourages me – is the unanimity of, among others, the CBI, TUC and The Times that Britain needs an industrial strategy. The very words are controversial. With them comes the baggage of past attempts and past failures'. (Heseltine, 2012: 4)

The Heseltine Report calls for an approach to stimulating economic growth which predates Margaret Thatcher's arrival in Downing Street in 1979. The extent to which the Report's 89 recommendations will be implemented by Prime Minister Cameron and his colleagues remains unclear, but the Report's initial reception suggests that they are rethinking their austerity strategy – a strategy that threatens to deliver electoral defeat if pursued until May 2015.

7 | *Choosing how to choose*

The AV ballot referendum

Since the Conservative–Liberal Democrat Coalition came to power in May 2010, campaigning for change has involved more than disputes about public policy. Institutional reform has been a prominent item on the political agenda. To date, the most noteworthy effort has involved a national referendum which asked the electorate if it wished to change the time-honoured Single-Member Plurality (First-Past-The-Post) electoral system in favour of the Alternative Vote (AV) system. The AV referendum, held on 5 May 2011, was the first national referendum held in the UK since 1975 when a vote on continued membership of the European Community took place. The AV referendum arose out of the agreement reached between the Conservatives and Liberal Democrats when they formed a coalition after the 2010 general election. Negotiations on this issue were difficult because the Conservatives had opposed changing the electoral system in their party manifesto where they had promised to keep the single-member plurality (first-past-the-post) system. In contrast, the Liberal Democrats had called for the Single Transferable Vote (STV) electoral system in their manifesto.[1]

The agreement that the two parties reached on holding a referendum on AV was an important element of the larger deal they made on the terms for forming a coalition government. Fundamentally, the Conservatives got what they wanted with regard to the economy and public-sector finances, namely Liberal Democrat support for a vigorous austerity programme. In return, the Liberal Democrats received support for holding a referendum on changing the electoral system. Although Liberal Democrat Leader, Nick Clegg, had labelled AV a 'miserable little compromise' before the 2010 election, he and his colleagues knew that it was a compromise that held promise of enabling them to do both 'good' and 'well'. The Liberal Democrats would do 'good' because democratically motivated institutional reform was a longstanding goal for the party which prided itself on advocacy of a progressive political agenda. Implementing AV would mean that elections very likely would produce a closer match between a party's popular vote total and its share of parliamentary seats, thus providing more equitable representation at Westminster.

At the same time, the Liberal Democrats would do 'well', because the balance of party support in Britain was such that holding elections under AV would enhance the prospect of hung parliaments. With no party able to win a majority of seats, the Liberal Democrats likely would hold the balance of power after any given election. Since obtaining their support would be the key to political power, the Liberal Democrats would be perpetual partners in governing coalitions, much as the Free Democrats have been in Germany or the Radical Socialists were in the French Fourth Republic. The Liberal Democrats believed that, if AV were implemented, they would be transformed from perpetual 'also rans' to the pivotal player in British party politics.

As part of their negotiations on forming a coalition, the Conservatives and the Liberal Democrats agreed on a compromise, which was to hold a referendum on adopting the Alternative Vote system, while acknowledging that they would campaign on opposite sides of the debate. It was a deal which neither party really wanted, but it was one which was reached to make the Coalition Agreement possible (Bogdanor, 2011; Norton, 2011). As ballot day approached and it became increasingly clear that the prospects of securing a Yes majority were fading, some Liberal Democrats claimed that the Conservatives had agreed informally that they would not campaign vigorously against AV. This undocumented charge carried little weight with the electorate, many of whom seemed indifferent to AV or electoral reform more generally.

The Parliamentary Voting Systems and Constituencies Bill, which introduced the enabling legislation for the referendum, went through Parliament in October 2010. At that time, Caroline Lucas, newly elected Green Party MP for Brighton, proposed an amendment to the Bill which would have offered voters a choice of three different electoral systems. But this was rejected and the deal agreed between the Conservatives and Liberal Democrats was preserved with AV and the existing first-past-the-post electoral systems as the only options for the voters to consider.

The referendum question originally read: 'Do you want the United Kingdom to adopt the "alternative vote" system instead of the current "first past the post" system for electing Members of Parliament to the House of Commons?' After criticism by the Electoral Commission that this question was difficult to understand, the wording was changed to read: 'At present, the UK uses the "first past the post" system to elect MPs to the House of Commons. Should the "alternative vote" system be used instead?' With this revised wording, the referendum was scheduled for 5 May 2011.

The referendum campaign

In his extensive cross-national study of referendums LeDuc (2003) concludes that referendum campaigns tend to follow a stylized three-stage pattern. At the beginning of the campaign the 'Yes' side is ahead, but large numbers of voters remain uncertain about which side to support. Then, as the campaign unfolds, there is a sizable, progressive shift in public opinion. In the end, the 'No' side ends up winning, often by a substantial margin. Survey evidence indicates that the dynamics of support-opposition to AV during the 2011 referendum campaign adhered closely to 'LeDuc's Law'. Figure 7.1a presents trends in vote intentions from January to early May 2011 using data from published public opinion polls and the BES monthly Continuous Monitoring Surveys (CMS). In January the Yes side held a slight lead and about one-third of the respondents said that they did not know how they felt about a change in the electoral system. Although the 'don't know' group decreased as the campaign progressed, it was still running at about one-fifth of those surveyed two weeks before the balloting. Concomitant with this decline among the undecideds, support for a No vote increased substantially as voting day approached.

This pattern is echoed in Figure 7.1b which displays data from the BES AV Referendum Study panel survey that tracks daily movements in support/opposition to the proposal in the month leading up to the vote. This figure indicates that in early April between one-fifth and one-quarter of the respondents were uncertain about what they would do, and it was only in the last fortnight of the campaign that the number of 'don't knows' fell below 15 per cent as the number intending to vote No surged upward. Figure 7.1b illustrates that this upward trend in No vote intentions over the month before the referendum was very strong, the linear correlation with time being fully +0.88, with the downward trend in the percentage of 'don't knows' being fully −0.93.

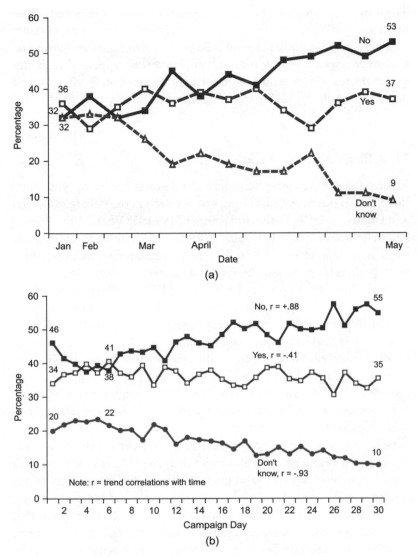

Figure 7.1 Dynamics of AV referendum vote intentions.
A. Referendum vote intentions, January 2011–May 2011.
B. Referendum vote intentions, 5 April– 4 May 2011.
Source: Figure 7.1a: BES Monthly Continuous Monitoring Surveys and published YouGov polls asking actual referendum question; Figure 7.1b: daily random samples from the pre-referendum wave of the BES AV referendum survey.

The downward trend in Yes vote intentions is less pronounced, albeit nontrivial (−0.41).

When balloting took place on 5 May the referendum proposal was decisively rejected − 32.1 per cent of the voters supported a change in the electoral system and 67.9 per cent opposed it. Turnout was a decidedly desultory 42.2 per cent (Electoral Commission, 2011).

Modelling referendum choice

Referendums have intrigued political scientists for many years and there are several overview volumes of research in the field (e.g. Bowler and Donovan, 1998; Butler and Ranney, 1994; de Vrees, 2007; Farrell and Schmitt-Beck, 2002; LeDuc, 2003). Alongside these collections, there is a number of case studies of particular referendums which have been held in various countries at different points of time (e.g. Blais *et al.*, 1996; Clarke and Kornberg, 1994; LeDuc, 2003, 2005; Marcussen and Zolner, 2001; Vowles, 1995). One important topic in this literature concerns the scheduling of these events. Why are referendums held? The dominant explanation sees referendums as the product of an elite-level game conducted by rational actors − that is, party strategists and leaders whose aim is to maximize their legislative representation (Benoit, 2004; Boix, 1999). Although interesting, these accounts tend to neglect the role of voters who are treated largely as spectators in elite-level contests.

Despite this emphasis on the behaviour of political elites, it is not difficult to conceive of ways in which voters might get involved in such games as players who demand electoral change or other institutional reforms. In this regard, previous research on the determinants of referendum voting has focused on two major types of explanation that might account for how voters behave in referendums. The first type of explanation involves what might be termed the 'merits of the case' − that is, judgments about the benefits and costs of passage or rejection of a referendum proposal. The motivating idea is quite simple − people will vote Yes if they believe that expected benefits of a proposal outweigh anticipated costs, and if they think that the costs will outweigh the benefits, they will vote no (see e.g. Blais *et al.*, 1996; Clarke and Kornberg, 1994; Clarke *et al.*, 2004a; Lupia, 1994). An extended version of the hypothesis encompasses broader political goals and values that will be furthered or inhibited by passing or rejecting a referendum proposal.

The second major type of explanation focuses on heuristics or cues that voters may employ to help them make their referendum choice. As discussed previously in this book and in our earlier studies of electoral choice in Britain and elsewhere, over the past two decades experimental economists and political psychologists have emphasized the importance of heuristics as guides to action in a broad range of decision-making situations (e.g. Gigerenzer, 2008; Gigerenzer *et al.*, 2011; Lupia, 1994; Lupia and McCubbins, 1998; Mondak, 1993; Sniderman *et al.*, 1991; see also Conlisk, 1996). In research on voting behaviour scholars have focused on the cueing properties of partisan attachments[2] and leader/candidate images. When deciding how to cast their ballots in a referendum, voters ask 'Who are the friends?' and 'Who are the enemies?' of the proposal and then consult their store of information about these individuals and groups. For example, when trying to decide what to do in the AV referendum, Conservative identifiers and people who had a positive image of party leader, David Cameron, likely would vote No because the Conservative Party and Mr Cameron supported the existing FPTP electoral system. Similarly, Liberal Democrat identifiers and those with positive images of party leader, Nick Clegg, would vote Yes because Clegg and his party endorsed AV.[3]

Other heuristics have been proposed as well. One of them is party performance, with voters using their evaluations of a party's performance as a cue whether they should accept or reject the position that party takes on a referendum proposal.[4] Yet another heuristic with considerable currency is risk orientation.[5] The hypothesis is straightforward: *ceteris paribus*, risk-acceptant people are more likely than risk-averse ones to vote Yes because they are more willing to take a chance on change. The focus on risk acceptance/aversion in studies of referendum voting comports well with research showing that people are likely to 'privilege the downside' when making decisions in many areas of life by emphasizing possible losses over possible gains (e.g. Kahneman, 2011; Kahneman *et al.*, 1982; Thaler, 1994), as well as the observation that major referendum proposals are typically defeated, often by wide margins.

Although cost-benefit calculations and heuristics are key variables in our referendum voting model, we also consider the role of mobilization efforts by groups who support or oppose the referendum proposal. In the case of the AV referendum, two umbrella groups were formed to mobilize supporters and opponents to the proposal. These groups were called 'Yes to Fairer Votes' and 'No to AV', respectively. In addition, we consider the impact of cognitive engagement. Following previous research (e.g. Dalton, 2008; Whiteley *et al.*, 2011), we hypothesize that well-educated and politically knowledgeable people are more likely to be exposed to positive messages about a referendum proposal such as AV which invoke broader democratic norms concerning the desirability of effective citizen involvement in the political process and public control over elected representatives. All else equal, such persons will be more likely to vote Yes than are their less knowledgeable and less well-educated fellow citizens. Finally, we specify several sociodemographic variables as statistical controls.

In summary, our AV voting model includes explanatory variables measuring: (i) perceived costs and benefits of AV and FPTP; (ii) broader goals and values associated with AV and FPTP; (iii) leader, partisan and party performance heuristics; (iv) risk orientations; (v) cognitive engagement (levels of political knowledge and formal education); (vi) sociodemographic controls (age, gender, income, residence in England, Scotland or Wales[6]). Since the dependent variable (voting for or against AV) is a dichotomy, a binomial logit model is used to estimate parameters of interest.

The data employed for the analyses which follow were gathered in conjunction with the Continuous Monitoring Survey (CMS) component of the 2010 BES.[7] The referendum survey employed a pre-post panel design, with 22 124 eligible voters being surveyed in 30 random daily replicates over the month preceding the balloting. In the week after the referendum, 18 556 of these individuals completed a second survey, yielding an 83.9 per cent panel retention rate.

The benefits and costs of AV

The pre-referendum wave of the referendum survey contained several 'agree-disagree' statements designed to ascertain views about the pros and cons of switching Britain's electoral system from first-past-the post (FPTP) to the Alternative Vote (AV).[8] Figure 7.2 shows that there was only one statement for which a large plurality favoured FPTP over AV – nearly half of the respondents (48.5 per cent) agreed that FPTP helps

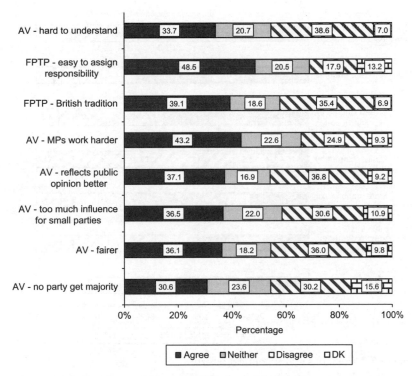

Figure 7.2 Perceptions of AV and FPTP electoral systems.
Source: CMS AV referendum survey.

voters to assign responsibility for policy successes and failures and less
than one in five (17.9 per cent) disagreed. In contrast, a substantial
plurality agreed with the idea that implementing AV would make MPs
work harder and less than one quarter disagreed. For all of the other
statements, the division of opinion was quite evenly balanced. For
example, there was an even division of opinion about AV being fairer
than FPTP, with 36.1 per cent agreeing and 36.0 per cent disagreeing.
Similarly, 30.6 per cent believed that no party could get a majority
if AV was implemented, but 30.2 per cent thought otherwise. Again,
slightly over one-third agreed that AV was hard to understand, but
nearly two-fifths disagreed. Overall, an average of 33.6 per cent gave
pro-AV responses to the statements and 35.8 per cent gave pro-FPTP
answers. An exploratory factor analysis (EFA) of responses to the eight
statements yields a single factor which explains 54.9 per cent of the

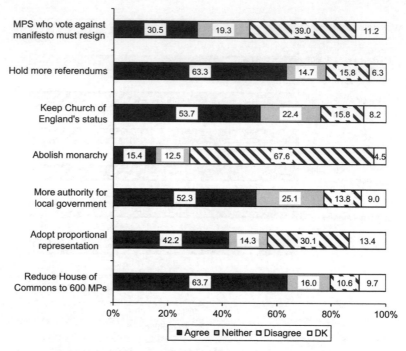

Figure 7.3 Opinions about political reforms.
Source: CMS AV referendum survey.

item variance. Factor scores from this EFA are used to measure the perceived benefits and costs of AV versus FPTP.

In addition to various specific benefits and costs of AV and FPTP, referendum voting is hypothesized to vary according to beliefs about the desirability of various kinds of political reform. Several agree–disagree statements were included in the CMS referendum surveys to tap these views.[9] Responses (see Figure 7.3) indicate that was substantial sentiment in favour of reform. Specifically, 63.3 per cent endorsed the idea of holding more national referendums to decide important issues and only 15.8 per cent were opposed. Similarly, 52.3 per cent agreed that more authority should be devolved to local government and only 13.8 per cent though this was a bad idea. Again, over three-fifths wanted to reduce the size of the House of Commons and one in ten disagreed. And, although division of opinion was closer, 42.2 per cent favoured proportional representation and 30.1 per cent were opposed.

Not all of the statements revealed strong sentiment for reform. In particular, fully two-thirds of the respondents disagreed with a statement about the desirability of abolishing the monarchy and a small majority said that they wanted to retain the Church of England's established status. Also, tempering evidence cited above indicating substantial support for proportional representation, when answering another question, over two-fifths said it was more important that one party obtain a majority of seats in parliament so it could govern on its own, with slightly over one-third answering that it was more important for a party's seat totals to match its vote totals.[10]

A second exploratory factor analysis was used to summarize these data on attitudes towards political reform. This analysis yielded three distinct factors that collectively explained 56.0 per cent of the item variance. Based on the pattern of item loadings, it is evident that the first of these factors captures attitudes towards proportion representation, whereas the second factor taps sentiments about enhanced democratization of the political process, and the third organizes feelings about traditional British institutions. The three sets of factor scores generated by this analysis are employed to measure orientations towards political reform.

Heuristics and political knowledge

Above, we have identified heuristics or cues that might influence voting in the AV referendum. In the run-up to the balloting, none of these heuristics advantaged the Liberal Democrats, AV's chief proponents. For example, a mere 3.0 per cent of the respondents in our April 2011 pre-referendum survey indicated that they thought the Lib Dems were the party best able to handle the issue they deemed most important (24.6 per cent chose the Conservatives, and 23.2 per cent chose Labour). Similarly, only 9.0 per cent thought of themselves as Liberal Democrat partisans, whereas 31.9 per cent and 25.6 per cent identified with Labour or the Conservatives, respectively). And, in sharp contrast to the situation during the 2010 general election campaign, Liberal Democrat leader, Nick Clegg, was heartily disliked in spring 2011 – his score on a 0 ('dislike') to 10 ('like') scale was only 3.7, nearly two full points what it had been a year earlier.[11] In contrast, Conservative Leader David Cameron's average like–dislike score, although far from brilliant, was 4.4, exactly what it had been in May 2010.

Labour's new leader, Ed Miliband, was also not especially popular – his average like–dislike score was 4.2. Still, this was half a point higher than the dismal score (3.7) recorded by his predecessor, Gordon Brown immediately before the 2010 general election.

Taken together, these data clearly show that none of the parties had a decisive 'heuristics advantage' when voters cast their ballots in the AV referendum. Perhaps particularly damaging for the Yes side was the fact that the cues being provided by the principal proponents of AV – the Liberal Democrats – were very weak. Nor could the Yes forces expect a strong boost from Labour. Labour had a small plurality share of party identifiers, but the party was divided on the merits of AV. Although new party leader, Ed Miliband, endorsed AV, he expressed little enthusiasm for it. And, as just noted, many voters had not warmed to him. Moreover, several senior Labour politicians, including erstwhile cabinet 'heavyweights' Margaret Beckett, John Prescott and John Reid, had voiced their opposition to changing the electoral system. Conservative heuristics had little pulling power either. The Conservatives had fewer identifiers than Labour, the Conservative edge as party favoured on important issues was very small, and their leader, David Cameron, generated little enthusiasm outside of the Tory heartlands.

As observed earlier, political knowledge is another potentially influential explanatory variable. Political knowledge is a key component in cognitive engagement models of voting turnout and civic involvement, and it is hypothesized to have an important mediating role affecting how voters use heuristics. Political knowledge has been measured in many different ways (e.g. Delli Carpini and Keeter, 1997; Luskin, 1987), but here we employ a five-item battery of questions concerning the British electoral system. None of these questions concerns the positions of parties or leaders on AV – measures of the latter will be employed later as part of our investigation of interaction effects involving leader images and 'heuristic-specific' political knowledge.

Responses to the electoral-system knowledge battery are displayed in Figure 7.4. They show that impressive majorities (82.3 per cent and 85.7 per cent, respectively) knew that the polls close at 10 pm and that any eligible voter could obtain a postal vote. A smaller, but still large, majority (72.7 per cent) knew that the voting age was not 16. In contrast, questions about the ability of Commonwealth citizens to vote and the existence of a 40 per cent turnout threshold for the results of the

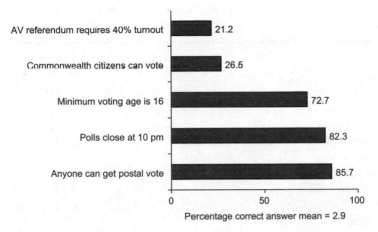

Figure 7.4 Electoral system knowledge: percentages giving correct answers.

AV referendum to be declared binding had far fewer correct answers (26.5 per cent and 21.2 per cent, respectively). Overall, the mean number of correct answers to the electoral-system knowledge battery was 2.9 (range 0 to 5). In the next section we will use the number of correct answers to the battery as an index of political knowledge when specifying the multivariate model of referendum voting.

Analyzing referendum voting

The results of the binomial logit analysis of referendum voting show that the model performs well; fully 88.6 per cent of the votes are correctly classified, this being a 71 per cent reduction in prediction errors compared to a naive-mode guessing approach (see Table 7.1). Consonant with these impressive numbers, the McKelvey R^2 is a very sizable 0.78. Regarding specific predictors, the coefficients reported in Table 7.1 indicate that judgments about the costs and benefits of AV had a highly significant effect ($p < 0.001$) on referendum voting, as did the three variables (proportional representation, citizen involvement, traditional institutions) measuring attitudes towards political reform. Signs on these coefficients indicate that, as expected, people who saw AV as having more benefits than costs and those who favoured proportional representation and greater citizen involvement in the political process were likely to vote Yes. In contrast, but also as anticipated,

Table 7.1 *Binomial logit model of Yes voting in Alternative Vote (AV) referendum*

Predictor	Model		Change in probability of voting Yes[†]
	β	s.e.	Δ
Costs-benefits of AV and FPTP	−2.04***	0.05	−0.98
Political reform:			
Proportional representation	0.91***	0.04	0.70
Citizen involvement	0.11***	0.03	0.15
Traditional institutions	−0.34***	0.03	−0.39
Leader images:			
Miliband	0.10***	0.01	0.19
Cameron	−0.11***	0.02	−0.22
Clegg	0.12***	0.02	0.24
Political knowledge	0.08**	0.02	0.08
Party best most important issue:			
Labour	0.14	0.09	ns
Conservatives	−0.15	0.10	ns
Liberal Democrats	0.26	0.22	ns
Other party	0.05	0.11	ns
Party identification:			
Labour	−0.06	0.09	ns
Conservatives	−0.48***	0.11	−0.08
Liberal Democrats	0.30**	0.12	0.07
Other party	−0.16	0.12	ns
Campaign contact:			
Yes to fairer votes	0.25**	0.09	0.04
No to AV	−0.14*	0.08	−0.03
Risk orientation	0.14***	0.04	0.05
Risk orientation squared	−0.02***	0.005	‡
Age	0.00	0.00	0.07
Education	0.14***	0.02	0.13
Gender	0.36***	0.06	0.07
Income	0.01	0.01	ns
Region:			
Scotland	−0.12	0.10	ns
Wales	−0.12	0.13	ns

Table 7.1 (cont.)

Predictor	Model		Change in probability of voting Yes[†]
	β	s.e.	Δ
Constant	−2.70***	0.23	
McKelvey R^2 =	0.78		
Percentage correctly classified =	88.6		
Lambda =	0.71		
Log-likelihood =	−3870.46		
AIC =	7794.92		
N =	15137		

*** $p \leq 0.001$; ** $p \leq 0.01$; * $p \leq 0.05$, one-tailed test.

ns – coefficient not significant, $P > 0.05$.

[†] change in probability of voting Yes as predictor varies from lowest to highest value with other predictors held at means in the case of continuous variables or 0 in case of dummy variables.

[‡] for risk orientation, change in probability is calculated for both risk and risk squared.

people who supported traditional British institutions (the Monarchy, the Church of England) were likely to vote No.

Heuristics were at work as well. Images of the three party leaders were influential and, as hypothesized, positive images of Clegg and Miliband were associated with an increased likelihood of a Yes vote, and a positive image of Cameron was associated with an increased likelihood of a No vote. Partisanship was influential too, with Liberal Democrat identifiers tending to vote Yes, and Conservative identifiers tending to vote No. And, although judgments about party performance on important issues were not influential, risk orientations were statistically significant. As Table 7.1 shows, the relationship is quadratic, with the signs on the risk terms indicating that, up to a point, increasing risk acceptance was associated with an enhanced probability of voting Yes. However, at the highest levels of risk acceptance, the relationship is reversed. This finding is consistent with the idea that AV was an acknowledged 'halfway' house in the universe of electoral reform.

As observed above, Nick Clegg himself had characterized AV as a 'miserable little comprise',[12] something he was reminded of during the campaign.

Political knowledge and campaign contact variables also work in anticipated ways. As Table 7.1 documents, electoral-system knowledge has the hypothesized positive effect on Yes voting; other things equal, more knowledgeable people were more enthusiastic about AV. This is also true for education; persons with higher levels of formal education were more likely to vote Yes. As for campaign contact, people contacted by the 'Yes to Fairer Votes' group campaigning for AV were more likely to respond with a Yes vote than were those who were not contacted by this group. In contrast, people contacted by the 'No to AV' group campaigning against AV were apt to vote No. And, net of all other considerations, men were more likely than women to support AV.

As noted in earlier chapters, the logit model's nonlinear function form inhibits easy interpretation of the strength of the effects of predictor variables. Accordingly, we provide intuition about their effects by constructing scenarios in which a predictor of interest is varied across its range while setting other predictors at their means in the case of continuous variables or at zero in the case of multiple-category dummy variables (i.e. party identification, party best on most important issue).[13] The results (Table 7.1, column 3) indicate that judgments about the costs and benefits of AV had a very impressive effect; as these judgments move across their range the probability of voting Yes changes by fully 0.98 points. The effects of attitudes towards proportional representation and traditional institutions were smaller, but still sizable, being 0.70 points for the former predictor and 0.39 points for the latter one. Leader heuristics exerted substantial effects as well; changes in feelings about Cameron, Clegg and Miliband were capable of altering the probability of voting Yes by 0.22, 0.24 and 0.19 points, respectively. The impact of partisan heuristics was considerably smaller – 0.08 points for Conservative identification and 0.07 points for Liberal Democrat identification. Changing risk orientations mattered little, altering the probability of a Yes vote by only 0.05 points.

Similarly small effects obtained for other predictors. Variations in electoral system knowledge and education could vary the probability of a Yes vote by 0.08 and 0.13 points, respectively. Campaign contact effects operated as well, with contact by the Yes to Fairer Votes increasing the probability of a Yes vote by 0.04 points. The impact of contact by No to AV was also very small, 0.03 points. Gender effects were also weak; in the scenario being considered, men were only 0.07 points more likely than women to vote Yes.

Overall, these results accord well with previous research on referendum voting. Merits of the case considerations and a variety of heuristics were clearly at work, with leader images being particularly influential among the latter. In the next section, we investigate the possibility that the effects of leader heuristics varied across the electorate, being mediated by variations in levels and types of political knowledge.

Party leader and political knowledge interactions

The preceding analysis documents that party leader heuristics behaved as hypothesized – controlling for all other factors, positive feelings about Ed Miliband and Nick Clegg enhanced the likelihood of voting Yes in the referendum and positive feelings about David Cameron diminished the likelihood of voting Yes. Reacting to similar results in other studies, some scholars have conjectured that the impact of leader heuristics varies across the electorate. The claim is that less politically knowledgeable people give greater weight to leader heuristics than do more knowledgeable individuals who have the cognitive resources to make decisions in accordance with the precepts of classic microeconomic-style utility maximization (e.g. Bartle, 2005; Mondak, 1993). People in the latter group are the political 'smart money' – having the requisite knowledge and ability, they downplay leader and other heuristics and 'do the math themselves'.

There is a rival hypothesis. Consonant with findings in experimental economics (Gigerenzer, 2008; Gigerenzer *et al.*, 2011; see also Clarke *et al.*, 2009b), it can be argued that politically sophisticated voters actually pay *more*, not less, attention to readily available cues, including those provided by partisan attachments and party leader images. Stated simply, sophisticated voters recognize that they do not have the knowledge and skills needed to make fully rational decisions. As per the discussion in Chapter 5, they are 'smart enough to know that they are not smart enough' (Clarke *et al.*, 2009a). They react by employing easily accessible cues provided by highly salient sources. In a Westminster-style democracy such as Great Britain, party leader images constitute one such source. By relying on leader cues, knowledgeable voters are the 'really smart money'.

It has been argued that reliance on leader cues to help make a political decision requires that voters *know* what the leader's position is on the choice under consideration (Karp, 1998). For example, to use their image of David Cameron as a heuristic when deciding how to cast their ballots in the AV referendum, voters need to know that the prime minister is opposed to AV. This argument is incorrect; in fact, all that is required is that voters *believe* that they know Mr Cameron's position. If they get the prime minister's position wrong, this would be no barrier to casting a Yes ballot because they believed that he wanted Britain to adopt AV. Every day millions of people act on false premises when making all sorts of decisions and there is no reason that the choices they make in elections or referendums should be exceptions.

However, there are reasons to expect that, in fact, accurate knowledge of a leader's position will be positively correlated with the strength of that leader's image as a heuristic. The idea is that voters may be interested in using leader images as cues in their decision-making process and are thereby motivated to seek knowledge on the leaders' positions on the choice at issue. Extending the 'really smart money' hypothesis discussed above, one may hypothesize that there exists a group of voters who want accurate information about leaders' positions so that they can use that information together with their leader images to help them make the decision of interest. In this regard, accurate information about leaders' positions on a highly salient topic such as a change in the country's electoral system typically is relatively easy to acquire. In fact, no special effort may be required – knowledge of where the leaders stand may be obtained *en passant* as voters peruse their daily newspapers or watch the evening news – the assumption being that the media typically (not invariably) provide accurate 'for' or 'against' information about major party leaders' positions on highly salient topics. Indeed, one might conjecture that, *ceteris paribus*, the ready availability of such knowledge enhances the likelihood that voters will use a leader heuristic (e.g. Zaller, 1992). If accurate knowledge of where leaders' stand on an important topic is easily acquired, why not use it and save the effort of seeking out additional information?

To summarize, there are three interaction hypotheses of interest. The first hypothesis is what we call the conventional 'smart money' hypothesis. According to this hypothesis, politically sophisticated

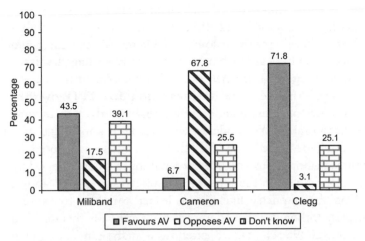

Figure 7.5 Knowledge of leaders' positions on AV.
Source: CMS AV referendum survey.

voters – here operationalized in terms of having a relatively rich store of factual political knowledge – give less weight to leader heuristics than do less sophisticated persons. The second, rival 'really smart money' hypothesis asserts the converse, namely that sophisticated voters give more weight to leader heuristics than do less sophisticated voters. The third hypothesis is a variant of hypothesis two: hypothesis three maintains that the *kind* of information that matters is knowledge about leaders' positions – sophisticated voters are more likely to have this knowledge and to use it to help them decide. 'Really smart' voters economize by using a readily available and accurate cue – for example, knowledge of a leader's position – in combination with their image of that leader to facilitate their decision-making task.

In the present context, these hypotheses are tested by incorporating party leader × political knowledge interaction effects in a multivariate model of referendum choice that is otherwise identical to the one analyzed above. Hypotheses 1 and 2 are tested using the measure of electoral system knowledge employed in that analysis (see Figure 7.4). In contrast, Hypothesis 3 is tested using variables that measure whether a voter knows the positions of Cameron, Clegg and Miliband on AV versus FPTP. In this regard, Figure 7.5 shows that sizable majorities of our survey respondents had accurate knowledge of where Cameron and Clegg stood on electoral system reform. Specifically, 67.8 per cent knew that Cameron opposed AV and slightly more, 71.8 per cent, knew that Clegg endorsed it. Ed Miliband's situation was considerably murkier. In keeping with his low profile in the AV campaign and the split among senior Labour party politicians regarding the desirability of jettisoning FPTP for AV, only 43.5 per cent of our survey respondents knew that Miliband was ready to throw FPTP over the side. For purposes of the interaction effect analyses, these three variables are dichotomized; respondents with accurate knowledge of a leader's position are scored 1 and all other respondents are scored 0.

These three dichotomous variables are multiplied by corresponding leader image variables. In the multivariate analyses presented above, we relied on the summary like–dislike leader variables to capture leader images. Although there is empirical warrant for this decision (Clarke *et al.*, 2009b: ch. 5), we extend the analysis by examining two additional aspects of leader image, namely *competence* and *trust* deemed important in previous research on heuristics (e.g. Lupia and McCubbins, 1998). Thus, we perform separate analyses for interaction effects involving three aspects of leader image – affect, competence and trust – with knowledge of various leaders' positions on AV.

It bears emphasis that interpretation of these interaction effects is not straightforward. Over the past decade, methodologists have discussed the intricacies of interpreting interaction effects in multivariate regression models, with most of these treatments focusing very heavily on the linear case (e.g. Brambor *et al.*, 2006; Kam and Franzese, 2007). Recently, Norton and his colleagues (Ai and Norton, 2003; Norton *et al.*, 2004; see also Berry *et al.*, 2010) have demonstrated that additional complexities arise for nonlinear models such as the binomial logit models of referendum voting of interest here. Consider the interaction of two variables X1 and X2. Following the analogy with what is done with linear models, one might be tempted to interpret the marginal effect for X1∗X2 as the derivative of $E(Y|XI∗X2,X)$ with respect to the interaction term (XI∗X2). However, as Norton *et al.* point out, the interaction effect in a logit (or probit) model is actually the cross-derivative with respect to X1 and X2.

Ai and Norton (2003: 124) note four important implications of this observation: (i) if the coefficient for the interaction effect in a model is zero, the interaction effect is not necessarily zero for all cases; (ii) the statistical significance of the interaction effect is not a simple t-test for the coefficient but rather varies across the cases in the analysis; (iii) the interaction effect is conditional on the full set of predictor variables in the model; (iv) the sign of the interaction effect is not necessarily the sign on the coefficient for the interaction effect but rather can vary depending on the values of the set of covariates in the model. Norton *et al.* (2004) provide statistical software that enables one to take (i)–(iv) into account when analyzing interaction effects in nonlinear models.[14]

Here, we employ the Norton *et al.* approach to analyze interactions between candidate images and political knowledge in our model of AV referendum voting. The model is otherwise identical to that discussed above (see Table 7.1). We begin by considering interactions between leader images measured using the 0–10 affect scale and the electoral system political knowledge index employed earlier. Given that the rival 'smart money' (Hypothesis 1) and 'really smart money' (Hypotheses 2 and 3) predict oppositely signed effects for the interaction between leader images and political knowledge, tests for the significance of the interaction effects are two-tailed ($p \leq 0.05$). The results (not shown) are consistent – all of the interaction effects for Cameron, Clegg and Miliband are statistically insignificant (results not shown in tabular form). There is no evidence that electoral system knowledge interacted with leader images to influence AV voting as per Hypotheses 1 or 2.

We next turn to Hypothesis 3, the variant of the 'really smart money' conjecture that involves knowledge of the positions on AV and FPTP held by various party leaders. Again, leader images are measured using the 0–10 affect scales. The analyses reveal that statistically significant interactions for Cameron and Miliband, with the signs of these effects being overwhelmingly in the expected directions (according to Hypothesis 3) for these two party leaders. As Figure 7.6 shows, fully 99.4 per cent of the Miliband interactions are significant ($p \leq 0.05$) and, as one would expect given his endorsement of AV, these effects are positive. Knowledge of Miliband's position on AV strengthens the positive impact of the Miliband image heuristic in the AV voting model. There are also a large number of significant effects for Cameron (for 59.0 per cent of the voters) and, as expected given his opposition to AV, all of these effects are negative. The case for Clegg is different; nearly all (99.8 per cent) of his interactions are statistically insignificant.

We next consider leader image × knowledge of leaders' AV position interactions that involve two alternative aspects of leader image, namely competence and trust.[15] Although there are strong correlations between various aspects of leader image,[16] it may be the case that the

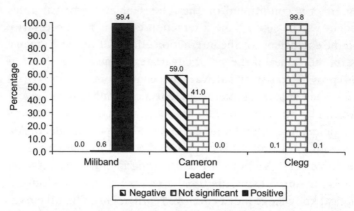

Figure 7.6 Summary of interaction effects – affective leader images multiplied by knowledge of leaders' positions on AV.

interaction effects of interest work differently for different components of leaders' images. As Figure 7.7a shows, the results for perceptions of leader competence are quite similar to those just described for leader affect – 73.3 per cent of the interactions involving perceptions of Miliband's competence and his position on AV are statistically significant and positive. Similarly, 89.5 per cent of the comparable interactions involving David Cameron are statistically significant and negative. However, the vast majority (97.1 per cent) of interactions involving Nick Clegg are again statistically insignificant.

For interactions involving the trust component of leader image, the situation is similar, with large majorities of the interactions for Miliband and Cameron being statistically significant (see Figure 7.7b). As expected, significant interactions involving Miliband are positive and those involving Cameron are negative. In addition, there are a sizable minority (30.4 per cent) of interactions that are statistically significant for Clegg. As anticipated, these effects are positive – that is, interactions between the 'trustworthy' component of Clegg's image and knowledge of his position on AV strengthen the likelihood of casting a Yes ballot. At least some of the people who trusted him and knew where he stood were more likely to endorse AV.

In sum, there are a sizable number of significant interactions between components of leaders' images and knowledge of their positions on AV versus FPTP. As Norton *et al.* have observed, the presence of such significant interactions can vary according to the values of various

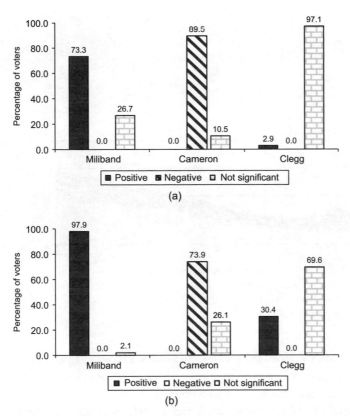

Figure 7.7 Summary of interaction effects – leader competence and trust multiplied by knowledge of leaders' positions on AV.
A. Competence
B. Trust

predictor variables. The point may be illustrated by plotting the Z-scores for the interaction between trust in David Cameron and knowledge of his position on AV-FPTP on a case-by-case (vote-by-voter) basis against the predicted probability of a Yes vote. The results show that the probability of a significant negative interaction is highest among persons who have only a relatively small probability of voting Yes and then diminish as that probability exceeds 0.6 (see Figure 7.8). Substantively, this pattern suggests that if the forces prompting a Yes vote are quite strong, perceptions of Cameron as a trustworthy leader and knowledge of his opposition to AV have little effect. The interaction of such perceptions and knowledge tend to matter most

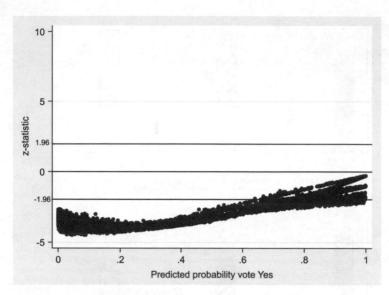

Figure 7.8 Interaction effects involving trust component of Cameron's image and knowledge of position on AV.

often when other factors are aligned against a Yes vote. In the latter circumstance trust in Cameron and knowledge of his opposition to AV combine to reinforce the tendency to vote No.

The comparable analysis for Nick Clegg (not shown in graphic form) reveals a similar, albeit substantially weaker pattern, with significant trust × knowledge interactions occurring when the overall probability of a Yes vote is small. However, in Clegg's case, these interactions are positive, enhancing the likelihood of endorsing AV. Finally, the analysis for Miliband underscores the possibility that interactions can be significant regardless of the overall probability of a Yes vote. In this regard, recall that the trust in Miliband × knowledge of his position on AV was significant and positive for nearly all voters (97.9 per cent), regardless of their probability of voting Yes. This point is illustrated in Figure 7.9. Substantively, this pattern suggests that *regardless* of the configuration of other factors at work in the campaign, Miliband could increase the likelihood of a Yes vote by informing the electorate that he favoured AV. Doing so would increase the probability of supporting AV among people who viewed Labour's new leader as trustworthy. Unfortunately for the supporters of AV, circa May 2011 many people

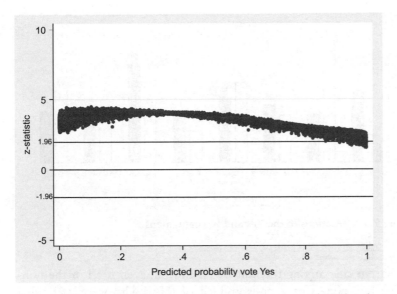

Figure 7.9 Interaction effects involving trust component of Miliband's image and knowledge of position on AV.

did not see him this way and he did not exert himself to make the case for the proposed electoral system.[17]

A public retrospective on the referendum

One of the most obvious aspects of the AV referendum was the dismal turnout – only 42.2 per cent of the electorate bothered to cast a ballot. Not only was this figure well off the already desultory level of participation (65.1 per cent) in the 2010 general election, it was also far below the 64.5 per cent turnout in the 1975 national referendum on Britain's continued membership in the European Community. One question raised by the low turnout in the 2011 referendum is whether the result would have been different if more people had gone to the polls. The CMS survey data answer this question negatively. When those who said that they did not turn out were asked how they would have voted, 19.1 per cent said Yes, 47.7 per cent said No and 33.3 per cent were unsure. Assuming the latter group was distributed proportionately among the Yes and No groups, the result would have been to produce a 28.2 per cent versus 71.8 per cent split in favour

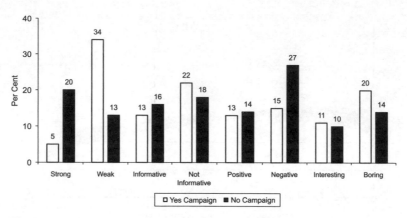

Figure 7.10 Reactions to the Yes and No campaigns.

of the No side among the nonvoters. Indeed, even if all of the non-voters had gone to the polls and all of those who were undecided had cast a Yes ballot, the referendum still would have failed, with the No side prevailing by a comfortable 12-point margin.[18] Although it is very unlikely that greater participation would have changed the outcome, the low turnout that did occur suggests substantial public disengagement and disaffection. The rival campaigns and their coverage in the media clearly failed to engage the electorate, with many people complaining only a week before the balloting that they were not well-informed about what they were being called upon to decide.[19]

In the wake of the referendum, negativity about the event was prevalent. When respondents in the CMS post-referendum survey were asked if there was a 'lot of mud-slinging' in the campaign, over three-fifths agreed and fewer than one in ten disagreed. Participants in this survey also were presented with four positive words and four negative ones and asked to give their reactions to the Yes and No campaigns. Figure 7.10 documents that negative responses overshadowed positive ones by a substantial margin. The tenor of these reactions was particularly evident for the Yes campaign, with only 5 per cent describing it as 'strong' and 34 per cent saying it was 'weak'. Similarly, 13 per cent or less indicated the Yes effort was 'informative', 'positive' or 'interesting', whereas 15 to 22 per cent said it was 'not informative', 'negative' or 'boring'. Overall, only 24 per cent designated one or more positive words to describe the Yes campaign and 53 per cent used one or more negative words. Reactions to the No campaign were only slightly more upbeat – overall, 34 per cent made one or more positive remarks, and 44 per cent made one or more negative ones.

In retrospect, it is difficult to escape the conclusion that the AV referendum was a decidedly unsuccessful exercise in direct democracy. Despite repeated efforts to inform people about the issues at stake, the rival campaigns failed to inform and engage much of the electorate. A majority of people did not go to the polls and, as observed, many judged the competing campaigns negatively. These judgments reflected the harsh tenor of widely publicized personal attacks launched by leading Yes and No advocates.[20] Quite possibly, an important result is that the campaigns and the referendum outcome have contributed to growing sense that the British political system is seriously in need of reform. The latter outcome would be doubly ironic; by conspicuously failing to achieve institutional change, the AV referendum may have heightened public appreciation of the need for reform, while making it more difficult to achieve. We consider this possibility in the concluding section.

What if? The consequences of AV

Part of the debate concerning the AV referendum involved speculation about what the consequences would be should AV be adopted. As discussed above, the Liberal Democrats and many more detached observers believed that AV would make it more difficult for any party to win a majority of parliamentary seats. As a result, the Liberal Democrats would be both 'king makers' and influential junior partners in the coalition governments that emerged after successive general elections. Although this scenario has considerable plausibility, it rests in the realm of counterfactuals and no one knows how likely Liberal Democrat hegemony under AV would be.

However, it is possible to use the 2010 BES survey data to investigate what would have happened if AV had been in place for this election. To this end, the post-election wave of the 2010 Rolling Campaign Panel Survey (RCPS) presented respondents with a hypothetical AV ballot and asked them to rank-order the parties. With these data it is possible to make inferences about the likely election outcome under AV. This analysis shows that AV would have produced a hung Parliament, with the Conservatives winning 283 seats (down 23 from the actual result),

Labour winning 248 (down 10), and the Liberal Democrats winning 89 (up 32) (see Sanders *et al.*, 2011b). Clearly, the Liberal Democrats would have benefited from AV. Also important, the projected shares are such that the Liberal Democrats could have formed a majority coalition with Labour as well as the Conservatives. Given the Liberal Democrats' general left-of-centre ideological stance and tradition of progressive politics, there would have been considerable pressure in the party to go with Labour. Whether Nick Clegg and his colleagues would have done so, particularly since it likely would have involved keeping Gordon Brown as prime minister, is unknown. But, unlike the situation produced by FPTP, the possibility of a Labour–Liberal Democrat coalition would have been strengthened in 2010 under AV.

In addition to opining about aggregate-level results, commentators have speculated about the consequences that adopting AV would have for individual-level voting behaviour. Perhaps holding elections under AV would change the calculus of electoral choice and a different set of factors would be critical for understanding why voters do what they do. Again, although it is impossible to say with certainty what would happen if AV were adopted, we can use the 2010 RCPS data on the rank-ordering of parties on a hypothetical AV ballot to investigate the effects of rival valence politics, spatial and sociodemographic models of electoral choice.

There is, of course, a large number of parties that compete in British general elections. The hypothetical AV ballot lists seven parties, including the Conservatives, Labour, the Liberal Democrats, as well as the SNP in Scotland and Plaid Cymru in Wales. Other minor parties such as UKIP, the BNP, the Greens and the Scottish Socialists are also included on the ballot depending upon which country is being considered. To keep the analysis reasonably simple and to permit generalizations across England, Scotland and Wales, we collapse the rank-orders into three categories: rank first, rank second, rank third or lower or not ranked. Determinants of this rank-ordered vote variable are analyzed using a rank-ordered logit model[21] (Long and Freese, 2006). Predictor variables include key valence politics indicators (leader images, party best on most important issue, party identification), spatial party-issue proximities, economic evaluations and emotional reactions to economic conditions and various sociodemographics (age, ethnicity, gender, country of residence (England, Scotland, Wales), private-public occupational sector, social class).[22] Similar to conditional and mixed

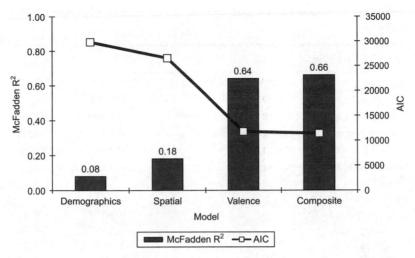

Figure 7.11 Performance of rival models of rank-ordering parties under AV electoral system.

logit models, there are two types of predictor variables in the rank-ordered logit model – alternative specific predictors and case specific predictors. Alternative specific predictors are variables that are characteristics of choices, whereas case specific variables are characteristics of voters making those choices. Here, leader images, party best on most important issues, and party-issue proximities are treated as alternative specific predictors. Other predictors are treated as case specific.

The analysis reveals that the valence politics model continues to exert dominant explanatory power, with its spatial and sociodemographic rivals lagging far behind. Specifically, the McFadden R^2s for these three models are 0.64, 0.18 and 0.08, respectively (see Figure 7.11). And, similar to the voting models considered in Chapter 5, a composite model that includes predictor variables from all three models performs slightly better with an R^2 of 0.66. Further evidence is provided by the AIC model selection statistics which are lower (i.e. better) for the valence politics model than for its spatial and sociodemographic competitors. Once more, and again quite typical, the AIC for the composite model is just slightly smaller for the composite model than for the valence politics model.

Table 7.2 presents parameter estimates for the several predictor variables in the composite rank-order logit model. Separate parameters

Table 7.2 *Rank-order logit model of party preferences on hypothetical AV ballot*

Predictor variables	β	s.e.
Alternative		
Specific predictors:		
Leader image	0.45***	0.01
Party best most important issue	0.94***	0.05
Issue-proximities	0.16***	0.01
Case-specific predictors:		
Conservative ranking:		
Party identification		
Conservative	1.83***	0.11
Labour	−0.85***	0.10
Liberal Democrat	−1.75***	0.12
Other party	0.15	0.13
Economic evaluations	−0.11**	0.04
Emotional reactions to economic conditions	−0.13***	0.03
Age	0.01***	0.002
Gender	−0.07	0.07
Social class	−0.20	0.08
Private/public-sector occupation	0.22***	0.07
Ethnicity	0.03	0.17
Region:		
Scotland	−0.26	0.14
Wales	0.12	0.17
Constant	0.78***	0.21
Labour ranking:		
Party identification:		
Conservative	−1.13***	0.12
Labour	1.71***	0.09
Liberal Democrat	−1.50***	0.11
Other party	0.04	0.14
Economic evaluations	0.05	0.04
Emotional reactions to economic conditions	−0.02	0.02
Age	0.001	0.002
Gender	−0.10	0.07
Social class	−0.39***	0.07
Private/public-sector occupation	0.01	0.07
Ethnicity	−0.17	0.15

Table 7.2 (cont.)

Predictor variables	β	s.e.
Region:		
Scotland	0.37***	0.12
Wales	0.23	0.16
Constant	0.27	0.20
McFadden R² =	0.66	

*** $p \leq 0.001$; ** $p \leq 0.01$; * $p \leq 0.05$; one-tailed test.
Note: ranking of Labour, Conservative and Liberal Democrat preferences; Liberal Democrat ranking is the reference category.

are estimated for Conservative and Labour rankings, with the Liberal Democrat rankings serving as the reference category. Among the alternative specific predictors, leader images, perceptions of party best on the most important issue and issue-proximities all have expected positive effects. Among the case-specific predictors, Conservative party identification increases the likelihood of ranking that party highly and Labour and Liberal Democrat party identifications decrease that probability. Economic evaluations and emotional reactions to the economy also behave as expected, with positive evaluations and reactions lowering the likelihood of ranking the Conservatives highly. In the Labour analysis, party identification again behaves as expected with Labour identifications raising the probability of a high Labour ranking and Conservative and Liberal Democrat rankings lowering that probability. Working-class voters and residents of Scotland are also more likely to rank Labour highly.

Viewed generally, findings from the rank-ordered logit analysis indicate that the relative strength of most determinants of voting would not change appreciably were AV to be adopted. Valence politics considerations continue to dominate, with spatial and sociodemographic predictors having much smaller roles. If anything, the strength of the spatial predictor is diminished in the present analysis compared to results of analyses of voting models under FPTP presented in Chapter 5 and elsewhere. This consideration aside, the calculus of electoral choice appears resistant to a shift from FPTP to AV.

Conclusion: the AV referendum reconsidered

On 5 May 2011 British voters had the opportunity to decide if their country should change its electoral system. This exercise in direct democracy is an example of the 'polity-shaping' referendums that have been employed with increasing frequency in mature democracies over the past two decades. Although a variety of explanations have been adduced in research on voting in these events, a number of studies have emphasized the importance of cost-benefit calculations and heuristics provided by partisan attachments and leader images. Analyses presented in this chapter testify that both types of variables affected the choices voters made in the AV referendum. Assessments of the 'pros' and 'cons' of AV and FPTP had very strong effects on voting, and both partisanship and leader images were influential as well. In these respects, the story of what shaped political choice in the AV referendum is a familiar tale.

However, there are aspects of the story that are less well known. Analyses using statistical methods appropriate for assessing interaction effects in nonlinear models reveal that the force of leader images was conditioned by levels of political knowledge. But, contrary to what some researchers have conjectured, leader image effects were not stronger among less knowledgeable voters. Also, basic factual knowledge about Britain's electoral system was not the kind of information that counted. What did matter was knowledge of leaders' positions on AV versus FPTP – that knowledge interacted with leader images such that the effects of those images were stronger among more knowledgeable voters. These effects obtained across various components of leader images, and were more widespread for David Cameron and Ed Miliband than for Nick Clegg.

The tenor of these findings is consistent with what we have termed the 'really smart money' hypothesis. Echoing research in experimental economics and political psychology, the core idea is that knowledgeable individuals make more, not less, use of readily available cues such as those provided by party leaders. In this regard, we observe that the salience of party leaders in the mass media encourages voters to form images of them as (in)competent, (un)likeable and (un)trustworthy, and knowledge of their positions on major issues typically can be acquired with little effort. Although it is possible that voters with inaccurate information about a leader's position might use that information in combination with their image of the leader when making a political choice, in the case of the AV referendum a large majority of people had accurate knowledge of at least one of the leaders' positions and, in turn, that knowledge boosted the impact of the leader image cue on referendum voting.

When considering how leader images affected the outcome of the AV referendum, it is clear that the Yes side was disadvantaged by negative public perceptions of its chief advocate, Nick Clegg. Although many people knew that the Liberal Democrat leader favoured AV, by May 2011 he had become decidedly unpopular, and many voters viewed him as less than competent and trustworthy. Given this negativity, it is conceivable that the Yes side would have done even worse had the political knowledge interaction effects involving Clegg's image as (un)trustworthy been more widespread.

Campaign strategists for the Yes side were very much aware of the Liberal Democrat Leader's image problem. They reacted by adopting a variety of curious, indeed bizarre, ways to make their case, while keeping Clegg 'out of sight' and, hopefully, 'out of mind'. Famous comedians (John Cleese, Eddie Izzard) were enlisted to serve as surrogate pitchmen for AV, and a YouTube video featuring terminally cute domestic cats was posted to explain the mechanics of AV and tout its democratic virtues.[23] Although entertaining, these campaign advertisements fell far short of what was needed to secure a Yes majority. Although they diverted voters' attention from Mr Clegg, Cleese, Izzard and their feline friends failed to make a compelling case for the merits of the proposed new electoral system.

Was the AV referendum much ado about nothing? Analyses designed to answer this question suggest that AV, if it had been in place for the 2010 general election, would have mattered in some ways, but not in others. At the aggregate level, a simulation of the 2010 election under AV yields a result that would warm a Liberal Democrat heart – substantially increasing the party's seat share at the expense of the Conservatives and, to a lesser extent, Labour. This result would have boosted the Liberal Democrats' bargaining power by putting it in a position to form a governing coalition with either of these parties. However, adopting AV basically would not have changed the relative weight of various factors affecting individual-level party support. Valence politics considerations would have continued to dominate as factors governing the choices voters made.

The decisive outcome of the AV referendum has settled the issue and the question of electoral reform is unlikely to be reopened for many years. If attempts are made to raise the issue again in the near future, opponents of reform will be able to say that the people have spoken and the question should no longer be up for discussion. Had the vote been closer, then supporters of STV or a fully proportional electoral system might be able to argue that this should be on the agenda in coalition negotiations if a future general election proves as inconclusive as the last one. However, the strength of opposition to change in the electoral system manifest in the 2011 AV referendum makes this unlikely.

Another effect of the resounding rejection of changing the electoral system might be to inhibit attempts at other constitutional reforms such as an elected House of Lords and the devolution of power from Whitehall to local communities. If so, this is unfortunate because data presented above indicate there is substantial public sentiment in favour of some types of institutional change. Although this does not mean that, for example, a referendum on having an elected upper chamber of Parliament would be successful, it does mean that the British public is not averse to considering ideas for alterations in existing political institutions and processes.

In addition, there is mounting evidence to suggest that the political institutions which generate support for British democracy are failing in comparison with an earlier era (Whiteley, 2012). Highly negative public reactions to the MPs' expenses scandal and the News of the World phone hacking crimes are stark indicators of widespread discontent and lack of trust with the institutions and key actors in the contemporary British state. This negativity is unlikely to dissipate in the near future.

It might be argued that a loss of trust in key institutions such as Parliament and the Executive may encourage further use of referendums in the future. If institutions and elite actors are no longer trusted, referendums might serve to generate the legitimacy needed for major decisions.[24] However, although our survey evidence suggests that there is substantial public support in the abstract for using referendums to decide important questions, the status quo bias discussed above is likely to be strong if people do not understand or are not engaged with the particular topic at issue. This tendency will be strengthened if they do not trust political leaders and political parties to provide guidance.

In this regard, at the time of the AV referendum, many voters were unfavourably disposed towards leaders of the three major parties, and the chief spokesperson for the Yes side, Liberal Democrat Leader, Nick Clegg, was genuinely unpopular.

There is a paradox that referendums are often called to settle constitutional questions that divide political parties, but almost by definition such questions are more likely to be seen as complicated – even esoteric – matters that are less relevant to the lives of ordinary people than 'bread-and-butter' issues concerning the economy, public services and crime. If so, holding referendums on constitutional topics may help to breed the kind of disaffection and disengagement evident in the 2011 AV ballot referendum. Holding a referendum on electoral reform in the context of a major economic crisis risked inviting the query: 'Why are they fiddling when Rome is burning?' It required more than a generation for a nationwide referendum to occur after the 1975 vote on continued British membership in the European Community. The same thing may happen again.

8 | *Performance politics and subjective well-being*

Public reactions to policy delivery are central to the valence model of electoral choice. Governments that succeed in delivering cherished public goods such as economic prosperity, low crime rates, effective health care and efficient public services can anticipate electoral success. In contrast, governments that fail to deliver satisfactory quantities of these goods can expect negative reactions from disgruntled electorates. Mechanisms linking policy performance with party support are generally left implicit in the valence model, since the assumption is that good performance automatically generates positive reactions from performance-oriented voters. However, it is an interesting question why people should behave in this way. The aim of this chapter is to examine this linkage, advancing the argument that successful policy delivery increases happiness or subjective well-being and failed policies have the opposite effect.

At the outset, it bears emphasis that the importance of subjective well-being is not restricted to the valence model of voting; rather, it also highly relevant for Downsian spatial models of party competition. Like their valence rivals, spatial models assume that voters are motivated by a desire to maximize utility. However, in spatial models well-being will be enhanced by the government implementing policies on position issues that divide electorates. Position issues animate both elite and mass political behaviour, and governments aim to deliver policies that some voters favour and others oppose. If the division of preferences on a particular policy is very close, large minorities of voters will not experience an increase, and may well experience a decrease in subjective well-being. In a 'spatial world' of fixed voter preferences and strategic politicians, there is no guarantee that government policy implementation will yield aggregate increases in life satisfaction. Minorities with intense preferences may be sorely disappointed with government policies and suffer sizable decreases in their sense of well-being.

Abstract implications of rival models of electoral choice aside, in practice it seems straightforward that being seen to promote voters' well-being is important for electoral success. However, there are implications for government behaviour that are not obvious. One such implication involves the observation that existing policies, even if they appear to be working well in some objective sense, may be doing little to make people happy. If alternative policies, regardless of their merits, promise to make more people happy, the government has an incentive to do things differently. In addition, it should not be assumed that successful policies are equally important in creating well-being and an important question is how different policies perform in this regard. For example, we do not know how crime prevention efforts compare with investment in health care or with anti-terrorism measures when it comes to influencing the public's sense of well-being. The general implication for party electoral strategies is that governments should try to maximize performance on those policies which have the largest impact on public well-being, something discussed more fully below. Equally, if effective government policy delivery is central to public well-being, it is important to know how this works. Can governments simply increase the public's sense of well-being by relying on a felicitous mix of directives from Whitehall or do they generate larger returns when they operate indirectly via local actors and organizations? Voters' reactions to policy pronouncements may be very different from their reactions to policy delivery 'on the ground'.

We begin this chapter by briefly reviewing the growing interdisciplinary literature on subjective well-being, paying particular attention to what is known about the impact of government and policy making. This review motivates a theoretical discussion of how policies might influence well-being. Next, we develop a multivariate model of the determinants of public well-being over a recent six-year period in Britain. Model parameters are estimated using data from the British Election Study's Continuous Monitoring Survey (CMS). We conclude the empirical analyses by exploring how subjective well-being is related to turnout and electoral choice.

Subjective well-being, government and policy-making

There is a growing body of research in the social sciences concerning life satisfaction or subjective well-being (Bok, 2010; Bruni and Porta,

2005, 2007; Easterlin, 2002, 2004, 2010; Frey, 2008; Frey and Stutzer, 2000, 2002, 2005; Helliwell, 2006; Lane, 2000; Layard, 2005). This literature explores different aspects of the relationship between individuals' sense of well-being and various social, economic and political conditions. These include relationships between well-being and economic prosperity (Di Tella *et al.*, 2003), family and marriage (Diener and McGovern, 2008), voluntary activity and participation (Helliwell and Putnam, 2007); economic growth and employment (Kenny, 1999; Winkelmann and Winkelmann, 1998), physical and psychological health (Layard, 2005); religion (Ferris, 2002) and governance (Inglehart *et al.*, 2008).

The relationship between subjective well-being and governance is particularly interesting for students of politics and public policy. For example, Frey and Stutzer (2000, 2005) studied how political participation influenced life satisfaction in Switzerland. They showed that levels of subjective well-being in Swiss cantons with high levels of political autonomy and opportunities for participation were higher than in cantons lacking these characteristics. It appears that having abundant opportunities to participate in political life help to make people happy. Inglehart and his collaborators (2008) looked at well-being in former communist countries in the years immediately after the fall of the Soviet Union. They found that levels of life satisfaction plunged in most of these countries in the early years after the Berlin Wall came down, but subsequently expanded as democracy in these countries took root. The larger message of these studies is that democratic governance can promote subjective well-being in a country's citizenry.

Regarding policy making, comparative research shows that there is a direct relationship between economic and social policies and subjective well-being (Pacek, 2009; Pacek and Radcliff, 2008; Radcliff and Pacek, 2001). Life satisfaction is high in countries such as Denmark and Sweden where social welfare provision is generous and lower in countries like Turkey where it is relatively meagre. Similarly, it is clear that economic growth and high levels of employment have significant positive impacts on subjective well-being (Kenny, 1999; Oswald, 1997). It also appears that governmental structures and processes influence well-being across the world, but the effects differ in developing and first-world countries. The honesty and efficiency of government appear to be quite important in developing countries where corruption is frequently a serious problem, whereas the quality of democratic processes is more important in the developed world (Helliwell, 2006; see also Helliwell and Haifang, 2008). In developing countries life satisfaction is linked closely to policy outcomes and the delivery of services, whereas in developed countries life satisfaction responds more strongly to the quality of democracy itself. Finally, there is recent evidence suggesting that effective policy-making has an impact on the life satisfaction of citizens over time (Whiteley *et al.*, 2010).

We begin by considering theoretical issues arising from the analysis of subjective well-being and policy making. This exercise suggests that policy making can influence well-being via a variety of mechanisms and policy domains. The analysis is dynamic and examines links between policy outcomes and subjective well-being over a period of six years, from 2004 to 2010. The primary focus is on modelling sense of life satisfaction at the individual level, but attention is also paid to the larger context in which policies evolve over time. In late 2007 the first signs of the approaching global financial crisis and subsequent recession became apparent in Britain when there was a run on the Northern Rock bank. This was the first run on a major British bank in 150 years. Following the near collapse of Northern Rock, the UK economy went into a severe recession alongside those of many other advanced industrial countries. Recovery did not begin until late 2009. This dynamic context enables us to evaluate the extent to which relationships between policy making and subjective well-being are influenced by the political and economic environments in which citizens find themselves.

Theoretical perspectives

As the preceding review of the literature suggests, it is now well established that government influences citizens' sense of well-being. This finding reflects a long-established premise of democratic theory that political system performance influences public happiness (e.g. Dahl, 1972; Pateman, 1970). However, the mechanisms by which this occurs are not well understood. One obvious mechanism which is highlighted by a long tradition of research on economic outcomes and party support is performance of the national economy. The general proposition is very straightforward – if governments deliver positive economic outcomes such as low inflation and unemployment rates coupled with vigorous and sustainable growth this should positively influence citizens' subjective well-being (Clarke *et al.*, 1998; Dorussen and Taylor, 2007; Duch and Stevenson, 2008; Lewis-Beck, 1988).

Early work on the political economy of party support identified sociotropic judgments as important factors in voters' electoral calculus (Clarke *et al.*, 1992; Kiewiet, 1983; Kinder and Kiewiet, 1981; Lewis-Beck, 1988; Norpoth *et al.*, 1991). These findings refer to voters' tendencies to reward governments for successfully managing the macroeconomy of growth, jobs and inflation. The focus is on national policy making rather than personal economic circumstances, although information of the latter type may help voters to form sociotropic judgments. Personal economic outcomes are thought to drive egocentric judgments which relate to an individual's financial circumstances and those of their immediate family. Both egocentric and sociotropic policy evaluations might influence subjective well-being, but they are different channels of influence. Such evaluations are not confined to the economy but rather can involve other policy domains as well.

Egocentric policy evaluations are likely to work differently from sociotropic ones since the former are products of people's personal experiences. If citizens ask the police to investigate a crime, or if they receive treatment from an NHS general practitioner, these are examples of egocentric policy delivery. At this level delivery effectiveness relies on 'street-level bureaucrats' – agents of the state who provide services 'on the ground' (Lipsky, 1980). These front-line employees who deliver public services to people possess a significant degree of discretion in their work. It seems likely that good or bad experiences when dealing with a street-level bureaucrat are likely to influence people's sense of well-being. In contrast, sociotropic policy judgments concern macro-level phenomena which may not reflect an individual's personal, day-to-day experiences. In addition, most citizens have direct contact with government only through street-level bureaucrats and rarely, if ever, interact with national or even ranking local officials who are responsible for the implementation of public policies.

Given these considerations, we expect that egocentric policy delivery is likely to be more important for subjective well-being than sociotropic policy delivery, although both might influence a person's sense of well-being (Whiteley *et al.*, 2010). However, it is not well understood which policies have the strongest effects on well-being and which ones have weaker effects. Also, it seems likely that the impact of sociotropic and egocentric policy delivery may vary across policy domains, but it is unclear, for example, if personal economic prosperity is more important than the state of the National Health Service in Britain, or if national crime prevention policies have a bigger impact than an individual's experience of crime in the streets.

Alongside the influence of egocentric and sociotropic evaluations on well-being in various policy areas, there is another channel of influence which links policy outcomes to subjective well-being. Affective reactions to policy delivery involve the role of emotions in influencing feelings of life satisfaction. 'Gut reasoning' (Popkin, 1991; see also Gigerenzer, 2008; Gigerenzer *et al.*, 2011; Sniderman *et al.*, 1991) or affective reactions have been advanced as a potent mechanism for helping citizens to make judgments about what their governments are doing. Such affective reasoning provides simple and efficient heuristics for judging policy delivery in contexts where voters lack the cognitive capacity and information needed to understand how the policy process works. For example, it is difficult for ordinary citizens to assess macroeconomic policy making, since experts disagree, oftentimes sharply, about relationships between monetary and fiscal policy and economic performance. In this situation voters find it difficult to use empirical evidence to attribute responsibility for policy outcomes to a particular party or leader. However, if voters rely on their feelings, this provides them with a 'fast and frugal' heuristic (Gigerenzer, 2008) for evaluating public policies and judging political performance. If people react positively to the economy, the state of the Health Service, crime rates and outcomes in various other policy domains, they can decide to reward the incumbent government without being concerned about the detailed mechanisms involved. All they know – and all they need to know – is that they feel good about the outcomes of policies that matter to them. According to this account, affective reactions to policy outcomes constitute a convenient, cost-effective heuristic for making political choices.

There is now a sizable literature on affective reasoning, and there is clearly an 'affect effect' which has numerous and diverse influences on political attitudes and behaviour (e.g. Marcus *et al.*, 2000; Neuman *et al.*, 2007; see also Conover and Feldman, 1986; Sniderman *et al.*, 1991). Such affective reasoning is not as well understood as cognitive reasoning where individuals calculate the costs and benefits of policies and react accordingly. As a result, there is a proliferation of theoretical frameworks and approaches in the psychological literature aimed at understanding the nature of affective reasoning (see Neuman *et al.*, 2007). Although the mechanisms at work are not well understood, it is likely that affective reasoning will influence citizens' subjective well-being, not least because well-being is itself primarily an affective phenomenon.

To summarize, we anticipate that the links between policy making and subjective well-being are complex and operate via cognitive and affective reasoning, the latter being useful for judging complex sociotropic policy outcomes. However, key relationships are likely to involve egocentric evaluations based on personal experiences generated as citizens deal with street-level bureaucrats whose job it is to provide policy delivery on the ground.

Modelling policy outcomes and subjective well-being

We analyze the relationship between policy outcomes and subjective well-being in contemporary Britain using the British Election Study's Continuous Monitoring Survey (CMS). With a representative national sample of over 1000 respondents per month cumulating to nearly 95 000 individuals surveyed between April 2004 and December 2010, the CMS contains indicators of cognitive, affective and egocentric evaluations of policy delivery in a variety of areas including the economy, health, education, immigration, anti-terrorism programmes, crime prevention and transportation. Policy domains used in the present analysis represent the top five most salient issues as identified in an open-ended question asking respondents to identify what they consider to be the most important problem facing the country.

Subjective well-being is measured in the CMS with the following question: 'Thinking about your life as a whole, are you very satisfied, fairly satisfied, a little dissatisfied, or very dissatisfied with your life as a whole?' Figure 8.1 shows the pooled responses to this question over the six-year period between 2004 and 2010. It is apparent that most people were fairly satisfied with their lives, with just over 10 per cent being very satisfied. There was also a sizable group who were dissatisfied, constituting just over one-third of all those surveyed. However, the satisfied outnumbered the dissatisfied by a sizable margin – a consistent finding in research on subjective well-being in various mature democracies (see Tov and Diener, 2009).

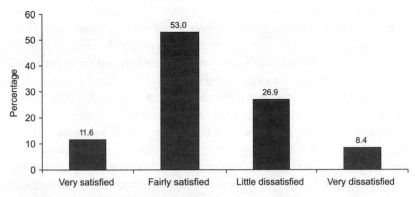

Figure 8.1 Life satisfaction in Britain, April 2004–December 2010.
Source: BES Continuous Monitoring Survey.

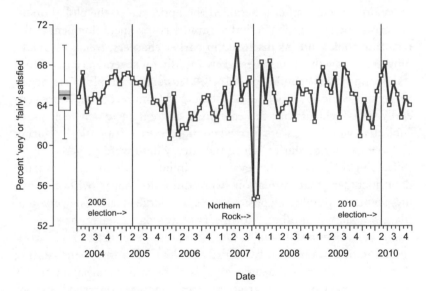

Figure 8.2 Dynamics of life satisfaction in Britain, April 2004–December 2010.
Source: BES Continuous Monitoring Survey.

The dynamics of life satisfaction are displayed in Figure 8.2 which shows the percentage of CMS respondents who were very or fairly satisfied with their lives in every month from April 2004 to December 2010. The series fluctuates over time but there is no long-term trend evident in the data, so there is no evidence to suggest that Britons are generally becoming either happier or unhappier over time. There are interesting dynamics in the data, particularly the abrupt drop in well-being in October and November 2007, when Britain experienced the widely publicized run on the Northern Rock bank. Although it was not known at the time, Northern Rock's travails signalled the start of what was to be a painful and protracted economic crisis. In the event, however, the 'Northern Rock effect' on life satisfaction was temporary as the British government rapidly stepped in and guaranteed the deposits of all the bank's customers by, in effect, nationalizing the institution. As Figure 8.2 shows, people's feelings of life satisfaction recovered quickly. Had the government not intervened, the effect might have been much longer lived.

Northern Rock's shock to the financial system was not an isolated anomalous event; rather it heralded the approach of the global financial crisis and the ensuing period of rapidly rising unemployment as the recession took hold. As discussed in earlier chapters, trends in unemployment show that joblessness grew rapidly for several months before stabilizing at the beginning of 2010.[1] Afterwards unemployment began to decline as the country gradually emerged from recession. More generally, it is evident that the economic context in which feelings of subjective well-being were formed changed rather dramatically during the six-year period during which the survey data were gathered.

Turning next to the policy evaluation indicators discussed above, the data document that evaluations were quite downbeat, with negative judgments outnumbering positive ones by a large margin on every item (data not shown in tabular form). This was particularly the case for crime, terrorism and immigration. The most pessimistic verdict concerned immigration, with two-thirds of the CMS respondents stating that policy delivery had deteriorated, with most of them saying that it had got a 'lot worse'. As far as the economy was concerned respondents were more pessimistic about the past than the future, although differences were not large.

Egocentric policy evaluations were measured differently than sociotropic ones. An initial filter question was asked to establish if a respondent had any direct experience in a specific policy area during the previous year. For example, if an individual or a member of their family had called the police about a crime in their home or their neighbourhood, this constituted personal experience. Respondents who answered yes to this question were then asked if they were satisfied or dissatisfied with the way that the officials had dealt with the problem. All of the policy domains, apart from the economy, were measured in this way. In the case of the economy, egocentric evaluations were assessed by means of retrospective and prospective questions about their personal financial circumstances.

Data generated by the egocentric policy evaluation indicators reveal that people were somewhat more optimistic about their own economic circumstances than those of the country as a whole (data not shown in tabular form). Economic pessimists still outnumbered optimists, but by smaller margins than observed in the data on sociotropic evaluations. Regarding other policy domains, seeking medical assistance was by far the most frequent in terms of the numbers of people involved. In this case the street-level bureaucrats are National Health Service employees such as doctors and nurses and overall evaluations of their performance were quite positive. In contrast, only minorities had sought assistance for a crime, had direct contact with immigrants, or had been exposed to anti-terrorist measures, for example, at airports. Overall, these people were more likely to be satisfied with their treatment than is apparent for comparable sociotropic evaluations. Personal experience in various policy domains is assessed rather differently from experiences mediated by others.

The affective-sociotropic reaction indicators were measured differently from cognitive-sociotropic and egocentric evaluations. Respondents were asked to choose from a set of eight words to describe their feelings about the policy domain under consideration. The list contained four positive and four negative words to describe their feelings. Figure 8.3 lists the percentages of survey respondents choosing positive ('hopeful', 'confident', 'proud', 'happy') and negative ('angry', 'afraid', 'disgusted', 'uneasy') words in various policy areas. Echoing the data on sociotropic evaluations, these percentages document that affective reactions were overwhelmingly negative. In every case the percentage of respondents choosing negative descriptors outnumbered the percentage choosing positive ones by a large margin. Crime appeared to generate the most negative feelings, closely followed by immigration and terrorism. The most positive scores concerned the National Health Service, with the economy attracting a limited number of positive comments. Overall, negative responses dominate in a way which is very different from those for the egocentric indicators. For the

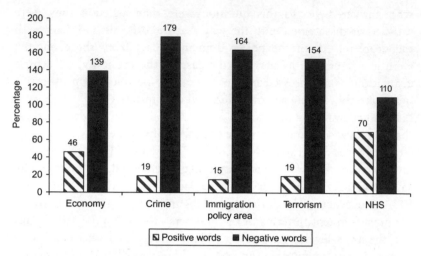

Figure 8.3 Emotional reactions to government performance in five policy areas.
Note: Total percentages of survey respondents mentioning one or more positive or negative words about various policy areas. Positive words are 'happy', 'hopeful', 'confident', 'proud'. Negative words are 'angry', 'disgusted', 'afraid', 'uneasy'.
Source: BES Continuous Monitoring Survey.

multivariate statistical analyses discussed below, affective reaction scales were created for each policy domain by subtracting the number of negative descriptors respondents chose from the number of positive descriptors they chose. The resulting scales ranged from −4 (negative) to +4 (positive).

Modelling subjective well-being

In light of the preceding discussion we begin our multivariate analysis of subjective well-being using the pooled CMS data from 2004 to 2010. The aim is to assess the explanatory power of rival models of life satisfaction. These models also include a number of control variables. In this regard, Layard (2005) highlights the 'Big Seven' factors which frequently emerge as important in empirical analyses of life satisfaction. These factors relate to family relationships, financial security, work experiences, personal relationships, community ties, health, and individual values. Here, family relationships are indexed by marital

Table 8.1 *Ordinal logit model of predictors of life satisfaction, pooled April 2004–December 2010 CMS surveys*

Predictor variables	Cognitive sociotropic	Affective sociotropic	Egocentric
Crime	0.09**	0.04**	0.16**
Immigration	0.09**	0.04**	0.09**
Health care	0.12**	0.09**	0.20**
Terrorism	0.10**	0.01**	0.16**
Economy	0.31**	0.20**	0.65**
Efficacy	0.004**	0.005**	0.004**
Trust	0.19**	0.19**	0.18**
Married	0.37**	0.35**	0.40**
Divorced	−0.17**	−0.19**	−0.15**
Unemployed	−1.06**	−1.03**	−0.94**
Retired	0.25**	0.27**	0.29**
Disabled	−0.82**	−0.80**	−0.72**
Education	0.04**	0.04**	0.04**
Occupational status	0.06**	0.05**	0.05**
Male	−0.11**	−0.14**	−0.06**
Income	0.10**	0.11**	0.09**
Age	−0.04**	−0.04**	−0.03**
Age squared	0.0004**	0.0004**	0.0003**
Ethnicity	−0.24**	−0.23**	−0.21**
McFadden R^2	0.09	0.09	0.12
Log-likelihood	−96485.3	−96357.9	−93413.6

Note: robust standard errors, $p \leq 0.01 = $ **.

status; financial security by household income; work experience by occupational status, employment, and retirement status; personal relationships and community ties by ethnic majority/minority status and interpersonal trust, the latter being a key indicator of social capital (Putnam, 2000); and health by disability status. Education is used to proxy personal values relevant to subjective well-being (see Frey and Stutzer, 2000, 2005). Controls for age and gender also are included.

Table 8.1 contains results of a pooled ordinal logit analysis which estimates the effects of the policy measures on life satisfaction, measured using the 'very dissatisfied' to 'very satisfied' scale discussed earlier. With a large sample such as the CMS survey data it is relatively easy for estimated effects to achieve statistical significance at conventional levels ($p \leq 0.05$), and they are all significant at the 0.01 level or greater. More telling, the signs of coefficients for the predictor variables are consistent with expectations. Thus, satisfaction with policy performance in relation to crime, immigration, health-care, anti-terrorism measures and the economy improves subjective well-being in all three models. In addition, the cognitive-sociotropic, affective-sociotropic and egocentric measures influence well-being in these models. Diagnostics suggest that the egocentric model has a better fit than its rivals. This is consistent with the hypothesis that direct experience is more important for subjective well-being than mediated experiences.

To provide a more comprehensive picture of the effects of various predictors we estimate a composite model that includes all the egocentric and sociotropic indicators. Figure 8.4 summarizes the results in terms of assessing the ability of various predictor variables to influence life satisfaction. The calculations providing data for this figure involve varying each predictor from its minimum to its maximum value, while holding other predictors at their means. In this way the ability of a particular predictor variable to change the probability of an individual being fairly or very satisfied with their life can be determined. It is apparent from Figure 8.4 that the egocentric policy variables have a larger impact on subjective well-being than do the sociotropic variables employed in the cognitive and affective models. Egocentric effects are all larger than sociotropic ones and, in particular, egocentric economic evaluations stand out as being important.[2]

With regard to cognitive and affective policy reactions, their effects in the composite model are quite similar to each other and they are relatively modest. But they all make a contribution to influencing subjective well-being, with affective reactions to economic conditions being more important than cognitive economic evaluations. When we examine the size of other policy effects in Figure 8.4 it is evident that health is second to the economy in its influence on well-being, closely followed by crime. In contrast, immigration and terrorism play smaller roles, although there is a significant effect of anti-terrorism measures in the egocentric model. The overall message is that policy outcomes in a variety of fields influence subjective well-being, but the performance of the street-level bureaucrats is particularly important in influencing people's sense of life satisfaction.

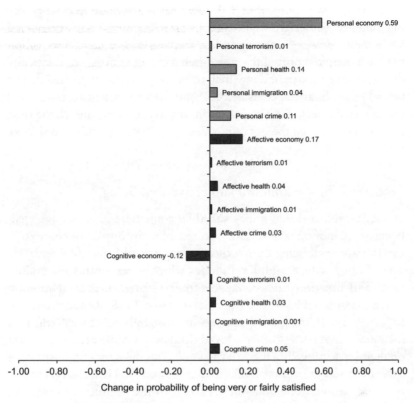

Figure 8.4 Effects of significant predictors on probability of being very or fairly satisfied with life.

The effects of various control variables are also consistent with expectations. As Table 8.1 shows, marriage increases subjective well-being and divorce reduces it. Working in a high-status occupation, having a good education and a receiving a generous income also improve life satisfaction. In contrast, poor health in the form of disability, unemployment and being a member of an ethnic minority significantly reduce life satisfaction. As the curvilinear specification[3] for age demonstrates, aging decreases subjective well-being but the effect lessens as people become elderly. In addition, retirement improves well-being, and it appears that men have a slightly lower sense of well-being than women. Finally, interpersonal trust has a particularly significant impact on well-being which attests to the importance of social and community ties.[4]

The model summarized in Table 8.1 estimates the effects of policy outcomes on subjective well-being in a statistic analysis of the pooled CMS data. However, as the earlier discussion indicates, the context in which people reported their well-being changed rather dramatically during the six-year period in which the survey data were gathered. The arrival of the financial crisis in 2007 and the subsequent recession had multifaceted effects on Britain's economy and society, and in the next section we examine the consequences for people's sense of subjective well-being.

Modelling the dynamics of subjective well-being

Having established that policy variables contribute to subjective well-being at the individual level, we next examine the impact of contextual variables on well-being during the six-year period from 2004 to 2010. This is done with a multilevel model which incorporates unemployment and inflation rates as aggregate-level predictors in a random intercepts ordered logit specification (see Hox, 1998; Raudenbush and Bryk, 2002).[5] In the pooled analysis discussed above, it was clear that if an individual became unemployed this had a sizable negative impact on their sense of well-being.[6] In the pooled model unemployment is an egocentric, i.e. individual-level, predictor variable. However, by incorporating national unemployment rates into the multilevel model, we can assess the aggregate-level impact of variations in joblessness as a contextual variable.

Earlier work has shown that subjective well-being is influenced by aggregate unemployment, but the effect is subject to a process of hedonic adaptation (Brickman and Campbell, 1971). This means that individuals gradually adapt to new levels of joblessness, and this produces a curvilinear relationship between unemployment rates and well-being assessments (Whiteley *et al.*, 2010). This 'new normal' effect is similar to that found in research on the relationship between income and well-being which shows that a windfall increase in income caused, for example, by winning a lottery, produces a temporary increase in life satisfaction but that the effect subsequently erodes (Easterlin, 2010).

Inflation is also included as an aggregate-level predictor in the model, although price increases were quite modest in Britain over the ten-year period up to 2010. Given this, it is likely that any negative psychological effects of inflation will be relatively small. Indeed, since inflation

Table 8.2 *Effects of aggregate-level predictors in multilevel ordinal logit model of life satisfaction, April 2004–December 2010*

Macro-level predictors	Sociotropic cognitive	Sociotropic affective	Egocentric
Bank run	−0.44**	−0.35**	−0.53**
Inflation	−0.02	−0.01	−0.03
Unemployment	−1.20*	−1.17**	−0.84*
Unemployment squared	0.15*	0.16**	0.11*
Maximum point of recession	−0.36**	−0.32**	−0.31**
General election 2005	−0.13	−0.08	−0.05
General election 2010	−0.33+	−0.20	−0.12
Pseudo R^2	0.23	0.26	0.27

Note: robust standard errors, ** $p \leq 0.01$; * $p \leq 0.05$; + $p \leq 0.10$.

was low for some years, modest price increases might actually be taken as a signal of economic buoyancy rather than difficulty, and thereby work to increase people's sense of life satisfaction. In either circumstance, inflation is unlikely to have a large impact on life satisfaction.

Additional control variables were included in the aggregate model to capture the impact of events that might influence the relationship between policy outcomes and subjective well-being. The run on the Northern Rock bank has already been mentioned and a dummy (0–1) variable was incorporated in the model to capture this effect. Similarly, the peaking of the recession in the early part of 2010 is also captured with a dummy variable, since it is possible that this high point of the misery associated with recession had an additional influence on well-being. Finally, possible effects of the 2005 and 2010 general elections are also investigated, again by specifying dummy variables.

Table 8.2 displays the aggregate-level effects in the multilevel model of life satisfaction, with the individual-level effects omitted since they are very similar to those in Table 8.1. The results confirm that unemployment has a nonlinear impact on subjective well-being. Not surprisingly, unemployment reduced individual well-being as the recession took hold, but subsequently people adjusted to the new levels of joblessness over time. In contrast, inflation does not have a significant effect, although the negative sign associated with the inflation coefficient is consistent with the expectation that citizens dislike rising prices. Regarding other predictors, the run on Northern Rock in 2007 had a temporary negative impact on well-being, as did the high point of the recession in early 2010. However, it does not appear that the 2005 and 2010 general elections influenced well-being.[7]

This analysis clearly shows that subjective well-being is influenced by government policies. Although the channels of influence are complex and work through a variety of policy domains it is readily apparent that egocentric evaluations are more important than sociotropic ones. This is particularly obvious regarding the economy, since egocentric economic evaluations tend to dominate the picture. Since the major focus in this book is on voting behaviour this raises the question: what is the relationship between voting intentions and subjective well-being in light of these findings? We know that policy performance influences both voting behaviour and subjective well-being. But does voting influence well-being, and if so how does it work? We consider this issue next.

Voting and subjective well-being

Initially, the relationship between voting and subjective well-being seems to be a rather tenuous one. However, there is an interesting literature which demonstrates a significant relationship between voting and satisfaction with democracy. In an influential paper Anderson and Guillory (1997) showed that individuals who reported voting for a party that won a national election were subsequently more satisfied with democracy in their country than those who voted for one of the losing parties. Other research has confirmed this finding as well as showing that democracy satisfaction is influenced by regime characteristics such as the rule of law, well-functioning regulation and low levels of corruption (Blais and Gélineau, 2007; Rohrschneider, 2002; Wagner *et al.*, 2009). This body of research suggests that there may be a relationship between subjective well-being and voting driven by similar factors as the relationship between voting and democratic satisfaction. If an individual's satisfaction with democracy increases as a result of their party winning an election, then it seems possible that their life satisfaction increases at the same time.

Anderson and Guillory (1997) also documented that losers were even less satisfied with democracy in countries with majoritarian or winner-take-all electoral systems like Britain, than in countries with proportional electoral systems. Similarly, winners were more satisfied in majoritarian systems than they were in proportional systems. These findings are not surprising since there tends to be more at stake in elections in countries with majoritarian systems where single-party governments are common. Elections in these countries have the potential to produce abrupt changes of policies more often than is the case in countries with proportional electoral systems. In countries with proportional electoral arrangements, sharp policy changes are less likely to occur because of the necessity of forming coalition governments that entail policy compromises. Thus, electoral systems mediate the relationship between democratic satisfaction and voting.

In studies of democratic satisfaction subjective well-being is often used as a predictor variable because it is seen as a possible determinant of democratic satisfaction and therefore needs to be incorporated in multivariate statistical analyses. If individuals have a predisposition to be satisfied with their lives for reasons discussed earlier then they are likely to be satisfied with democracy. It is possible, although unlikely, that democratic satisfaction influences life satisfaction as well. This is because life satisfaction is much more fundamental and central for most people than satisfaction with a political regime. This is particularly true for the large majority of people who are at most only tangentially involved in the political process. Accordingly, we rule out reciprocal relationships between these variables on theoretical grounds.

There are two mechanisms by which voting might influence subjective well-being. The first relates to turnout and the second to party choice. As far as turnout is concerned, we have examined rational choice models of turnout in earlier studies (Clarke *et al.*, 2004b, 2009b). In the general incentives model of political participation analyzed in those studies a key selective incentive encouraging people to vote is the feeling of personal satisfaction they receive from participating in an event like an election. This is a 'process incentive' in the sense that satisfaction comes from taking part in an election rather than voting for a particular party. Process incentives for participation are well known in the electoral behaviour literature (e.g. Brennan and Buchanan, 1984; Seyd and Whiteley, 1992).

One of the process incentive indicators in the BES in-person post-election survey in 2010 is the Likert-scaled statement: 'I feel a sense of satisfaction when I vote'. If we focus on the individuals who are very satisfied with their lives (see Figure 8.5), we can see that there is a

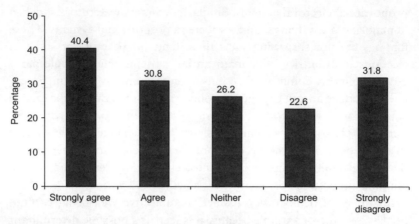

Figure 8.5 Responses to the statement 'I feel a sense of satisfaction when I vote' and percentages very satisfied with life.
Source: BES 2010 post-election in-person survey.

strong relationship between this and feeling a sense of satisfaction with voting. Respondents who are very satisfied with life are much more likely to agree with the statement than to disagree with it, suggesting that there is an association between life satisfaction and process incentives to participate. Individuals who are satisfied with life are more likely to vote.[8] This relationship illustrates clearly why people will vote even when there is no direct payoff from doing so in terms of electoral outcomes. Narrowly defined rational choice accounts of voting predict that people will not participate if their involvement makes no difference to the outcome. This is the well-known 'paradox of participation' (Riker and Ordeshook, 1968). But if people experience a sense of well-being simply by participating in the process they will vote anyway, showing that narrowly constructed rational choice accounts are inadequate for explaining turnout.

A second aspect of the relationship between voting and subjective well-being concerns party choice and is related to the earlier discussion of satisfaction with democracy. Individuals are likely to be more satisfied with their lives if they vote for a winning party for two reasons. There are affective and cognitive reasons for increased well-being arising from winning. The affective dimension is the idea that supporting a winner makes people feel good for its own sake, much as supporters of a football team feel good when their team wins. The cognitive

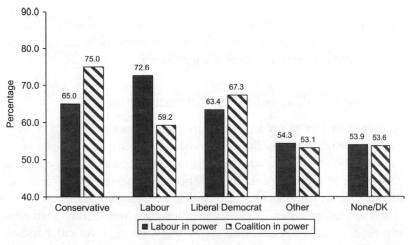

Figure 8.6 Percentages very or fairly satisfied with life by voting intentions during periods of Labour and Coalition government, April 2004–August 2012. *Source:* BES Continuous Monitoring Survey, April 2004–August 2012.

dimension is somewhat more complex – in this case winning an election is related to both valence and spatial issues. Regarding valence issues, individuals will feel greater well-being in anticipation that their preferred party will do a better job of delivering on policies like promoting economic prosperity and reducing crime than their opponents would have done. Regarding spatial issues, life satisfaction is improved by voters' perceptions that their party will deliver policies with which they agree.

Figure 8.6 illustrates the relationship between life satisfaction and voting intentions in the CMS survey data. The figure displays the relationship using pooled data from April 2004 to April 2010 when Labour was in power, as well as the same relationship with pooled data from June 2010 to August 2012 when the Conservative–Liberal Democrat Coalition was in power. It is clear that more Labour voters reported being satisfied with life when the party was in power than when it was in opposition. A similar relationship obtains for Conservative and Liberal Democrat supporters, who were more satisfied with life after the 2010 general election than they were beforehand. This simple, but striking, association between vote intentions and life satisfaction suggests that findings in studies of democracy satisfaction may be at least partially a product of how supporting governing versus opposition parties affects life satisfaction. Having one's party in power not only enhances satisfaction with a democratic political regime, it also promotes a sense of subjective well-being.

Conclusion: policy, politics and life satisfaction

This chapter has examined the relationship between subjective well-being in Britain and public policy outcomes over time. The strongest effects of policy delivery are found in egocentric models with personal experience of crime, health, immigration and anti-terrorism measures all playing important roles. However, the economy tends to dominate the picture when it comes to influencing well-being, with egocentric economic effects being particularly strong. Notwithstanding these effects, reactions to performance in other policy domains, notably health care and crime, also influence well-being. Reactions to immigration and anti-terrorism measures have statistically significant but relatively minor impacts.

Contextual effects are also at work. When the run on the Northern Rock bank in 2007 heralded the arrival of the financial crisis and subsequent recession, individual subjective well-being responded rapidly. Gordon Brown's government wisely responded to this crisis by underwriting the bank and its immediate effects on life satisfaction soon abated. Subsequently, the rise in unemployment had a further depressing effect on sense of well-being, although this weakened once the worst of the recession was past, suggesting that voters were gradually adjusting to the experience of heightened unemployment.

Analyses also indicate that voting influences life satisfaction – a relationship which is suggested by existing work on electoral effects on satisfaction with the practice of democracy in various countries. There is a measurable effect of voting for a winning party on life satisfaction in much the same way as there is on democratic satisfaction. Without gainsaying the value of existing studies of the causes and consequences of democracy satisfaction, present findings indicate the value of paying greater attention to the political behavioural sources of subjective well-being.

Future studies should also focus more closely on links between valence policy evaluations and subjective well-being. One interesting line of enquiry concerning our understanding of valence politics involves public reactions to the performance of local-level policy providers – street-level bureaucrats – who have been largely neglected in the voting literature up to this point. The heavy emphasis on national political leaders in voting research in Britain and elsewhere has tended to obscure how direct service providers influence valence issue evaluations and subjective well-being. The significance of these street-level bureaucrats has clear policy implications. A government which neglects the performance of its direct service providers is less likely to receive electoral rewards than one that supports these agents of the state and fosters their policy-delivery efforts. This is because street-level bureaucrats have influential roles mediating governmental impacts on citizens' sense of subjective well-being. Life satisfaction and policy performance 'on the ground' go hand-in-hand.

9 | Valence politics, austerity policies and electoral prospects

In *Affluence, Austerity and Electoral Change in Britain* we have investigated factors affecting electoral choice and change in modern Britain. Beginning with the landslide 1997 general election that brought Tony Blair's New Labour Party to power, analyses show that the valence politics model that emphasizes party performance judgments, party leader images and flexible partisan attachments does much to account for voting decisions and patterns of party support in inter-election periods. Spatial models of party competition that focus on distances between parties and voters on positional issues dividing the electorate are relevant, but their effects are secondary. Sociological models featuring social class or other sociodemographic characteristics have much weaker effects. As discussed in Chapters 2 and 3, the valence politics model dominated throughout the Blair years and its explanatory power continued unabated during Gordon's Brown's premiership.

Chapters 4 and 5 demonstrate that valence politics considerations also did much to shape the choices voters made in the 2010 general election – the contest that ended the New Labour era and set the stage for a Conservative–Liberal Democrat Coalition Government. The impact of leader images was dramatically illustrated by the first-ever leaders' debate when voters' highly favourable reactions to Nick Clegg's performance boosted the Liberal Democrats' standing in the polls and reconfigured the election campaign. Analyses show that both the Air War – the national campaign in the media – and the Ground War – local campaigns across the country – were important for understanding voting behaviour in 2010.

The persistent significance of valence forces over the 1997–2010 period is noteworthy because of the major economic crisis that began in Britain with the failure of the Northern Rock bank in autumn 2007. As the crisis unfolded, it obliterated the comfortable affluence of the Blair years and precipitated the most serious recession since the Great Depression of the 1930s. The deep and protracted downturn encouraged David Cameron, George Osborne and their Conservative colleagues to advocate deep cuts to public sector spending to 'rebalance' Britain's economy. The resulting combination of hard times and promises of stringent austerity by one of the major parties did not decrease the impact of valence politics variables on party support in the 2010 election. And, as discussed in Chapter 6, the pattern persisted after the election when the Conservative–Liberal Democrat Coalition Government came to power. Although one might conjecture that the Coalition Government's painful policies would translate the hypotheticals and abstractions of tax–spend preferences asked in public opinion surveys into concrete position issues that would divide the electorate and drive party support, Chapter 6 documented the continuing pre-eminence of valence forces after the 2010 election.

The general importance of leader images and partisan attachments for understanding political choice was illustrated in Chapter 7 where we investigated the determinants of voting in the May 2011 referendum to change Britain's single-member plurality electoral system to the Alternative Vote. Although referendum voting was strongly influenced by straightforward 'merits of the case' considerations and more general beliefs about the desirability of institutional reform, voters' attitudes towards the leaders and parties taking opposing stands on the proposal were important. In the event, the likelihood of a Yes vote was seriously inhibited by widespread antipathy towards Liberal Democrat Leader, Nick Clegg who was a vociferous proponent of changing Britain's electoral system. Enjoying widespread popularity after his performance in the first leaders' debate during the 2010 election campaign, Clegg fell from favour when he and other senior Liberal Democrats joined the Coalition Government and promptly reneged on their widely publicized pledge to oppose university fee increases. During the subsequent May 2011 referendum campaign, Clegg's badly tarnished image negated his ability to advocate the case for AV effectively. The dominance of the valence politics triumvirate of leader images, party performance evaluations and flexible partisan attachments was also evident in analyses of how voters would have ranked their party preferences had an AV ballot been used in the 2010 general election.

Chapter 8 investigated important relationships between policy performance in areas such as the economy, health care, education and the provision of national and personal security and voters' sense of subjective well-being. These analyses help to 'close the loop' in the theory of valence politics, linking the theory to larger ideas that do much to animate political discourse in Britain and other democracies. Rather than simply assuming that policy performance matters for people's satisfaction with their lives, analyses of data gathered in monthly CMS surveys revealed that performance judgments in several major policy domains affect subjective well-being. Contextual effects are also evident, with the Northern Rock bank failure and the subsequent onset of the economic crisis providing a natural experiment for testing these effects. Importantly, these analyses demonstrate that policy performance 'close to home' matters; voters' egocentric judgments – their beliefs about how policy delivery affects them and their families – are a major determinant of the political economy of life satisfaction in contemporary Britain.

In the following sections of this chapter we first place these British findings in comparative perspective. Then, we return to the British case, focusing on the political economy of public reactions to the Coalition's Government's austerity policies. We conclude by considering the implications of these reactions for party support and the outcome of the next general election.

Crisis economics and party support in comparative perspective

The most striking international development in the last five years is the return of deep and protracted economic recession across much of the developed world. Early twenty-first-century optimism, as expressed by leading policy makers such as Alan Greenspan and Ben Bernanke in the United States and Gordon Brown in Britain, that the spectre of recession, let alone depression, had been consigned to the history books evaporated in the wake of widely unexpected economic developments. Starting in late 2007, the much-heralded 'Great Moderation' of the business cycle gave way to a nearly catastrophic financial meltdown followed by a deep and protracted recession. As discussed in earlier chapters, Britain has been significantly affected by the ongoing crisis. But, Britain is hardly alone – the crisis has affected the economies of virtually all of the mature democracies. In particular, the crisis of the Eurozone has severely impacted several countries in the European Union, Britain's most important trading partner.

In this final chapter we examine the implications of the return of depression-style economics for the politics of democratic societies in general, focusing particularly on the electoral consequences of this development. The current recession raises the spectre that incumbent governments of whatever political persuasion will be thrown out of office as electorates become increasingly dissatisfied with their performance. In Britain, this possibility has significant implications for the electoral prospects of the Conservative–Liberal Democrat Coalition Government.

To address these topics, we first evaluate the impact of recession on the evaluations of government performance in Britain and 22 other European countries. For this purpose, we use European Social Survey (ESS) data gathered in 2010. Our focus is on public perceptions of governmental performance in managing the economic crisis. The aim is to identify the extent to which incumbents have lost the confidence of electorates since the start of the crisis in 2008. To provide perspective on trends in government performance evaluations over time, earlier ESS data also are employed.

We next consider how the recession has influenced satisfaction both with incumbent governments and with democracy more generally. The latter is an interesting issue since it addresses the question of whether or not a severe economic downturn has the effect of undermining support for democratic regimes as distinct from support for political authorities, that is, incumbent governments. In this regard, there are possibly important implications involving the rise of radical right and anti-system parties in several European democracies (Arzheimer, 2009). This may be particularly important in societies where democracy has only been recently established. Next, we return to Britain and examine the dynamics of public attitudes towards the economic crisis. The chapter concludes by considering the political economy of austerity in Britain and elsewhere.

A key issue for students of electoral politics is to determine how toxic recessionary economics is for the reputations of governments in contemporary democracies. There is abundant anecdotal evidence to suggest that it is very damaging for incumbents. For example, Nicholas Sarkozy failed in his bid to be re-elected President of France in 2012, and ruling coalition governments were thrown out of office in the Netherlands in 2010 and in Denmark in 2011. And, as discussed in earlier chapters, Labour was soundly defeated in the 2010 British general

election. But, there are counter examples. In Germany, the CDU/CSU –
a member of the governing coalition – fared very well in the 2009 Ger-
man Bundestag elections and party leader, Angela Merkel, remained
Chancellor. In Canada, the governing Conservative Party increased its
vote and seat shares in the 2011 federal election, thereby securing a
parliamentary majority. And, in the United States, Barack Obama won
a second term in the White House in the 2012 presidential election.
Clearly, the continuing economic doldrums have not proved fatal for
all incumbents.

More generally, between 2008 and 2012 there were 34 national legislative elections in the 27 member states of the European Union. In
no less than 20 of these elections, incumbent parties or ruling coalition governments were defeated, and political leaders were replaced.[1]
Although incumbents were re-elected in the remaining cases, the com-
position of ruling coalition governments often changed, and quite frequently they lost votes in these elections. It appears that the economic
crisis has made life difficult for incumbents in all of the advanced
democracies, although the extent of the effect has varied across
countries.

A central focus of this chapter is to examine the reaction of voters
to the performance of their governments in dealing with the economic
crisis. There is a question in the 2010 European Social Survey which
asked: 'Now thinking about the [country] government, how satisfied
are you with the way it is doing its job?' This question provides a
general indicator of what Europeans thought about the performance
of their governments some two and a half years after the crisis began.
Individuals were asked to code their responses on an 11-point scale
varying from zero (extremely dissatisfied) to ten (extremely satisfied).
Figure 9.1 shows the overall distribution of responses across the 23
European countries in the survey.[2] It can be seen that there were
large differences in the scores. About one in eight of the respondents
accorded their governments a zero rating and a majority (57 per cent)
gave scores less than the mid-point (5) on the scale. Only about one-
quarter (26 per cent) of those surveyed offered scores above the mid-
point and the mean was a mediocre 3.8. Clearly, satisfaction with the
government performance was not especially high.

Figure 9.2 displays the mean satisfaction with government performance scores for each of the 23 countries considered individually.
There was wide variation, with Greeks giving the lowest ratings with

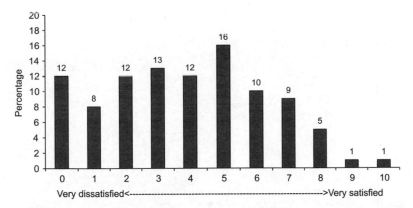

Figure 9.1 Satisfaction with government performance in 23 European countries, 2010.
Source: 2010 European Social Survey.

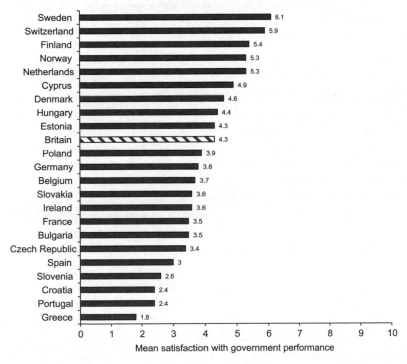

Figure 9.2 Mean satisfaction with government performance in 23 European countries, 2010.
Source: 2010 European Social Survey.

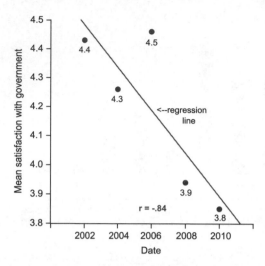

Figure 9.3 Changing levels of satisfaction with government in 21 European countries, 2002–10.
Source: 2002–10 European Social Surveys.

an average score of only 1.8, and the Swedes giving the highest ratings with an average of 6.1. British respondents accorded their government a mean rating of 4.3, which is above average for the 23 countries considered as a whole.[3] It can readily be seen that there is a north–south division in the data with northern European democracies like Denmark and Norway having much higher scores than southern European countries like Greece, Portugal and Spain. In addition, former communist countries like the Czech Republic and Bulgaria are well below average compared with firmly established democracies such as Switzerland and Sweden.

The 'satisfaction with government performance' question has been asked in each of the biannual European Social Surveys since the project was initiated in 2002, so we can get an overall picture of how evaluations of incumbents have changed over the first decade of the twenty-first century. The data are displayed in Figure 9.3. This figure shows that in the pre-crisis era (2002–06), satisfaction with government performance remained quite stable, with an overall mean score of just below 4.5. Then, there was a sizable decline in performance satisfaction in 2008 (to 3.9) and a further decline (to 3.8) in 2010. As Figure 9.3 shows, the arrival of the economic crisis correlates strongly (r = −0.84)

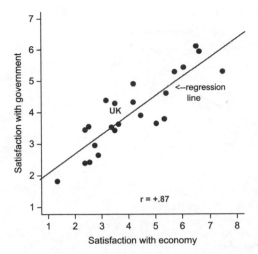

Figure 9.4 Satisfaction with government performance and satisfaction with economy in 23 European countries, 2010.
Source: 2010 European Social Survey.

with a decided decrease in satisfaction with government performance across Europe.

We can investigate the effects of the economic downturn on satisfaction with the performance of the government with the help of another question in the European Social Survey. This question asked: 'On the whole how satisfied are you with the present state of the economy in [country]?' Once again, responses were coded on an 11-point (0 to 10 scale). The relationship between mean responses to this question and government satisfaction ratings for the 23 countries appears in Figure 9.4. The relationship is very strong ($r = +0.87$), indicating that judgments which voters made about the performance of their governments were strongly influenced by perceptions of the performance of the economy.

Regarding the electoral consequences for incumbents, we examine the relationship between voting for incumbent parties and satisfaction with governmental performance. This is shown in Figure 9.5 where the vertical axis measures the percentage of respondents in the 2010 ESS who voted for incumbent parties. Since respondents were asked to report their vote in the previous national election which took place before satisfaction with the current government was measured, the

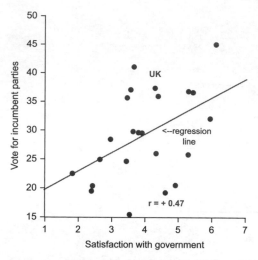

Figure 9.5 Electoral support for incumbent parties and satisfaction with government performance in 23 European countries, 2010.
Source: 2010 European Social Survey.

analysis should be interpreted with caution. That said, the association between the two variables is positive and quite strong (r = +0.47) – as expected, higher levels of satisfaction with government performance are related to higher vote shares for incumbent parties.

In the next section we focus on satisfaction with government at the individual level in these 23 countries. The aim is to delineate factors which influence government satisfaction, paying particular attention to the role of economic performance.

Modelling satisfaction with government

The central theme of the literature on the political economy of party support is that a successful economic performance by governments brings electoral rewards to incumbent parties, whereas unsuccessful economic performance has the opposite effect (e.g. Clarke *et al.*, 1992; Duch and Stevenson, 2008; Key, 1968; Lewis-Beck, 1988; Norpoth *et al.*, 1991; van der Brug *et al.*, 2007). This theme also long has been salient in research on the political cultural bases of public support for democracy (e.g. Almond and Verba, 1963; Easton, 1965; Lipset, 1963). A key idea in these early studies which reappears in more recent research is that strong economic performance can help to reinforce and consolidate democracy in regimes making the transition from authoritarianism to democracy, and weak performance can undermine democratic consolidation (Diamond, 1999; Fails and Pierce, 2010; Rose and Mishler, 1996). As one researcher argued, stable democracies depend on citizens regarding democracy as 'the only game in town' (di Palma, 1990) and they are inclined to do this if democratic consolidation is accompanied by economic prosperity.

Another important line of research examines the effects of political institutions and political participation on satisfaction with democracy (Anderson and Guillory, 1997; Mishler and Rose, 2001; Wells and Krieckhaus, 2006). Recent studies have shown that institutional arrangements tend to influence democratic norms rather than the reverse process of democratic norms sustaining institutions (Fails and Pierce, 2010). But the absence of deep, protracted recessions in the period since the end of the Second World War through 2007 inhibited research on the impact of severe economic crises on public satisfaction with democracy. Depression-era economic conditions cannot be recreated in a laboratory.

As Figure 9.5 shows, circa 2010 there is a sizable aggregate relationship (r = +0.47) between satisfaction with government performance and voting for incumbent parties in the 23 European democracies. Thus, it seems likely that variables which influence voting behaviour such as leadership evaluations, partisanship and valence issues are likely to play an important role in influencing satisfaction with government performance as well and, by extension, satisfaction with democracy more generally. Partisanship in particular is likely to have a direct effect on (dis)satisfaction with government performance, but also an indirect effect via perceptual screening effects that encourage individuals to focus on good news and ignore bad news about the parties they support (Campbell *et al.*, 1960).

Ideology is another factor likely to influence satisfaction with political authorities and democracy in European countries (Palfrey and Poole, 1987). The effects of ideology are apt to be linked to the partisan affiliations of incumbents, with left-leaning voters being more critical of centre-right parties in power and right-leaning voters more sympathetic to them. The reverse applies for right-leaning voters when centre-left governments are in power. But ideology can have an independent influence on government and democratic satisfaction apart from partisanship. Persons with left-of-centre ideological beliefs are apt to be more critical of the status quo in democracies than those with right-of-centre beliefs, something which is likely to be reinforced by the economic crisis. Historically, critiques of capitalism have been the linchpin of leftist ideologies and the current crisis – involving traumatic shocks to the interlocking financial systems of major mature democracies – invites interpretation as an exemplar of the pathologies of contemporary political-economic arrangements.

As the earlier discussion indicated, policy performance is likely to be one of the most important influences on the public's satisfaction with government and democratic politics. This is apparent from Figure 9.4, but confidence in government is not only a matter of economic performance. The valence politics model suggests that other policy domains such as health, crime, education and welfare are important as well. In addition, position issues central to Downsian spatial theories of party competition should influence government performance judgments and democratic satisfaction. People should have confidence both in governments and in the practice of democracy if policies are delivered that are closely aligned with their preferences on divisive position issues. If, for example, government is delivering the balance of taxation and public spending which an individual prefers, that should produce high levels of satisfaction with both government and with democracy more generally. However, a wealth of empirical evidence presented in earlier chapters and previous research indicates that spatial issues are likely to be overshadowed by valence considerations when voters make performance judgments.

The 2010 European Social Survey (ESS) permits a limited test of these conjectures. Regarding partisanship, the ESS asks respondents if they feel close to a political party. Data generated by this question provide a useful proxy measure of partisan attachments, enabling us to determine if voters identify with a governing party, an opposition party, or no party at all. In this way the influence of partisanship on government and democratic satisfaction can be estimated. Concerning valence issues, satisfaction with the economy has already been discussed and it is likely to have a strong influence. In addition, there are questions about satisfaction with health care, the education system and the police's handling of crime. These can all be included as measures of reactions to valence issues in models of satisfaction with government performance and the practice of democracy more generally.

With the recession in mind, a question in the ESS enquired about respondents' personal economic circumstances. Respondents were asked to indicate the extent to which they believed that their income was adequate to make ends meet in the current economic climate.[4] A variable based on responses to this question was included in the analyses of incumbent government and democracy satisfaction as well as an interaction between this variable and the 11-point scale measuring evaluations of the national economy. The interaction term enables us to determine if these variables reinforce each other as influences on government and democratic satisfaction.

Regarding leadership evaluations, there were no direct measures of public evaluations of individual political leaders in the ESS. However, a proxy measure is provided in the form of a question that asks respondents to indicate their trust in politicians. Once again this is measured with an 11-point scale varying from 0 ('no trust at all') to 10 ('complete trust'). A related question on trust in political parties also is included, since it throws light on the impact of institutional trust on satisfaction with government and democratic performance. Finally, the impact of ideology is gauged with responses to a question which asked respondents to score themselves on an 11-point 'left-right' scale, where a low score indicates left-leaning and a high score, right-leaning, orientations.

The impact of spatial issues can only be measured indirectly in the ESS since there are no questions which ask respondents to compare their own positions on a particular issue with those of political parties. However, there are questions about various controversial issues such as immigration, income inequality, gay rights and environmental problems.[5] While not being able to test spatial distances directly with these items, it is nonetheless possible to determine if attitudes about these position issues influence satisfaction with incumbent governments and the practice of democracy more generally. These issues are controversial across Europe as a whole and should provide insight into the impact of spatial issues.

The models of satisfaction with government performance and the practice of democracy are displayed in Table 9.1. In addition to the predictor variables just discussed, the models include several sociodemographics. Parameter estimates are generated by OLS regression analyses of the data from 23 countries in the ESS. The table presents standardized regression coefficients and the analyses show that

Table 9.1 *OLS regression model of determinants of satisfaction with government and democracy in 23 European countries, 2010*

	Satisfaction with government	Satisfaction with democracy
	β	β
Feels close to an incumbent party	0.14***	0.06***
Feels close to an opposition party	−0.08***	−0.01***
Satisfaction with economy	0.31***	0.25***
Satisfaction with education	0.07***	0.17***
Satisfaction with health care	0.02***	0.07***
Satisfaction with police	0.04***	0.08***
Trust in politicians	0.23***	0.15***
Trust in political parties	0.10***	0.11***
Attitudes towards immigration	0.03***	0.05***
Attitudes towards the environment	0.03***	0.01
Attitudes towards gay rights	−0.01***	0.04***
Attitudes towards inequality	−0.03***	−0.04***
Left-right ideology	0.08***	0.04***
Perceptions of income adequacy	−0.02***	−0.03***
Economic satisfaction * income adequacy	0.06***	0.01
Age	−0.04***	−0.06***
Age squared	0.06***	0.06***
Gender	−0.00	0.02***
Ethnic minority	0.01***	0.00
Unemployed	0.00	−0.01**
Education	0.01+	0.02***
Social class	−0.00	0.01
Income	−0.00	0.02***
R^2	0.54	0.47

*** $p < 0.001$; ** $p < 0.01$; * $p < 0.05$; + $p < 0.10$; one-tailed test.
Note: standardized regression coefficients.
Source: 2010 European Social Survey; N = 43 961.

satisfaction with the economy is easily the most important predictor. This variable has a coefficient of 0.31 in the government satisfaction model and 0.25 in the democratic satisfaction model. The egocentric economic evaluation measure, which captures an individual's perceptions of the adequacy of their incomes, has predictable effects – individuals who feel under financial pressure are less likely to be satisfied with the incumbent government and the state of democracy.

Moreover, as the interaction term shows, the effects of these ego centric economic evaluations on satisfaction with the government vary in strength depending on sociotropic evaluations – that is, judgments about the performance of the overall economy. However, as Table 9.1 indicates, the interaction effect is not significant in the analysis of satisfaction with democracy more generally.

Together with the economy, other valence issues exert significant effects. Satisfaction with health care, education and the police all help to explain satisfaction with both government performance and also the practice of democracy in the 23 European countries. In the government satisfaction model, the second largest coefficient is the one for trust in politicians, the measure indexing evaluations of political leadership. This variable also has a large and statistically significant coefficient in the democratic satisfaction model. These results are consonant with the valence politics hypothesis that political leadership is a key factor in explaining the extent of citizen satisfaction with the performance of their governments and the workings of their political systems.

Effects associated with trust in political parties are also important and play a similar role in both models. Related effects concern partisanship, but in this case support for an incumbent party positively influences evaluations of governments and democracy, whereas support for an opposition party negatively influences these evaluations. In the case of satisfaction with governments, this finding is anticipated but it is perhaps surprising that it carries over into democratic satisfaction, albeit weakly.

Turning next to proxy measures of spatial variables, attitudes towards immigration influence both satisfaction variables. People who believe immigrants make a positive contribution to the economy are likely to be more satisfied with their government and also their political system. In the case of attitudes towards the environment, individuals who are optimistic that science will solve environmental problems tend to be more satisfied with their governments, although this measure has no effect on democratic satisfaction. Regarding attitudes towards gay rights, supporters of such rights tend to be more critical of the government than opponents, although the opposite is true in relation to democratic satisfaction. Finally, supporters of greater income equality are more critical of both the government-of-the-day and democracy more generally.

Demographics play a larger role in the democratic satisfaction model than the government satisfaction model. Older respondents tend to be more critical than the young, although the quadratic specification (age + age squared) shows that this effect weakens for older individuals. More highly educated respondents are supportive of the incumbent government and democracy more generally, although this effect appears more robust for democratic satisfaction. Income has no impact on government satisfaction but it does influence democratic satisfaction and a similar point can be made about gender and unemployment. Men tend to be more supportive of democracy than women and, as might be expected, the unemployed are less supportive than those with jobs.

Overall, these models are similar to vote choice models and this is because of the importance of performance in influencing support for incumbents as distinct from opposition parties. However, the strength of the relationship between evaluations of performance of the economy and satisfaction with government indicates that continuing hard times are playing a significant role in the decline in satisfaction with incumbent governments observed in Figure 9.3. In the next section we focus the discussion once again on Britain, focusing on links between economic evaluations and support for political parties.

Public reactions to austerity in Britain

Findings in the previous section show that Britain is not unusual in the way voters have responded to current economic travails. We have seen that evaluations of the state of the economy help to explain support for incumbent governments across Europe as a whole. We examined the plans and performance of Britain's Coalition Government up to the mid-term of the present Parliament in Chapter 6. Analyses presented there indicated that subjective economic evaluations influence party support and, in turn, these evaluations are driven by a number of factors. In this section we investigate public attitudes to the Coalition's austerity strategy in greater detail and consider some of the wider issues raised by it.

Public reactions to the Coalition's austerity programme during the first eight months of 2012 are illustrated in Figure 9.6.[6] Exactly half of Britons accept the necessity for budget reductions – 50 per cent of the respondents in the CMS surveys agreed with the statement that public-sector cuts are essential, whereas 23 per cent disagreed, and 27 per cent were unsure. However, almost as many (45 per cent) agreed with the

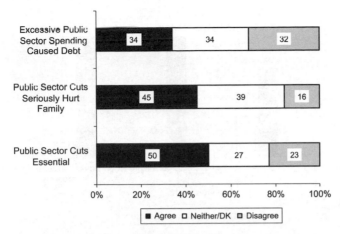

Figure 9.6 Attitudes towards public-sector cuts, January–August 2012.
Source: January–August 2012 BES CMS surveys.

proposition that the cuts were likely to result in substantial harm to their families, and only 16 per cent disagreed. The extent of division in public opinion is perhaps most evident in responses to the statement that excessive public spending causes sovereign debt. As shown in Figure 9.6, the 2012 CMS respondents divided nearly equally over the impact of public spending on debt, with 34 per cent agreeing that excessive public-sector spending caused it and 32 per cent disagreeing. A similarly even division of opinion is apparent in responses to a question asking for summary judgments about the anticipated effects of the public-sector cuts – 37 per cent stated that the cuts will strengthen the economy, slightly more (41 per cent) thought they will weaken it, and 22 per cent were unsure (data not shown).

Although still very much divided, additional analyses document that opinion has been trending gradually against the policies since the austerity measures were initially introduced by the Coalition Government in June 2010. Since then, agreement that budget reductions are essential has fallen gradually from 68 per cent to 50 per cent, while agreement that the cuts are causing serious difficulties for respondents' families has risen from 41 to 45 per cent. In addition, the percentage agreeing that excessive public spending is the main cause of Britain's debt has fallen from 45 per cent in June 2010 to 34 per cent in August 2012.

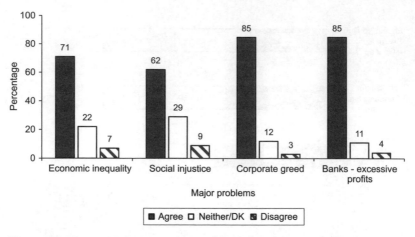

Figure 9.7 'Occupy Britain': major problems facing Britain today, January–August 2012.
Source: January–August 2012 BES CMS surveys.

Negative attitudes towards prevailing social and economic conditions suggest why critics of austerity have gained traction. Echoing the strident rhetoric of 'Occupy' protestors, large majorities of respondents in the January–August 2012 CMS surveys identify economic inequality, social injustice, corporate greed and excessive bank profits as major problems in contemporary Britain.[7] As Figure 9.7 illustrates, 71 per cent and 62 per cent, respectively, believe economic inequality and social justice are serious problems, and less than 10 per cent in each case disagree. Opinions about major financial institutions are even harsher, with fully 85 per cent stating that banks are enjoying excessive profits and corporate greed is a major problem. Only 3 per cent and 4 per cent, respectively, disagree with these propositions.

There is also evidence that many people blame British banks for the economic crisis. Figure 9.8 documents that this is not a recent phenomenon. Rather, starting in autumn 2008 over six CMS respondents in ten (61 per cent) blamed the banks for the situation, with this number increasing to seven in ten (71 per cent) by August 2012. The percentages assigning responsibility to government, although hardly trivial, are considerably smaller – 40 per cent in October 2008 and 45 per cent in 2012. As also shown in Figure 9.8, the percentage blaming the European Union has trended sharply upward, from 22 per cent to 46 per cent. Again, however, the latter number is considerably smaller than those for domestic banks. Overall, the numbers in

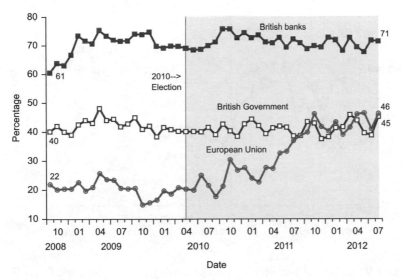

Figure 9.8 Trends in attributions of responsibility for economic crisis, October 2008–August 2012.
Source: October 2008–August 2012 CMS surveys.

Figures 9.7 and 9.8 clearly testify that the arguments of movements such as Occupy Britain that blame capitalist financial institutions for the serious social and economic difficulties confronting the country are echoing widespread sentiments in British public opinion.

Starting in October 2008, the British Election Study began asking CMS respondents to use a 0–10 scale (with 0 designated as 'very unlikely' and 10 designated as 'very likely') to forecast the likelihood that the economic crisis would be resolved in the year ahead. From the outset, CMS respondents have been quite bearish, with the initial average score being 4.0 on the 0–10 scale. And, as Figure 9.9 illustrates, pessimism has increased substantially over time – in August 2012 the average score had dropped to a dismal 2.1. Nor is there much volatility in these gloomy assessments. Indeed, since the austerity-minded Conservative–Liberal Democrat Coalition came to power in May 2010, the monthly average has never exceeded 3.0.

What are the sources of this widespread and deepening economic pessimism? In the spirit of the late V.O. Key (1966), a straightforward answer is: 'People are not fools! – they are bearish because the economy is in perilous shape and shows no sign of reviving any time soon'.

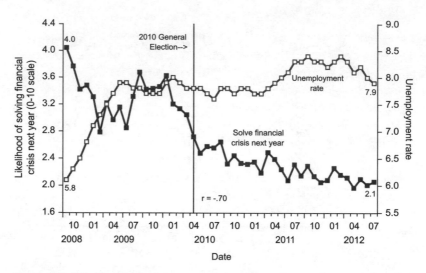

Figure 9.9 Likelihood of solving economic crisis and unemployment, October 2008–August 2012.
Source: October 2008–August 2012 CMS surveys.

Given a continuing barrage of bad news and commentaries highlighting future uncertainties, it does not surprise that many people are less than sanguine about resolving the crisis in the foreseeable future. In this regard, perhaps no single indicator carries as much weight in the public mind as the unemployment rate – monthly jobless numbers provide a widely publicized and easily understood measure of how hard times are. As discussed in earlier chapters, UK unemployment figures now have been depressing for an extended period of time – rising from 5.8 per cent in October 2008 to 8.4 per cent in October 2011 before retreating slightly (to 7.9 per cent) in August 2012. As Figure 9.9 shows, the correlation between public expectations of solving the crisis in the next year and the unemployment rate is strongly negative ($r = -0.70$).

If people use unemployment figures as a convenient heuristic for assessing the economy's present state and future prospects, then it should be possible to model the relationship between forecasts for solving the crisis and the jobless rate as an error correction process (Enders, 2009). This error correction model enables us to estimate the long-run equilibrium relationship between unemployment and perceived economic prospects and to identify factors prompting short-run deviations from this equilibrium relationship. These factors may help to explain variation in people's economic forecasts, but over the long run, expectations for solving the crisis should evolve in dynamic equilibrium with the length of lines at Jobs Centres. Here, we specify four such 'other factors'.

The first factor is the Chancellor of the Exchequer's 2009–12 budget speeches which have delivered a depressing litany of claims about the necessity for varying mixtures of spending cuts and tax hikes. Second is the former Labour Government's March 2009 announcement of a massive quantitative easing programme to jump-start the faltering economy. Third is the presence since May 2010 of the austerity-minded Conservative–Liberal Democrat Coalition Government. As discussed in Chapter 6, Prime Minister David Cameron and Chancellor George Osborne have made the ailing economy and the need for stringent austerity measures the touchstone of their economic strategy. Covering the Government's pronouncements and adding their own embellishments, the news media have regularly reminded viewers that times are tough. For their part, Ed Miliband, and his Shadow Chancellor, Ed Balls, have responded to this 'doom and gloom' by arguing that times are indeed hard and quick relief is unlikely because the Government insists on pursuing an ill-advised neo-Thatcherite economic agenda. A fourth factor is the widely publicized November 2010 and November 2011 demonstrations prompted by the Government's decision to raise university tuition rates by upwards of 300 per cent. Characterized by violent confrontations between marchers and police, the 2010 protests dramatized the costs that the new austerity policies would entail for millions of British families. The 2011 protests were both smaller and tamer, but reminded people of the financial burdens they were being asked to shoulder.

In summary, the time series error correction model of public forecasts of whether the economic crisis will be solved over the forthcoming year is:

$$\Delta \text{SOLVE}_t = \beta_0 + \beta_1 \Delta \text{UNEMP}_{t-1} - \alpha_1(\text{SOLVE}_{t-1} - c_1 \text{UNEMP}_{t-1})$$
$$+ \beta_2 \text{BUDGET09}_{t-1} + \beta_3 \text{BUDGET10}_{t-1}$$
$$+ \beta_4 \text{BUDGET11}_t + \beta_5 \text{BUDGET12}_{t-1} + \beta_6 \text{QE}_{t-1}$$
$$+ \beta_7 \text{COALITION}_{t-1} + \beta_8 \text{PROTEST}_{t-1} + \varepsilon_t \qquad (9.1)$$

Table 9.2 *Error correction model of public opinion about the economic crisis, October 2008–August 2012*

Predictor variables	β	s.e.
Change in unemployment rate (t-1)	−0.86***	0.21
Error correction mechanism (t-1)	−0.65***	0.09
Unemployment rate (t-1)- ECM	0.30***	0.08
2009 Budget statement (t-1)	−0.24*	0.14
2010 Budget statement (t-1)	−0.32*	0.14
2011 Budget statement (t)	−0.28*	0.14
2012 Budget statement (t-1)	0.02	0.14
2009 Quantitative easing (t)	−0.45***	0.14
2010 General election (t)	−0.66***	0.09
Protests/strikes (t-1)	−0.22**	0.09
Constant	3.69***	0.67

Adjusted $R^2 = 0.63$
N = 46
*** $p \le 0.001$; ** $p \le 0.01$; * $p \le 0.05$; one-tailed test.
Source: October 2008–August 2012 CMS surveys.

where:

 SOLVE = forecast for solving the economic crisis
 UNEMP = unemployment rate
 BUDGET09 – BUDGET12 = annual budgets
 QE = quantitative easing
 COALITION = Coalition Government elected
 PROTEST = protests
 Δ = differencing operator
 ε_t = stochastic error term ($N (0, \sigma^2)$, t is time, and α, c and βs are parameters to be estimated.

Model parameters are estimated using nonlinear least squares and aggregate CMS data for the October 2008–August 2012 period.

As reported in Table 9.2, this model can account for a large percentage of the variation in public opinion about the likelihood of the economic crisis (adjusted $R^2 = 0.63$). Indicative of the power of the error correction mechanism operating between public forecasts for solving the crisis and monthly unemployment rates, the adjustment parameter (α) is −0.65, p < 0.001. This signifies that a shock to the system, from whatever source, is eroded at a rate of nearly 65 per cent in each subsequent month by the long-run cointegrating relationship between optimism/pessimism about resolving the crisis and the unemployment rate. Unemployment also has large short-term effects, with a 1 per cent increase in joblessness being sufficient to lower forecasts by nearly one full point ($\beta = -0.86$, $p < 0.001$) on the 0–10 scale.

Other factors are operative as well. As expected, annual budgets, the initial round of quantitative easing, the student protests, and the replacement of Labour by the Conservative–Liberal Democrat Coalition all worked to dampen public forecasts that the economic crisis would soon be resolved. The impact of the presence of the Coalition Government is especially noteworthy. Specified as an ongoing (permanent) effect, the presence of the Coalition has worked to reduce economic forecasts by -0.66 points each month. Effects of the first round of quantitative easing and the widely publicized protests are smaller (βs $= -0.45$ and -0.22, respectively), but statistically significant. The effects of the annual budget statements are also negative and statistically significant for every year except 2012.

Overall, the model provides a parsimonious explanation of the bearish public forecasts about the future course of the economic crisis. As hypothesized, unemployment is the key heuristic, with forecasts for the economy and the joblessness rate constituting a powerful error correction process. Since autumn 2008, that process has adjusted the effects of various shocks, the largest being the replacement of Gordon Brown's Government by an avowedly austerity-minded Coalition Government determined to 'rebalance' the British political economy via deep cuts in public spending.

Cut the public sector, occupy Britain

Growing scepticism about the likelihood of solving the economic crisis has parallels in widespread concern with socioeconomic inequality (reflected in the Occupy Britain Movement) and gradually diminishing support for the public-sector cuts. We suggest that these latter two attitudes can be explained not only by the perceived likelihood of solving the economic crisis, but also by partisan affiliations, cognitive and emotional reactions to economic conditions, and sociodemographic factors such as age, education, gender, income, social class and country of residence (England, Scotland, Wales).

Table 9.3 *OLS regression models of perceptions of social-economic inequality and opinions about public-sector cuts, January–August 2012*

Predictor variables	Socio-economic inequality		Public-sector cuts	
	β	s.e.	β	s.e.
Economic evaluations	−0.22***	0.01	0.29***	0.01
Economy-emotional reactions	−0.11***	0.01	0.04***	0.01
Likelihood solve crisis	−0.03***	0.004	−0.01**	0.004
Socio-economic inequality	xx	xx	−0.13***	0.01
Party identification:				
Conservative	−0.19***	0.03	0.61***	0.03
Labour	0.18***	0.03	−0.37***	0.02
Liberal Democrat	0.22***	0.04	0.11***	0.03
Other party	−0.01	0.03	0.09***	0.03
Age	0.01***	0.0002	0.003***	0.0001
Education	0.01	0.01	−0.02**	0.006
Gender	0.02	0.02	0.05**	0.02
Income	−0.01***	0.002	0.00	0.002
Social class	−0.02	0.02	0.01	0.02
Country:				
Scotland	0.09**	0.03	−0.17***	0.03
Wales	0.12**	0.04	−0.04	0.04
Constant	−0.31***	0.06	−0.08**	0.05
$R^2 =$	0.22		0.42	
N = 8563				

xx – variable not included in model.
*** $p \leq 0.001$; ** $p \leq 0.01$; * $p \leq 0.05$, one-tailed test.

Table 9.3 summarizes OLS regression analyses of perceived socio-economic inequality and support for the public-sector cuts,[8] using CMS survey data collected between January and August 2012. We expected that perceptions of socio-economic inequality would reflect partisan divisions, with Conservative identifiers rejecting the notion that inequality is a major problem and Labour identifiers endorsing the idea. Expectations regarding Liberal Democrat identifiers are less certain – on one hand, they might support their Coalition partner and reject the idea that inequality is a serious problem; on the other hand, the party has a long tradition of championing progressive policies and institutional reform, suggesting widespread rank-and-file sensitivity to socio-economic inequality. The results (see Table 9.3) indicate the latter hypothesis receives empirical support: as anticipated, Conservative party identification has a negative impact ($\beta = -0.19$, p < 0.001) on perceived socio-economic inequality, whereas both Labour and Liberal Democrat party identifications have positive effects (βs = 0.18 and 0.22, respectively, p < 0.001).

Regarding other predictors, as expected positive economic evaluations, positive emotional reactions to the economy, and a belief that the economic crisis soon would be solved all had negatively signed coefficients indicating that people who were sanguine about the economy tended to be less concerned about inequality as a major issue than were those who were pessimistic. Forecasts of the likelihood of solving the economic crisis had the anticipated negative effect on perceptions of socio-economic inequality – as anticipated, people who were optimistic about resolving the crisis tended to be less concerned with inequality as a major problem. Only a few sociodemographic variables had significant effects – older people, those with lower incomes and residents of Wales all had greater concerns about inequality.

If individuals had consistent belief systems, it might be expected that predictor variables with positive effects in the socio-economic inequality model – concern over inequality – would have negative effects in the public-sector cuts support model, and vice versa. In the 'support for cuts' model, we included the variable reflecting concern over socio-economic inequality.[9] This predictor exhibits the expected negative relationship ($\beta = -0.13$, p < 0.001), indicating that people concerned about inequality tend to oppose the cuts. We also anticipated that identifiers with one of the Coalition parties would be more likely than Labour partisans to support the cuts and this proved to be the case. Effects for Conservative and Liberal Democrat identifiers were positive, whereas the effect of Labour partisanship was negative.

Economic evaluations, emotional responses to economic conditions and forecasts of the likelihood of solving the crisis also had statistically significant effects. Positive economic evaluations and positive emotional reactions to the economy were associated with greater support for public-sector cuts (Table 9.3, column 2). The remaining predictor, forecasts for solving the crisis had a negative impact on support for the public-sector cuts. This result may reflect the fact that many of those who expect the economy to recover quickly may have concluded that the size and scope of public-sector cuts are excessive and counterproductive.

Bears bite

Since the Coalition Government came to power in May 2010, public opinion about Conservative Leader David Cameron and that of Liberal Democrat Leader Nick Clegg has become increasingly negative. As Figure 9.10, Panel A shows, affect for both Cameron and Clegg stood at a healthy 5.1 points one month after they took office. In the ensuring months, their scores have trended downward, falling to 3.7 for Cameron and 3.1 for Clegg in August 2012. Nor is it simply the case that people do not like them, perhaps because they are administering bitter, but needed, medicine to heal the ailing economy. Rather, as documented in Figure 9.10, Panel B, both leaders' competence ratings have fallen sharply – in Cameron's case from a high 6.2 points to a mediocre 4.5 points. Clegg has fared worse, with his competence score moving sharply downward from 5.6 to merely 3.1. Rightly or wrongly, there is a growing sense in the electorate that the Coalition leaders are not able to handle the country's affairs effectively.

It might be conjectured that these downward trends are rooted in widespread perceptions that the economic crisis is not about to end anytime soon. The Coalition's austerity policies may be justified as being necessary to cure Britain's economic malaise. But, as discussed above, public forecasts that the economic crisis will soon be resolved in the foreseeable future have become increasingly pessimistic as unemployment has remained high and Chancellor George Osborne's 'bad news' budgets have become a familiar feature of Government rhetoric. It is plausible that the growing bearishness is the motor driving increasingly negative judgments about government leaders. In the language of econometrics, this suggests the existence of a cointegrating relationship between public forecasts for solving the economic crisis and images voters have of Messrs Cameron and Clegg. That cointegrating relationship can be specified as a simple error correction model. Recalling that Clegg suffered a barrage of negative publicity in autumn 2010 for reneging on his pledge to oppose increases in university fees, we also include a dummy variable in the model to index the effect of

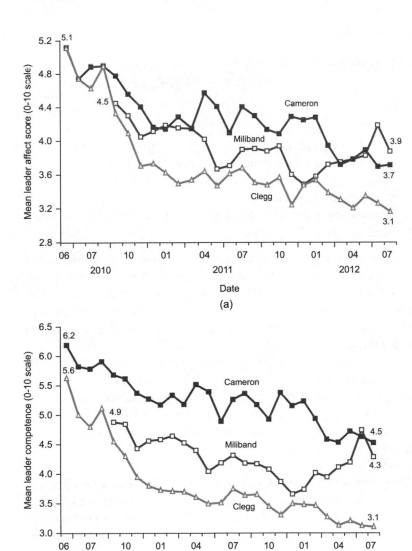

Figure 9.10 Party leader images, June 2010–August 2012.
A. Leader affect ratings.
B. Leader competence ratings.
Source: June 2010–August 2012 CMS surveys.

that event. The model is:

$$\Delta \text{LIMAGE}_t = \beta_0 + \beta_1 \Delta \text{SOLVE}_t - \alpha_1(\text{LIMAGE}_{t-1}$$
$$- c_1 \text{SOLVE}_{t-1}) + \beta_2 \text{UNIFEE}_t + \varepsilon_t \qquad (9.2)$$

where:

LIMAGE = Cameron or Clegg's affect or competence rating
SOLVE = forecast for solving the economic crisis
UNIFEE = university fee increases announced
Δ = differencing operator
ε_t = stochastic error term (N $(0, \sigma^2)$, t is time, and α, c and βs are parameters to be estimated.

Parameter estimates are obtained using nonlinear least squares of aggregate CMS data for the June 2010 to August 2012 period. The analysis documents the hypothesized cointegrating relationships, with Table 9.4 Panel A showing that Cameron's affect and competence ratings have tended to move in tandem with public judgments about the likelihood of solving the economic crisis. The short-term effects of these judgments are such that a downward movement of 1 point on the 0–10 scale would cost Cameron slightly over half a point in his affect rating and over four-fifths of a point in his competence rating. The long-term effects for affect and competence are −0.66 and −0.69, respectively, thereby indicating that shocks to Cameron's image, from whatever source, are quickly eroded in subsequent months by judgments about the economic crisis.

Effects for Clegg are similar, but stronger. The short-term effects of a downward movement in forecasts for solving the economic crisis are nine-tenths of a point for affect and a full point for competence. The long-term effects are −0.71 and −0.59, respectively, again indicating that negative judgments about the crisis have played a powerful long-run role in driving down his affect and competence ratings. In addition, unlike Cameron (see Table 9.4, Panel A), Clegg's image was tarnished by his widely publicized and much criticized U-turn on university fees, which cost him a half point in affect and four-tenths of a point in competence (Table 9.4, Panel B).

In earlier chapters, we have discussed the power of leader images in valence politics models of electoral choice and models of party support in inter-election periods. This is why the downward trends in

Table 9.4 *Error correction models of Coalition leaders' images, June 2010–August 2012*

	Affect		Competence	
	β	s.e.	β	s.e.
A. Cameron's image				
Predictor variables				
Change in financial crisis forecast (t)	0.55*	0.29	0.85**	0.35
Error correction mechanism (t-1)	−0.66***	0.18	−0.69***	0.19
Financial crisis forecast – ECM (t-1)	−1.40***	0.47	−1.84*	0.53
University fee increase (t)	−0.12	0.15	−0.04	0.16
Constant	0.81	0.84	0.73	0.97
Adjusted R²	0.28		0.30	
N = 25				
B. Clegg's image				
Predictor variables				
Change in financial crisis forecast (t)	0.89***	0.21	1.01***	0.23
Error correction mechanism (t-1)	−0.71***	0.13	−0.59***	0.11
Financial crisis forecast – ECM(t-1)	−1.12***	0.32	−1.57***	0.40
University fee increase (t)	−0.51***	0.15	−0.40***	0.14
Constant	1.24*	0.59	0.42	0.58
Adjusted R²	0.63		0.65	
N = 25				

*** $p \leq 0.001$; ** $p \leq 0.01$; * $p \leq 0.05$; one-tailed test.

the Coalition leaders' affect and competence ratings are very important. As shown, these trends reflect the electorate's increasing pessimism about resolving the now protracted economic crisis. That pessimism is bad news for Cameron, Clegg and their parties. Leader images do much to drive electoral choice and the Coalition's current low numbers in opinion polls are harbingers of the future peril they may encounter.

However, despite the negativity expressed about Cameron and Clegg, their political futures are not necessarily bleak. In this regard, Figure 9.10 documents that many voters continue to have reservations about Labour leader, Ed Miliband. Miliband's initial affect rating in the October 2010 CMS was a mediocre 4.5 and since then it trended downward, reaching 3.9 in August 2012. His competence scores have been equally uninspiring. The significance of leader images suggests that this lack of enthusiasm for Miliband – should it continue – may give Cameron, Clegg and their Coalition colleagues a useful opening in the run-up to the next general election.

Another opening may be provided by economic evaluations. Either by luck or design, Britain's economic prospects may well improve before the next election. If, for whatever reason, the economy does regain its health, Cameron and Clegg will quickly claim that they were right all along and their austerity medicine did the trick. Whether their claim is valid will not matter much. With a stronger economy comes more jobs and analyses presented in this chapter demonstrate that the latter will be key to transforming bearish economic forecasts into bullish ones. In turn, increasingly bullish attitudes will help Cameron and Clegg to refurbish their images as competent leaders deserving of public affection and respect – and the electoral support that will bring.

Conclusion: austerity policies and valence politics

The massive public-sector cuts they have implemented carry both risks and opportunities for the governing Coalition and its lead partner, the Conservative Party. An economic recovery would give the Conservatives and Prime Minister Cameron the opportunity to claim that their 'smaller government' approach that 'rebalances' the public and private sectors is exactly the medicine the ailing British economy needed after over a decade of Labour 'big government' excess. However, if the current combination of high unemployment and negligible-to-negative growth persists, Labour and other political parties will be able argue that the austerity-driven cuts have been senseless and cruel – beneficial only to a very small percentage of Britons, many of them wealthy Conservative supporters in the City of London. These charges would resonate with antipathy to banks and bankers that extends far beyond supporters of the 'Occupy' movement.

Viewed globally, the analyses presented above suggest that support for the Coalition Government's austerity policies eventually may be undermined by a lack of visible results in the real economy. A substantial segment of the British populace in the mid-term of the current government believe that public-sector cuts are essential for the country's long-term economic health but, increasingly the view that the cuts are causing serious difficulties for families is leading many people to say 'enough is enough'. Sustained high levels of unemployment propelled by public-sector job cuts put mounting pressure on the welfare budget and are unlikely to be regarded kindly by either frustrated job-seekers or those workers who have been fired during the economic downturn. Furthermore, confidence in Britain's ability to solve the economic crisis has been falling as persistently high unemployment figures cue voters that the problem is unlikely to be fixed any time soon. Faced with a continuing lack of jobs, a 'double-dip' recession and an episodic, but recurrent, flood of bad news about conditions in Greece, Spain and other EU countries, the British public is being sorely tempted to conclude that the Coalition Government's austerity policies are ineffective and unjust. This explains the pattern in public opinion discussed in Chapter 6 showing that the Coalition's reputation for economic competence is a wasting asset.

Valence politics considerations are having important effects on the evolution of public attitudes towards the economic crisis and the austerity measures that have been implemented to combat it. Perceptions of socio-economic inequality are less likely when individuals evaluate the economy positively, when they experience positive emotional reactions to economic conditions, and when they believe that a near-term solution to the crisis is at hand. But, at present, bullish Britons are hard to find – rather, most are decidedly bearish about prospects for solving the economic crisis any time soon. This prevailing pessimism is coupled with widely shared beliefs that Britain is blighted by a toxic mix of corporate greed, excessive bank profits, economic inequality and social injustice. According to this view, Gordon Gekko is not just an 'over-the-top' Hollywood caricature of an atypically rapacious banker; rather his real-life counterparts populate the City. They may not be the 'masters of the universe' described in *Liar's Poker* (Lewis, 1989) and many subsequent stories of Wall Street excess, but they dominate Britain's economy and politics to the detriment of millions of ordinary people.

The dark nature of present-day British public opinion is noteworthy but it does not necessary signal an impending revolution or, less dramatically, the sure defeat of Prime Minister Cameron and his Coalition colleagues at the next general election. At the time of writing in the mid-term of the present Parliament the election is more than two years away, and it is possible that conditions will improve before voters are asked to choose. Perhaps Hayek really does trump Keynes and the Government's austerity policies will eventually work as advertised. But the analyses in Chapter 6 indicate that negative expectations do have pernicious economic consequences and, if so, the Coalition's neo-conservative political economy experiment may end in tears.

In any case, the fact that valence politics variables have powerful effects in the vote intention models discussed in earlier chapters indicates that attitudes towards spending cuts and socio-economic inequality, however important, will not be the sole drivers of party support when voters go to the polls. Rather than respond reflexively to conditions around them, British voters, like their counterparts elsewhere, place economic difficulties and the policy responses they engender in a broader context with images of party leaders, partisan attachments and global assessments of party performance. As documented above, differing positions regarding the austerity policies are exerting substantial effects on party support, but these attitudes have not negated the force of other valence politics considerations. Reactions to the evolving state of the economy coupled with mutable partisan attachments and more general evaluations of party and leader performance can be expected to animate electoral choice in the years ahead.

More generally, the weakness and mutability of partisanship, unfavourable valence policy outcomes and political leaders who appear unable to deal with the present crisis, combine to suggest the possibility of further fragmentation of Britain's party system. We have already discussed the challenge to the Conservatives from UKIP and the substantial loss of support for the Liberal Democrats and their leader, Nick Clegg, in earlier chapters. Labour has benefited to some extent but, party leader, Ed Miliband has not been enthusiastically received and many voters remain unconvinced that Labour has the policy remedies needed to revitalize the country's now long-ailing economy and their leader has the ability to do the job. As a result, Labour is not as far ahead in the polls as it was in the run-up to the 1997 general election that brought Tony Blair, Gordon Brown and New Labour to power. To date, there is considerable 'push' away from the Coalition but little 'pull' in any other direction. British party politics are in flux and the 2015 general election may contain surprises for all of us.

Appendix A
Design of the 2010 British
election study

The design of surveys conducted in the 2010 British Election Study is displayed in Figure A.1. The figure shows there are three distinct components: the in-person pre-campaign and post-election panel survey, the multiwave rolling campaign panel study (RCPS) and the monthly Continuous Monitoring Surveys (CMS). The first of these surveys repeated the classic in-person probability sample which has been the staple of the BES since the first study was conducted by Butler and Stokes in 1963. Although the BES originally included inter-election panel components, this design was replaced in the 1980s by a single post-election survey with no pre-campaign component. The latter design was changed in 2001 when the Essex team assumed responsibility for the study. For the first time the in-person survey consisted of a pre-campaign and a post-election panel survey.

In 2010, fieldwork for the in-person survey was performed by BMRB, under supervision of Study Director, Nick Howat. As Figure A.1 shows, the 2010 pre-campaign survey consisted of slightly less than 2000 respondents. These respondents were approached again immediately after the election, and the post-election sample was increased by a top-up survey giving a total of 3075 respondents. The top-up component was included to increase the representative quality of the survey given that a panel design was employed.

The second component of the 2010 study was the rolling campaign panel survey (RCPS). The RCPS, which was conducted via the internet by YouGov under the direction of Study Director, Joe Twyman, was much larger than the face-to-face survey. The initial sample size was nearly 17 000 respondents, approximately 4000 of whom had been interviewed earlier as part of the 2005 BES RCPS. This panel component makes it possible to track a subset of respondents from immediately prior to the 2005 general election through to the period after the 2010 election. The very large sample of the 2010 RCPS made it possible to contact over 500 respondents each day during the

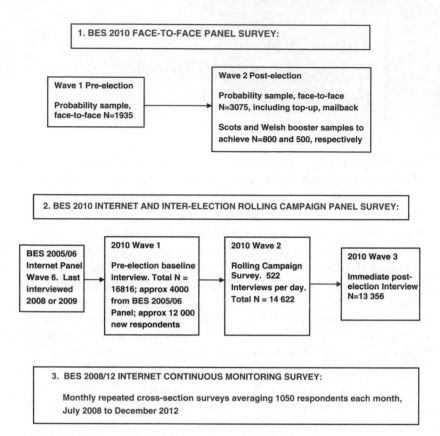

Figure A.1 Design of the 2010 British Election Study.

30 days of the official campaign from 8 April to 5 May 2010. The data generated by these 'daily replicate' surveys provides a finely grained tracking record of dynamics of public opinion throughout during the official campaign. The results are discussed in detail in Chapter 4. A third wave of the RCPS was conducted immediately after the general election. This wave focuses on gathering reports of voting behaviour, voter contact by political parties and reactions to the election outcome.

The third component of the 2010 BES was the Continuous Monitoring Survey (CMS) which was conducted from July 2008 to December 2012. In fact, the CMS started in April 2004 and for the period through June 2008 it was funded with a research grant from the National Science Foundation (US). The aim of the CMS is to track trends in public opinion and voting intentions in inter-election periods, since many important events and conditions which might influence election outcomes can occur months or even years before polling day. The CMS has been used to monitor public reactions to policy delivery in key areas such as the economy, health, education, crime, anti-terrorism efforts and transport. CMS data are used extensively throughout the book. For example, they are used in Chapters 2 and 3 to study factors affecting the dynamics of party support throughout the Blair and Brown years. Then, the data are used in Chapter 5 to analyze the stability of major explanatory variables in models of electoral choice. In Chapter 7 CMS data are employed to monitor shifts in opinion in the run-up to the May 2011 referendum on the Alternative Vote and to analyze voting in the referendum. Also important, the CMS has enabled us to track public reactions to the economic crisis that began in Britain in the autumn of 2007 with the run on the Northern Rock bank. In Chapters 6, 8 and 9, we use CMS data to document how the crisis has affected public reactions to the Coalition Government's austerity programme and the larger political economy of the Great Recession era.

The research design of the 2010 BES thus is considerably more complex than earlier BES which featured a single post-election face-to-face survey. This is for a reason which is apparent in the title of this book. Political party support and election outcomes have dynamic properties, with important shifts in public opinion taking place long before the election is called and again during the official campaign in the immediate run-up to polling day. The design of the 2010 BES captures changes in key variables which explain why individuals vote the way that they do and it facilitates modelling effects of the political-economic context in which these shifts occur. The design of the 2010 BES enables researchers to study the impact of the dramatic shift from affluence to austerity which has occurred in recent years on electoral change in Britain.

Appendix B
Measurement

This appendix describes key variables in several models analyzed in various chapters. For additional information, please contact Harold Clarke: clarke475@msn.com. BES data, questionnaires and technical information are available for free download at: http://bes2009–10.org.

Key variables

Voting in the 2010 General Election: Respondents were asked: (a) 'Talking to people about the General Election on May 6th, we have found that a lot people didn't manage to vote. How about you – did you manage to vote in the General Election?' If a respondent indicated voting, they were asked: (b) 'Which party did you vote for in the General Election?' In the binomial logit analyses of Labour voting, Labour voters are scored 1 and voters for all other parties are scored 0. In the multinomial logit analyses of opposition party voting Conservative voters are scored 1, Liberal Democrat voters are scored 2, voters for all other parties except Labour are scored 3, and Labour voters are scored 4.

Partisanship: Partisan attachments are measured using the first question in the standard BES party identification sequence: 'Generally speaking, do you think of yourself as Labour, Conservative, Liberal Democrat or what?' Party identification variables are a series of 0–1 dummies with 'no' and 'don't know' responses designated as the reference category.

Party performance on most important issue: The party performance variables are a series of 0–1 dummies for the Conservatives, Labour and the Liberal Democrats with 'none' and 'don't know' responses designated as the reference category.

Leader affect: 'Using a scale that runs from 0 to 10, where 0 means strongly dislike and 10 means strongly like, how do you feel about

David Cameron/Ed Miliband/Nick Clegg'? Respondents saying 'don't know' were assigned the mean score.

Leader competence: 'Using a scale that runs from 0 to 10 where 0 means a very incompetent leader and 10 means a very competent leader, how would you describe David Cameron/Ed Miliband/Nick Clegg'. Respondents saying 'don't know' were assigned the mean score.

Economic evaluations: Questions are worded as follows: (a) personal retrospective – 'How does the financial situation of your household now compare with what it was 12 months ago?'; (b) personal prospective – 'How do you think the financial situation of your household will change over the next 12 months?'; (c) national retrospective – 'How do you think the general economic situation in this country has changed over the last 12 months?'; (d) national prospective – 'How do you think the general economic situation in this country will develop over the next 12 months?' Responses are: 'get/got a lot better'; 'get/got a little better'; 'stay the same'; 'get/got a little worse'; 'get/got a lot worse'. For purposes of analysis, the response categories are coded: lot better = 5, little better = 4, stay the same/don't know = 3, little worse = 2, lot worse = 1.

Emotional reactions to economic conditions: Questions are worded as follows: (a) 'Which, if any, of the following words describe your feelings about the country's general economic situation? (Please tick up to FOUR)'; (b) 'Thinking of the same list of feelings, do any of them describe your feelings about the financial situation of your household? (Please tick up to FOUR)'. The words are: angry, happy, disgusted, hopeful, uneasy, confident, afraid, proud. A word is scored 1 if mentioned and 0 if it is not mentioned. Overall national and personal emotional reactions to economic condition variables are constructed by subtracting the number of negative words mentioned from the number of positive words mentioned.

Emotional reactions to the Afghanistan War: Respondents were asked to describe their emotional reactions to the Afghanistan War using a set of eight words. The words are: angry, happy, disgusted, hopeful, uneasy, confident, afraid, proud. A word is scored 1 if mentioned and 0 if it is not mentioned. Overall emotional reactions to the war are measured by subtracting the number of negative words mentioned from the number of positive words mentioned.

Issue–party proximities: Respondents are asked the following question: 'Using the 0 to 10 scale below, where the end marked 0 means that government should cut taxes a lot and spend much less on health and social services, and the end marked 10 means that government should raise taxes a lot and spend much more on health and social services, where would you place yourself on the scale?' Respondents were then asked where they would place the Conservatives, Labour, the Liberal Democrats, the SNP (in Scotland) and Plaid Cymru (in Wales). Respondents also were asked: 'Some people think that reducing crime is more important than protecting the rights of people accused of committing crimes. Other people think that protecting the rights of accused people, regardless of whether they have been convicted of committing a crime, is more important than reducing crime. On the 0–10 scale below, where would you place your own view?' Respondents also were asked where they would place various political parties on the scale. The issue-proximity variables are the average absolute distances between the respondent and each of the parties on the two dimensions. Respondents with 'don't know' answers are recoded to the mean for that specific respondent-party distance.

Liberal Democrat manifesto issues: Respondents were asked: 'Please indicate if you agree or disagree with the following policy proposals . . . (a) 'Exempt the first £10,000 of earnings from income tax'; (b) 'Charge a "mansion tax" on properties worth over £2 million'; (c) 'Scrap Britain's Trident nuclear deterrent'; (d) 'Limit tax relief on pensions to the basis rate of tax'; (e) 'Introduce new eco taxes including a fuel tax for airline flights'; (f) 'Have Britain co-operate more closely with the European Union'. Response categories were: 'strongly agree' = 5, 'agree' = 4, 'neither agree nor disagree' / 'don't know' = 3, 'disagree' = 2, 'strongly disagree' = 1. An exploratory factor analysis of items (a) to (f) yielded a two-factor solution that explained 56.8 per cent of the item variance. Based on patterns of factor loadings the factors were labelled 'Liberal Democrat political proposals' and 'Liberal Democrat economic proposals'. Factor scores for the two factors were used in the multivariate analysis of voting behaviour in Chapter 5.

MPs expenses scandal: Respondents were asked the following questions: (a) 'The reports on MPs expense claims prove that most MPs are corrupt', (b) 'The way some MPs have claimed expenses makes me very angry', (c) 'Despite all the press coverage, what MPs claim for expenses really isn't that important', (d) 'Most MPs did nothing wrong – they were just claiming expenses that the rules allow', (e) 'MPs who have abused their expense claims should be required to resign immediately'. Response categories are: 'strongly agree', 'agree', 'neither agree nor disagree' / 'don't know', 'disagree', 'strongly disagree'. Categories are scored from 1 to 5 with high scores assigned to categories indicating disapproval of MPs behaviour. An exploratory factor analysis of the resulting 5 variables yields a one-factor solution explaining 57.4 per cent of the item variance. The factor scores from this analysis are used to measure reactions to the scandal.

Sociodemographics: Age is measured as age in years or as a set of 0–1 dummy variables for the following age brackets: 18–25, 26–35, 36–45, 46–55, 56–65; respondents 66 years of age and older are treated as the reference category; **education** is age leaving school scored as a series of ordinal categories ranging from '15 or less' and 'don't know' = 1 to '19 or older' or 'still at university', 'still in school' = 5; **gender** is a dummy variable with men scored 1 and women 0; **income** is a set of ordinal categories ranging from 'less than £5000 per year' to 'more than £100 000 per year'; **country of residence** is two 0–1 dummy variables for Scotland and Wales with England as the reference category. **Region of residence** is a series of 0–1 dummy variables for East Anglia, Midlands, North, South East, South West, Scotland and Wales with Greater London as the reference category; **private/public-sector occupation** is scored private sector = 1 and public sector, not ascertainable = 0. Respondents not supplying requisite information were scored using spouse's data if available; **social class** is measured by dividing respondents into white-collar and blue-collar occupations (or former occupations for retired persons), with the white-collar group scored 1 and the blue-collar group scored 0. In cases where a respondent did not supply requisite occupational information and the respondent had a spouse, the spouse's information was used; **trade union membership** is measured: member = 1, nonmember = 0.

Tactical voting: Tactical voting is measured using responses to the following question: 'People give different reasons for why they vote for one party rather than another. Which of the following best describes your reasons?' (a) 'the party had the best policies', (b) 'the party had the best leader', (c) 'I really preferred another party but it stood no chance of winning in my constituency'. Respondents choosing (c) are considered tactical voters and are scored 1; all other voters are scored 0.

Notes

Chapter 1

1 See e.g. Beech and Lee, 2008; Blair, 2010; Mandelson, 2010; Rawnsley, 2010; Seldon, 2007; Seldon and Lodge, 2010; Seldon *et al.*, 2007.
2 The electorate in 2010 consisted of 45 610 369 people (see Kavanagh and Cowley, 2010: 351).
3 It is important to note that large minorities did not identify with any social class. See Clarke *et al.* (2004b: ch. 5).
4 See www.internetworldstats.com.

Chapter 2

1 Although there are earlier studies, the systematic study of voting behaviour in national elections is often dated from the publication of *The American Voter* (Campbell *et al.*, 1960; see also Campbell *et al.*, 1954).
2 The literature on economic voting is voluminous. For review, see Dorussen and Taylor (2007). See also Clarke *et al.* (1992) and Norpoth *et al.* (1991).
3 A useful summary of empirical research on spatial models is Adams *et al.* (2005).
4 See Chapter 5 for details.
5 For example, the correlation between Labour vote intention and Labour identification between June 1997 and May 2007 is $r = -0.88$.
6 Initial analyses showed that inflation, the other standard objective economic measure (whether measured in levels or changes; lagged or unlagged), had no effect in any of the models that we tested.
7 Johansen's (1996) unrestricted cointegration rank test indicates that there is a single cointegrating vector for these three time series variables. Both the trace statistic test ($\chi^2 = 32.56$, p $= 0.02$) and the max eigenvalue test ($\chi^2 = 22.46$, p $= 0.03$) reject the null of no cointegrating vectors in favour of one or more cointegrating vectors. These tests fail to reject the null of a single cointegrating vector in favour of two or more cointegrating vectors. For the latter cases, the test statistics are $\chi^2 = 10.10$ (trace test), p $= 0.27$ and $\chi^2 = 7.25$, p $= 0.46$ (max eigenvalue test).

8 For example, the fuel crisis effect was worth 7.10*.47 − 3.34 points in October; 3.34*.47 = 1.57 points in November; and 1.57*.47 = 0.74 of a point in December.
9 See, for example, Sanders and Gavin (2004).

Chapter 3

1 Previous analyses have established that this inter-election panel sample is representative of UK public opinion as measured in regular monthly cross-section opinion polls (Sanders *et al.*, 2011a).
2 The AIC (Akaike Information Criterion) is computed as: -2*loglikelihood + 2k where k is the number of model parameters. See Burnham and Anderson (2002).
3 Results available from the authors on request.
4 The results of using the binomial/multinomial approach are substantially the same as those reported here.
5 There is no corresponding measure for respondents' assessments of Liberal Democrat management competence on the economy and NHS.
6 Attitudes towards British involvement in Iraq were quite stable at the individual level over time. We included an identical intervention question in our 2005 post-election panel wave survey. Of 4894 respondents, only 214 (4%) switched from either approval to disapproval or from approval to disapproval of the intervention between the pre- and post-election survey waves.
7 In the 2010 pre-election internet survey 45% identified the economy in general as the most important issue. This figure increased to 52% when those citing either unemployment, inflation or consumer debt are included. See Chapter 5, Figure 5.2.
8 Adding Iraq casualties variables to the model in Table 3.5 produces non-significant results.
9 For example, the global leadership effect was 5.46 points (6.91*.79) in November; and 4.31 points in December. By July 2009, the effect was less than a single point, and by the end of the year it had disappeared.

Chapter 4

1 According to the Continuous Monitoring Survey voting intentions in April 2009 were Conservatives 42.5%, Labour 27.5%, Liberal Democrats 19% and others 11%.
2 A website called mydavidcameron.com was set up to do this.
3 Constituency boundary changes between 2005 and 2010 mean that the analysis cannot be done for exactly the same geographically defined sets

of constituencies over the 2005–10 time interval. However, analysing 2010 marginality and 2010 spending yields a very similar correlation ($r = -0.62$).

4 General election turnout in the 15 general elections held between 1945 and 1997 averaged 76.2%. Turnout fell to 59.4% in 2001 before increasing slightly to 61.4% in 2005.

5 This measure is based on a set of 11 point like–dislike scales, where 0 means that respondent strongly dislikes the party and 10 means that they strongly like it. For example if the individual gives Labour a score of L_i and the Conservatives a score of C_i on the scale, then the party differential is given by $(L_i - C_i)^2$. The party differential for all respondents and all parties can then be derived from:

$$\text{Party differential} = \sum_{(i=1)}^{n} \sum_{(j=1)}^{m} (x_{ij} - x_{ik})^2$$

Summed over n individuals and m political parties.

6 Newspapers endorsing the Conservatives were the *Daily Mail/Scottish Daily Mail, Daily Star/Daily Star of Scotland, Daily Telegraph, Daily Express, Financial Times*, the *Sun* and *The Times*. The *Daily Mirror* endorsed Labour and the *Guardian* and *Independent* endorsed the Liberal Democrats.

7 This variable scored 1 if a respondent judged that a particular party had the best campaign, -1 if they judged that the party had the worst campaign and 0 if they 'didn't know'.

Chapter 5

1 The AIC discounts a model's explanatory power by taking into account the number of parameters in the model. $\text{AIC} = -2^*\text{LL} + 2K$ where LL is the model log-likelihood and K is the number of parameters.

2 Voting for various minor parties is also analysed but not shown in the table.

3 CMS surveys were not conducted in May 2005, September 2006 and May 2010.

4 The principal components analysis explained 43% of the variance in the six measures and all factor loadings exceeded 0.55.

5 The positive descriptors were happy, hopeful, confident and proud and the negative descriptors were angry, disgusted, uneasy and afraid.

6 Early work on multilevel modelling suggested that one could be confident in parameter estimates when the number of second-level cases was as small as 30 (e.g. Kreft, 1996; see also Hox 1998; Kreft and DeLeuw, 1998; Raudenbush and Bryk, 2002). However, simulations reported by Maas

and Hox (2005) indicate that standard errors tend to become unreliable when the second-level N is less than 50.
7 As discussed in Chapter 2, analyses in Clarke *et al.* (2009b: ch. 4) indicate that the negative effects of the Iraq War on Labour voting in the 2005 election operated principally by tarnishing Tony Blair's image.

Chapter 6

1 There is an inverse relationship between the price of bonds (which are essentially IOUs) and interest rates. If an individual buys a bond worth £100 with a return of 5.0% that means they would receive £105 at the end of the year if interest rates remain unchanged. But if interest rates increase to 10.0% that halves the price of new bonds in the markets since at the new interest rate a bond costing £50 will provide a return of £5.
2 The dynamic factor analysis is implemented using Stata 12's state space form model. See Drukker and Gates (2011).
3 The economic evaluation and emotional reactions to economic conditions variables are discussed in Appendix B.
4 The wording of the CMS question used to measure expectations about the national economy is presented in Appendix B.
5 In an amusing article Hendry (1980) illustrated the danger of spurious regressions by showing that there was a very strong and statistically significant relationship between inflation and cumulative rainfall in the UK in the 1960s and 1970s.
6 The log transformation has the effect of reducing volatility and thereby promoting variance stationarity in a series of interest.
7 The Dickey-Fuller test statistics for the undifferenced variables are: national economic expectations $= -1.68$, inflation $= -2.36$, unemployment $= -0.79$. The critical value ($p < 0.05$) $= -2.89$ and so we fail to reject the null hypothesis of nonstationarity. For the differenced variables the test statistics are: national economic expectations $= -9.37$, inflation $= -5.11$, unemployment -4.49, so we reject the null of nonstationarity.
8 Each equation in the VAR has three continuous variables operating at three lags, three dummy variables, an error correction term and an intercept. Thus, each of the three equations in the VAR system has 14 coefficients. This illustrates the point that although VAR is a very flexible modelling strategy that avoids imposing possibly misleading parameter constraints, it does require a reasonably long time series to implement.
9 The maximum eigenvalue test statistic for one as opposed to no cointegrating vectors is $\chi^2 = 30.98$ and the critical value is $\chi^2 = 21.13$, so we reject the null of no cointegrating vectors. However, the test statistic for

two cointegrating vectors as opposed to one cointegrating vector is $\chi^2 = 10.18$ and the critical value $\chi^2 = 14.22$, so we fail to reject the null of one cointegrating vector.

10 Figure 9.8 in Chapter 9 presents data showing that over two-fifths of the respondents in monthly CMS surveys conducted since October 2008 blame the government for the economic crisis.

Chapter 7

1 A useful reference on AV, STV and other electoral systems is Farrell (2011). Unlike AV, STV enhances the proportionality of representation by using multi-member constituencies.

2 As elsewhere in this volume, partisan attachments are measured using the first question in the standard BES party identification sequence: see Appendix B for details.

3 In their manifesto for the 2010 general election, the Liberal Democrats had advocated the Single Transferable Vote (STV). See Liberal Democrats (2010). In the post-election negotiations that led to the Conservative–Liberal Democrat election, the two parties compromised with an agreement to hold a referendum on the Alternative Vote.

4 Party performance evaluations are based on responses to a question concerning which party is best able to handle the issue the respondent deemed most important. See Appendix B for details.

5 In the analyses below, risk orientation is measured using the following question: 'In general do you dislike taking risks, or do you like taking risks? Please use the scale below where 0 means "really dislike taking risks" and 10 means "really like taking risks" to indicate how you generally feel about taking risks'.

6 Measures of sociodemographic variables are discussed in Appendix B.

7 Similar to the other BES CMS surveys, the 2011 AV referendum survey was conducted via the internet. See Chapter 1.

8 The wording of these statements is: (1) 'If Britain adopts the Alternative Vote system for general elections, then no party could ever get a majority of seats in the House of Commons'; (2) 'The Alternative Vote electoral system is fairer because it produces a closer correspondence between parties' percentage share of votes and the number of seats they get in Parliament'; (3) 'The Alternative Vote electoral system gives too much influence to small political parties'; (4) 'The Alternative Vote electoral system will produce electoral outcomes that more accurately reflect the political opinions of the British public than the present First-Past-The-Post electoral system does'; (5) 'The Alternative Vote electoral system

makes MPs work harder for their constituents because they need the support of a majority to get them elected'; (6) 'The First-Past-The Post electoral system should be kept because it is an important part of Britain's political tradition'; (7) 'The Alternative Vote electoral system is too hard for the average person to understand'; (8) 'The First-Past-The-Post electoral system helps voters to know which party is responsible for policy success or failure'. Responses to the statements were scored: 'strongly agree' = 5, 'agree' = 4, 'neither agree nor disagree' / 'don't know' = 3, 'disagree' = 2, 'strongly disagree' = 1.

9 These statements are: (a) 'The number of Members in the House of Commons should be reduced from 650 to 600 MPs'; (b) 'The UK electoral system should be changed to proportional representation so that the percentage of seats that a party gets in Parliament is the same as the percentage of the votes that it receives in a general election'; (c) 'Local governments should have more decision-making authority compared to the central government in London'; (d) 'The monarchy should be abolished so that the UK can be a republic'; (e) 'The Church of England should keep its status as the official established church in England'; (f) 'The UK should have more national referendums to decide important political issues'; (g) 'Members of Parliament who vote against their own party's election manifesto should be required to resign and seek re-election'. Response options are: 'strongly agree' = 5; 'agree' = 4; 'neither agree nor disagree/don't know' = 3; 'disagree' = 2; 'strongly disagree' = 1.

10 The question wording is: 'Thinking about the outcomes of general elections, which of these statements is more important to you?' Response options are: (a) 'That one party get more than half the seats in parliament so it can govern on its own' =1; (b) 'That every party's percentage of seats in parliament is the same as their percentage of the vote' = −1; (c) 'Don't know' = 0.

11 See Appendix B for wording of questions measuring affect for the party leaders.

12 www.guardian.co.uk/politics/2011/feb/05/av-get-clegg-campaign

13 The analysis is conducted using the Stata CLARIFY program (Tomz *et al.*, 1999).

14 Greene (2010) accepts that Norton *et al.*'s technical analyses are correct, but argues that their approach to interpreting interaction effects is not useful unless one has articulated specific hypotheses that one wishes to test. Here, we are testing specific hypotheses.

15 Respondents were asked if the words 'competent' and 'trustworthy' described Cameron, Clegg and Miliband 'very well', 'quite well', 'not

very well' or 'not very well at all'. The responses were scored 'very well' = 5, 'quite well' = 4, 'not very well' = 2, 'not very well at all' = 1. Respondents saying they 'did not know' were given a score of 3.

16 The average inter-item correlation (r) between the affect, competence and trust components of Cameron's image is 0.78. Correlations for Clegg and Miliband are 0.68 and 0.73, respectively.

17 Only 20.7% said they thought the word 'trustworthy' described Clegg 'very well' or 'quite well'. For Cameron and Miliband, the comparable numbers were 35.9% and 31.8%, respectively. The percentage who said the word 'competent' described Clegg 'very well' or 'quite well' was 22.6, as compared to 49.5 for Cameron and 31.4 for Miliband.

18 This calculation uses the survey distribution of Yes supporters, no supporters and undecideds among declared nonvoters to apportion the actual percentage of nonvoters (57.8%) to the Yes and No voter groups. The entire undecided group (33.2%) among declared nonvoters is assumed to vote Yes.

19 A majority (51%) of respondents in a BPIX survey conducted just over a week before the referendum said that they only partially understood AV or did not understand it at all.

20 Illustrative are the heated exchanges between Conservative spokesperson Baroness Warsi and Liberal Democrat cabinet minister Chris Huhne concerning campaign financing and whether AV or FPTP would do the most to facilitate the fortunes of extremist parties such as the BNP.

21 The rank-ordered logit model should not be confused with the standard ordered logit model. We estimate parameters in the rank-ordered logit model using Stata 12's ROLOGIT procedure.

22 Measures of these predictor variables are discussed in Appendix B.

23 'Is Your Cat Confused About the Referendum on the Alternative Vote on 5th May'. See www.youtube.com/watch?v=HiHuiDD_oTk

24 Recently, Hugh-Jones (2011) has developed formal models that suggest institutions of direct democracy can increase trust in elected officials.

Chapter 8

1 There are different measures of unemployment produced by the Office of National Statistics in Britain. For the analyses in this chapter we use the claimant count, which is the number of people claiming unemployment benefits.

2 The cognitive macroeconomy variable has switched signs in this simulation because it is collinear with the personal economic measure.

3 The curvilinear age effect is specified as a quadratic, that is, age in years + age in years squared.

4 In the simulation income increases the probability of being very or fairly satisfied by 0.26 points and interpersonal trust increases it by 0.28 points.
5 The multilevel ordered logit model is:

$$Y_{ij} = \pi_{ij} + \Sigma\,\pi_{ijk}\,X_{ijk} + e_{ij}$$
$$\pi_{ij} = \beta_{jk} + \Sigma\,\beta_{qjk}\,W_{qjk} + r_{qjk}$$

where Y_{ij} is life satisfaction of individual i at time j, and X_{ijk} are the k predictors and π_{ijk} the coefficients in the level one model. The intercept π_{ij} in the level one model is then the dependent variable in the level two model where W_{qjk} are the level two predictors and β_{qjk} the level two coefficients.
6 If the simulations reported in Figure 8.3 are extended they show that if the individual becomes unemployed the probability of them being fairly or very satisfied with life falls by 0.23 points.
7 The 2010 election variable achieves significance at the 0.10 level in the cognitive-sociotropic model but this is not a robust result which appears in other specifications.
8 Note that there were only 34 cases of individuals who strongly disagreed with the statement 'I feel a sense of satisfaction when I vote' and who were very satisfied with life. This explains the anomalous results for the 'strongly disagree' category in Figure 8.5.

Chapter 9

1 See the European Election Database (http://www.nsd.uib.no/european_election_database).
2 These are Belgium, Bulgaria, Switzerland, Cyprus, Czech Republic, Germany, Denmark, Estonia, Spain, Finland, France, United Kingdom, Greece, Croatia, Hungary, Ireland, Netherlands, Norway, Poland, Portugal, Sweden, Slovenia and Slovakia. Data were also collected for three non-European countries which are not included in this analysis.
3 Note that the fieldwork for the British survey was done after the general election of 2010 and so the higher than average scores could in part be attributed to the honeymoon of the Coalition Government.
4 The question asks: 'Which of the descriptions on this card comes closest to how you feel about your household's income nowadays?' The response categories are: 1 – Living comfortably on present income; 2 – Coping on present income; 3 – Finding it difficult on present income; 4 – Finding it very difficult on present income.
5 The immigration question asked: 'Would you say it is generally bad or good for [country's] economy that people come to live here from other countries?' The economic inequality question asked if respondents agree

or disagree with the statement: 'The government should take measures to reduce differences in income levels'. The gay rights question asked for responses to the statement 'Gay men and lesbians should be free to live their own life as they wish'. Finally, the environmental problems question seeks responses to the statement: 'Modern science can be relied on to solve our environmental problems'.

6 Question wording is as follows: 'Please indicate how far you agree or disagree with each of the following statements: (i) The Government's cuts in public expenditure are essential for the long-term health of the UK economy; (ii) The cuts in public expenditure that the Government proposes are likely to cause serious financial difficulties for me and my family; (iii) Excessive public spending is the main cause of Britain's debt'. Response categories: strongly agree, agree, neither agree nor disagree, disagree, strongly disagree, don't know. Wording of the fourth question is: 'Which of the following statements come closest to your view about the overall impact of the proposed public expenditure cuts?' (a) 'The public expenditure cuts will strengthen Britain's economic growth and international competitiveness'; (b) 'The public expenditure cuts will damage Britain's economy by pushing it further into recession'; (c) 'Don't know'.

7 Respondents were asked: 'Here are some things people are saying about economic and social conditions in Britain these days. Please indicate if you agree or disagree': (a) 'Economic inequality is a major problem in Britain'; (b) 'Social injustice is a major problem in Britain'; (c) 'Corporate greed is a major problem in Britain'; (d) 'British banks are making excessive profits at the expense of ordinary people'. Response categories: strongly agree, agree, neither agree nor disagree, disagree, strongly disagree, don't know.

8 The dependent variables (socio-economic inequality and support for public-sector cuts) in these regression analyses are factor scores based on principal components analyses of the questions cited in notes 6 and 7 above. The socio-economic inequality analysis explains 65.4% of the item variance, with an average factor loading of 0.81 (range 0.78–0.86). The public-sector cuts analysis explains 54.2% of the item variables, with an average factor score of 0.72 (range 0.52–0.85).

9 The measure of attitudes towards socio-economic inequality is the factor score variable described in note 8.

Bibliography

Achen, C. (1992). Social psychology, demographic variables, and linear regression: breaking the iron triangle in voting research. *Political Behavior*, **14**: 195–211.

Adams, J. F., Merrill, S. III, and Grofman, B. (2005). *A Unified Theory of Party Competition*. New York: Cambridge University Press.

Ai, C. and Norton, E. C. (2003). Interaction terms in logit and probit models. *Economics Letters*, **80**: 123–9.

Alesina, A. and Rosenthal, H. (1995). *Partisan Politics, Divided Government and the Economy*. New York: Cambridge University Press.

Almond, G. and Verba, S. (1963). *The Civic Culture: Political Attitudes and Democracy in Five Nations*. Princeton, NJ: Princeton University Press.

Anderson, C. and Guillory, C. A. (1997). Political institutions and satisfaction with democracy: a cross-national analysis of consensual and majoritarian systems. *American Political Science Review*, **91**: 66–81.

Ansolabehere, S. and Schaffner, B. F. (2011). Re-examining the validity of different survey modes for measuring public opinion in the U.S.: findings from a 2010 multi-mode comparison. Paper presented at the AAPOR Annual Conference, Phoenix AZ, 12–15 May.

Arzheimer, K. (2009). Contextual factors and the extreme right vote in Western Europe, 1980–2002. *American Journal of Political Science*, **53**: 259–75.

Bartle, J. (2005). Homogeneous models and heterogeneous voters. *Political Studies*, **53**: 653–75.

Beck, U. (1992). *The Risk Society*. London: Sage Publications.

Beech, M. and Lee, S. (2008). *Ten Years of New Labour*. London: Palgrave-Macmillan.

Benoit, K. (2004). Models of electoral system change. *Electoral Studies*, **23**: 363–89.

Berry, W. D., DeMeritt, J. H. R. and Esarey, J. (2010). Testing for interaction in binary logit and probit models: is a product term essential? *American Journal of Political Science*, **54**: 248–66.

Bjornskov, C., Dreher, A. and Fisher, J. A. V. (2007). The bigger the better? evidence of the effect of government size on life satisfaction around the world. *Public Choice* 130: 267–92.

Black, D. (1958). *The Theory of Committees and Elections*. Cambridge: Cambridge University Press.

Blair, T. (2010). *A Journey*. London: Hutchinson

Blais, A. (2000). *To Vote or Not to Vote: The Merits and Limits of Rational Choice Theory*. Pittsburgh: University of Pittsburgh Press.

Blais, A. and Gélineau, F. (2007). Winning, losing and satisfaction with democracy. *Political Studies*, 55: 425–41.

Blais, A., Gidengil, E., Nevitte, N. and Johnston, R. (1996). *The Challenge of Direct Democracy: The 1992 Canadian Referendum*. Montreal: McGill-Queen's University Press.

Bogdanor, V. (2011). *The Coalition and the Constitution*. Oxford: Hart Publishing.

Boix, C. (1999). Setting the rules of the game: the choice of electoral systems in advanced democracies. *American Political Science Review*, 93: 609–24.

Bok, D. (2010). *The Politics of Happiness: What Government Can Learn from the New Research on Well-Being*. Princeton, NJ: Princeton University Press.

Bowler, Shaun and Todd Donovan (1998). *Demanding Choices: Opinion, Voting and Direct Democracy*. Ann Arbor: University of Michigan Press.

Brambor, T., Clark, W. and Golder, M. (2006). Understanding interaction models: improving empirical analyses. *Political Analysis*, 14: 63–82.

Brennan, G. and Buchanan, J. (1984). Voter choice and the evaluation of political alternatives. *American Behavioral Scientist*, 28: 185–201.

Brickman, P. and Campbell, D. T. (1971). Hedonic relativism and planning the good society. In M. H. Appley, ed., *Adaptation-Level Theory: A Symposium* (New York: Academic Press), pp. 287–305.

Bruni, L. and Porta, P. L. (2005). *Economics and Happiness: Framing the Analysis*. Oxford: Oxford University Press.

Bruni, L. and Porta, P. L. (eds.) (2007). *Handbook on the Economics of Happiness*. London: Edward Elgar.

Buiter, W. H. (1990). *International Macroeconomics*. Oxford: Clarendon Press.

Burnham, K. P. and Anderson, D. R. (2002). *Model Selection and Multimodel Inference: A Practical Information-theoretic Approach*, 2nd edn. New York: Springer-Verlag.

Butler, D. and Ranney, A. (eds.) (1994). *Referendums Around the World: The Growing Use of Direct Democracy*. London: Macmillan.

Butler, D. and Stokes, D. (1969). *Political Change in Britain: Forces Shaping Electoral Choice*. New York: St Martin's Press.

Butler, D. and Stokes, D. (1974). *Political Change in Britain: Forces Shaping Electoral Choice*, 2nd edn. London: Macmillan.

Campbell, A., Gurin, G. and Miller, W. (1954). *The Voter Decides*. Evanston, Il: Row, Peterson.

Campbell, A., Converse, P., Miller, W. and Stokes, D. (1960). *The American Voter*. New York: John Wiley & Sons, Inc.

Carmines, E. G. and Stimson, J. A. (1989). *Issue Evolution: Race and the Transformation of American Politics*. Princeton: NJ. Princeton University Press.

Cartwright, E. (2011). *Behavioral Economics*. London: Routledge.

Charemza, W. W. and Deadman, D. F. (1997). *New Directions in Econometric Practice*, 2nd edn. Cheltenham: Edward Elgar.

Clarke, A. E., Frijters, P. and Shields, M. A. (2008). Relative income, happiness and utility: an explanation of the Easterlin paradox and other puzzles. *Journal of Economic Literature*, **46**: 95–144.

Clarke, H. D. and Kornberg, A. (1994). The politics and economics of constitutional choice: voting in Canada's 1992 national referendum. *Journal of Politics*, **56**: 940–62.

Clarke, H. D. and McCutcheon, A. (2009). The dynamics of party identification reconsidered. *Public Opinion Quarterly*, **73**: 704–28.

Clarke, H. D. and Stewart, M. C. (1994). Prospections, retrospections and rationality: the 'Bankers' model of presidential approval reconsidered. *American Journal of Political Science*, **38**: 1104–23.

Clarke, H. D. and Whitten, G. D. (2013). Hard choices in hard times: valence voting in Germany 2009. *Electoral Studies* **32**, forthcoming.

Clarke H. D., Elliott, E. W., Mishler, W., Stewart, M. C., Whiteley, P. F. and Zuk, G. (1992). *Controversies in Political Economy: Canada, Great Britain, the United States*. Boulder, CO: Westview Press.

Clarke, H. D., Stewart, M. and Whiteley, P. (1998). New models for New Labour: the political economy of Labour party support, January 1992–April 1997. *American Political Science Review*, **92**: 559–76.

Clarke, H. D., Ho, K. and Stewart, M. C. (2000). Major's lesser (not minor) effects: prime ministerial approval and governing party support in Britain since 1979. *Electoral Studies* **18**: 255–74.

Clarke, H. D, Kornberg, A. and Stewart, M. (2004a). Referendum voting as political choice: the case of Quebec. *British Journal of Political Science*, **34**: 345–55.

Clarke, H. D., Sanders, D., Stewart, M. C. and Whiteley, P. (2004b). *Political Choice in Britain*. Oxford: Oxford University Press.

Clarke, H. D., Kornberg, A. and Scotto, T. J. (2009a). *Making Political Choices: Canada and the United States.* Toronto: University of Toronto Press.

Clarke, H. D., Sanders, D., Stewart, M. C. and Whiteley, P. (2009b). *Performance Politics and the British Voter.* Cambridge: Cambridge University Press.

Clarke, H. D., Stewart, M., Sanders, D. and Whiteley, P. (2011). Valence politics and electoral choice in Britain. *Journal of Elections, Public Opinion and Parties,* 21(2): 237–53.

Clarke, H. D., Kornberg, A., Scotto, T. J. and Stewart, M. C. (2012). Political choices in hard times: voting in the 2010 U.S. House elections. *Journal of Elections, Public Opinion and Parties,* 22: 139–65.

Coalition Progamme for Government (2010). http://www.direct.gov.uk/ prod_consum_dg/groups/dg_digitalassets/@dg/@en/documents/ digitalasset/dg_187876.pdf

Coleman, J. S. (1988). Social capital in the creation of human capital. *American Journal of Sociology,* 94: 95–120.

Conlisk, J. (1996). Why bounded rationality? *Journal of Economic Literature,* 34: 669–700.

Conover, P. and Feldman, S. (1986). Emotional reactions to the economy: I'm mad as hell and i'm not going to take it any more. *American Journal of Political Science,* 30: 50–78.

Conservative Party (2010). *Invitation to Join the Government of Britain: The Conservative Manifesto 2010.* http://conservativehome.blogs.com/ files/conservative-manifesto-2010.pdf

Converse, P. E. (1964). The nature of belief systems in mass publics. In D. Apter, ed., *Ideology and Discontent* (Glencoe, IL: The Free Press), pp. 206–61.

Converse, P. E. (1969). Of time and partisan stability. *Comparative Political Studies,* 2: 139–72.

Crewe, I. (1986). On the death and resurrection of class voting: some comments on how Britain votes. *Political Studies,* 35: 620–38.

Crossman, R. (1963). Introduction to Bagehot. In W. Bagehot, *The English Constitution* (London: Fontana), pp. 1–57.

Dahl, R. A. (1972). *Polyarchy: Participation and Opposition.* New Haven: Yale University Press.

Dalton, R. J. (2008). *Citizen Politics: Public Opinion and Political Parties in Advanced Industrial Societies,* 5th edn. Washington, DC: Congressional Quarterly Press.

Dalton, R. J. (2013). *The Apartisan American: Dealignment and Changing Electoral Politics.* Washington, DC: Congressional Quarterly Press.

Dangerfield, G. (1935). *The Strange Death of Liberal England*. New York: Capricorn Books.

Delli Carpini, M. X. and Keeter, S. (1997). *What Americans Know about Politics and Why It Matters*. New Haven: Yale University Press.

Denver, D., Hands, G., Fisher, J. and McAllister, I. (2002). The impact of constituency campaigning in the 2001 general election. In L. Bennie *et al.*, eds., *British Elections & Parties Review*, vol. 12 (London: Frank Cass), pp. 80–94.

de Vrees, C. H. (ed.) (2007). *The Dynamics of Referendum Campaigns*. London: Palgrave Macmillan.

Diamond, L. (1999). *Developing Democracy: Towards Consolidation*. Baltimore, MD: The Johns Hopkins University Press.

Diener, M. L. and McGovern, M. B. (2008). What makes people happy? In M. Eid and R. J. Larsen, eds., *The Science of Subjective Well-Being* (New York: The Guilford Press).

di Palma, G. (1990). *To Craft Democracies: An Essay in Democratic Transitions*. Berkeley, CA: University of California Press.

Di Tella, R., MacCulloch, R. and Oswald, A. (2003). The macroeconomics of happiness. *Review of Economics and Statistics*, 85: 809–27.

Dorussen, H. and Taylor, M. (eds.) (2007). *Economic Voting*. London: Routledge.

Downs, A. (1957). *An Economic Theory of Democracy*. New York: Harper & Row.

Druckman, J. and Parkin, M. (2005). The impact of media bias: how editorial slant affects voters. *Journal of Politics*, 67: 1030–49.

Drukker, D. M. and Gates, R. M. (2011). State space methods in Stata. *Journal of Statistical Software*, 41: 1–24.

Duch, R. and Stevenson, R. T. (2008). *The Economic Vote: How Political and Economic Institutions Condition Election Results*. New York: Cambridge University Press.

Easterlin, R. (ed.) (2002). *Happiness in Economics*. London: Edward Elgar.

Easterlin, R. (2004). Explaining Happiness. *Proceedings of the National Academy of Sciences*, 100: 1176–83.

Easterlin, R. (2010). *Happiness, Growth and the Life Cycle*. Oxford: Oxford University Press.

Easton, D. (1965). *A Systems Analysis of Political Life*. New York: John Wiley & Sons, Inc.

Electoral Commission (2011). *UK General Election Campaign Spending Report*. London: Electoral Commission.

Enders, W. (2009). *Applied Econometric Time-Series*. New York: John Wiley & Sons, Inc.

Erikson, R. S., MacKuen, M. B. and Stimson, J. A. (2002). *The Macro-Polity*. New York: Cambridge University Press.

Fails, M. D. and Pierce, H. N. (2010). Changing mass attitudes and democratic deepening'. *Political Research Quarterly*, **63**: 174–87.

Fair, R. (1978). The effect of economic events on votes for president. *Review of Economics and Statistics*, **60**: 159–73.

Fair, R. (2004). *Estimating How the Macroeconomy Works*. Cambridge, MA: Harvard University Press.

Farrell, D. (2011). *Electoral Systems: A Comparative Introduction*. London: Palgrave Macmillan.

Farrell, D. and Schmitt-Beck, R. (eds.) (2002). *Do Political Campaigns Matter: Campaign Effects in Elections and Referendums*. London: Routledge.

Ferris, A. L. (2002). Religion and the quality of life. *Journal of Happiness Studies*, **3**: 199–215.

Fieldhouse, E. and Cutts, D. (2008). Diversity, density and turnout. *Political Geography*, **27**: 530–48.

Fiorina, M. P. (1981). *Retrospective Voting in American National Elections*. New Haven: Yale University Press.

Fisher, J. and Denver, D. (2008). From foot-slogging to call centres and direct mail: a framework for analysing the development of district-level campaigning. *European Journal of Political Research*, **47**: 794–826.

Franklin, C. (1992). Measurement and the dynamics of party identification. *Political Behavior*, **14**: 297–309.

Frey, B. S. (2008). *Happiness: A Revolution in Economics*. Cambridge MA: MIT Press.

Frey, B. S. and Stutzer, A. (2000). Happiness, economy and institutions. *Economic Journal*, **110**: 918–38.

Frey, B. S. and Stutzer, A. (2002). *Happiness and Economics*. Princeton, NJ: Princeton University Press.

Frey, B. S. and Stutzer, A. (2005). Happiness research: state and prospects. *Review of Social Economy*, **62**: 207–28.

Gallagher, M. and Mitchell, P. (eds.) (2005). *The Politics of Electoral Systems*. Oxford: Oxford University Press.

Gelman, A., King, G. and Boscardin, W. J. (1998). Estimating the probability of events that have never occurred: when is your vote decisive? *Journal of the American Statistical Association*, **93**: 1–9.

Gigerenzer, G. (2008). *Rationality for Mortals: How People Cope with Uncertainty*. Oxford: Oxford University Press.

Gigerenzer, G., Hertwig, R. and Pachur, T. (eds.) (2011). *Heuristics: The Foundations of Adaptive Behavior*. Oxford: Oxford University Press.

Gomez, B. and Wilson, M. (2001). Political sophistication and economic voting in the American electorate: a theory of heterogeneous attribution. *American Journal of Political Science*, 45: 899–914.

Gomez, B. and Wilson, M. (2006). Cognitive heterogeneity and economic voting: a comparative analysis of four democratic electorates. *American Journal of Political Science*, 50: 127–45.

Goodhart, C. A. and Bhansali, R. J. (1970). Political economy. *Political Studies*, 18: 43–106.

Granger, C. W. J. (1969). Investigating causal relations by econometric models and cross-spectral methods. *Econometrica*, 3: 424–38.

Granger, C. W. J. and Newbold, P. (1974). Spurious regressions in econometrics. *Journal of Econometrics*, 2: 111–20.

Green, D. P., Palmquist, B. and Schickler, E. (2002). *Partisan Hearts and Minds: Political Parties and the Social Identities of Voters*. New Haven: Yale University Press.

Greene, W. (2003). *Econometric Analysis*, 5th edn. New York: Prentice-Hall.

Greene, W. (2010). Testing hypotheses about interaction terms in nonlinear models. *Economics Letters*, 107: 291–96.

Gurr, T. R. (1970). *Why Men Rebel*. Princeton, NJ: Princeton University Press.

Heath, A. F., Jowell, R. M. and Curtice, J. K. (1985). *How Britain Votes*. Oxford: Pergamon Press.

Heath, A. F., Jowell, R. M. and Curtice, J. K. (1987). Trendless fluctuation: a reply to Crewe. *Political Studies*, 35: 256–77.

Heath, A. F., Evans, G., Field, J. and Witherspoon, S. (1991). *Understanding Political Change: The British Voter 1964–1987*. Oxford: Pergamon Press.

Helliwell, J. (2006). Well-being, social capital and public policy: what's new? *Economic Journal*, 116: C34–C45.

Helliwell, J. and Haifang, H. (2008). How's your government? International evidence linking good government and well-being. *British Journal of Political Science*, 38: 595–619.

Helliwell, J. and Putnam, R. D. (2007). The social context of well-being. In F. A. Huppert, N. Baylis and B. Kaverne, eds., *The Science of Well-Being* (Oxford: Oxford University Press), pp. 435–60.

Hellwig, T. T. (2001). Interdependence, government constraints and economic voting. *Journal of Politics*, 63: 1141–62.

Hendry, D. F. (1980). Econometrics – alchemy or science? *Economica* 47: 387–406.

Hennessey, P. (2000). *The Prime Minister: The Office and its Holders Since 1945*. London: Penguin Books.

Heseltine, M. (2012). No stone unturned in pursuit of growth. Independent Report. www.bis.gov.uk/heseltine-review.

HM Treasury (2010). Budget 2010. London: HM Treasury.

Ho, K., Clarke, H. D., Chen, L-K. and Weng, D. L-C. (2013). Valence politics and electoral choice in a new democracy: the case of Taiwan. *Electoral Studies*, **32**, forthcoming.

Hox, J. (1998). Multilevel modeling: when and why. In I. Balderjahn, R. Mathar and M. Schader, eds., *Classification, Data Analysis and Data Highways* (New York: Springer Verlag), pp. 147–54.

Hugh-Jondes, D. (2011). Explaining institutional change: why elected politicians implement direct democracy. In H. Saskia, W. de Jong, J. Gijsenberg and T. Howen, eds., *Creative Crises of Democracy* (Brussels: Peter Lang).

Inglehart, R., Foa, R., Peterson, C. and Welzel, C. (2008). Development, freedom and rising happiness: a global perspective (1981–2007). *Perspectives on Psychological Science*, **3**: 264–85.

Iyengar, S. (1991). *Is Anyone Responsible? How Television Frames Political Issues*. Chicago: University of Chicago Press.

Jennings, M. K. and Niemi, R. G. (1974). *The Political Character of Adolescence*. Princeton, NJ: Princeton University Press.

Johansen, S. (1991). Estimation and hypothesis testing of cointegration vectors in Gaussian vector autoregressive models. *Econometrica* **59**: 1551–80.

Johansen, S. (1996). *Likelihood-based Inference in Cointegrated Vector Autoregression Models*. Oxford: Oxford University Press.

Johnston, R. J., Pattie, C. J. and Allsopp, J. G. (1988). *A Nation Dividing? The Electoral Map of Britain 1979–1987*. London: Longman.

Johnston, R. J., Rossiter, D. J., Pattie, C. J., Dorling, D. F. L., MacAllister, I. and Tunstall, H. (1999). Changing biases in the operation of the UK's electoral system, 1950–1997. *British Journal of Politics and International Relations*, **1**: 133–64.

Johnston, R. J., Pattie, C. J., Dorling, D. F. L., MacAllister, I., Tunstall, H. and Rossiter, D. J. (2000). The neighbourhood effect and voting in England and Wales: real or imagined?, in P. J. Cowley, D. R. Denver, A. T. Russell and L. Harrison, eds., *British Elections and Parties Review* (London: Frank Cass), pp. 47–63.

Johnston, R. J., Propper, C., Burgess, S., Sarker, R., Bolster, A. and Jones, K. (2005). Spatial scale and the neighbourhood effect: multinominal models of voting at two recent British general elections. *British Journal of Political Science*, **35**: 487–514.

Kahneman, D. (2011). *Thinking Fast and Slow*. New York: Farrar, Straus and Giroux.

Kahneman, D., Slovic, P. and Tversky, A. (eds.) (1982). *Judgment under Uncertainty: Heuristics and Biases.* Cambridge: Cambridge University Press.

Kam, C. D. and Franzese, R. J. Jr (2007). *Modelling and Interpreting Interactive Hypotheses in Regression Analysis.* Ann Arbor: University of Michigan Press.

Karp, J. (1998). The influence of elite endorsements in initiative campaigns. In S. Bowler, T. Donovan and C. J. Tolbert, eds., *Citizens as Legislators: Direct Democracy in the United States* (Columbus: The Ohio State University Press), pp. 149–65.

Kavanagh, D. and Cowley, P. (2010). *The British General Election of 2010.* London: Palgrave Macmillan.

Kenny, C. (1999). Does growth cause happiness or does happiness cause growth? *Kyklos,* 52: 3–26.

Key, V. O. (1966). *The Responsible Electorate: Rationality in Presidential Voting, 1936–1960.* Cambridge, Mass: Belknap Press.

Keynes, J. M. (1936). *The General Theory of Employment, Interest and Money.* London: Macmillan.

Kiewiet, R. D. (1983). *Macroeconomics and Micropolitics: The Electoral Effects of Economic Issues.* Chicago: University of Chicago Press.

Kinder, D. R. and Kiewiet, R. D. (1981). Sociotropic politics: the American case. *British Journal of Political Science,* 11: 129–62.

King, A. (ed.) (2002). *Leaders' Personalities and the Outcome of Democratic Elections.* Oxford: Oxford University Press.

Kornberg, A. and Clarke, H. D. (1992). *Citizens and Community: Political Support in a Democratic Society.* New York: Cambridge University Press.

Kreft, I. G. G. (1996). Are multilevel techniques necessary? An overview, including simulation studies. Unpublished manuscript, California State University at Los Angeles.

Kreft, I. G. G. and de Leeuw, J. (1998). *Introducing Multilevel Modeling.* Thousand Oaks, CA: Sage Publications.

Krugman, P. (2012). *End This Depression Now!* New York: W.W. Norton.

Labour Party (2010). *The Labour Party Manifesto: A Future Fair For All.* http://labour.org.uk/manifesto

Lakeman, E. (1974). *How Democracies Vote: A Study of Electoral Systems.* London: Faber & Faber.

Lane, R. E. (2000). *The Loss of Happiness in Market Economies.* New Haven: Yale University Press.

Layard, R. (2005). *Happiness: Lessons from a New Science.* London: Penguin.

Layard, R. (2006). Happiness and public policy: a challenge to the profession. *Economic Journal*, 116: C24–C33.

LeDuc, L. (2003). *The Politics of Direct Democracy: Referendums in Global Perspective*. Toronto: Broadview Press.

LeDuc, L. (2005). Saving the pound or voting for Europe? *Journal of Elections, Public Opinion and Parties*, 15: 169–96.

Lewis, M. (1989). *Liar's Poker*. New York: W.W. Norton.

Lewis-Beck, M. S. (1988). *Economics and Elections: The Major Western Democracies*. Ann Arbor, MI: University of Michigan Press.

Lewis-Beck, M. S. and Nadeau, R. (2011). Economic voting theory: testing new dimensions. *Electoral Studies*, 30: 288–94.

Lewis-Beck, M. S. and Paldam, M. (2000). Editorial: Economic voting, an introduction. *Electoral Studies*, 2: 113–20.

Lewis-Beck, M. S., Nadeau, R. and Bélanger, E. (2012). *French Presidential Elections*. New York: Palgrave Macmillan.

Liberal Democrats (2010). *Liberal Democrat Manifesto 2010*. http:// network.libdems.org.uk/manifesto2010/libdem_manifesto_2010.pdf

Lipset, S. M. (1963). *Political Man: The Social Bases of Politics*. New York: Doubleday.

Lipsky, M. (1980). *Street Level Bureaucracy: Dilemmas of the Individual in Public Services*. New York: Russell Sage Foundation.

Long, J. S. and Freese, J. (2006). *Regression Models for Categorical Dependent Variables Using Stata*, 2nd edn. College Station, TX: Stata Press.

Luevano, P. (1994). *Response Rates in the National Election Studies 1948–1992*. Technical Report 44. Ann Arbor, MI: American National Election Study.

Lupia, A. (1994). Shortcuts versus encyclopedias: voting in California insurance reform elections. *American Political Science Review*, 88: 63–76.

Lupia, A. and McCubbins, M. (1998). *The Democratic Dilemma: Can Citizens Learn What They Really Need to Know?* New York: Cambridge University Press.

Lupia, A., McCubbins, M. and Popkin, S. (eds.) (2000). *Elements of Reason: Cognition, Choice and The Bounds of Rationality*. New York: Cambridge University Press.

Luskin, R. (1987). Measuring political sophistication. *American Journal of Political Science*, 31: 856–99.

Maas, C. J. M. and Hox, J. J. (2005). Sufficient sample sizes for multilevel modelling. *Methodology*, 1: 86–92.

Mandelson, P. (2010). *The Third Man*. London: Harper Press.

Marcus, G. E., Neuman, W. R. and MacKuen, M. (2000). *Affective Intelligence and Political Judgment*. Chicago: University of Chicago Press.

Marcussen, M. and Zolner, M. (2001). The Danish EMU referendum 2000. *Government and Opposition*, 36: 379–401.

McKenzie, R. and Silver, A. (1968). *Angels in Marble: Working Class Conservatives in Urban England*. London: Heinemann.

Merrill, S. III and Grofman, B. (1999). *A Unified Theory of Voting: Directional Proximity Spatial Models*. New York: Cambridge University Press.

Mill, J. S. (1987). *Utilitarianism and Other Essays*. London: Penguin Classics.

Miller, W. E. and Shanks, J. M. (1996). *The New American Voter*. Cambridge, MA: Harvard University Press.

Mishler, W. and Rose, R. (2001). Political support for incomplete democracies: realist vs. idealist theories and measures. *International Political Science Review*, 22: 303–20.

Mondak, J. (1993). Source cues and policy approval: the cognitive dynamics of public support for the Reagan agenda. *American Journal of Political Science*, 37: 186–212.

Muller, E. N. (1979). *Aggressive Political Participation*. Princeton, NJ: Princeton University Press.

Murray, J. (2012). A small model of the UK economy. Working paper number 4. London: Office of Budgetary Responsibility.

Nadeau, R., Martin, P. and Blais, A. (1999). Attitudes towards risk-taking and individual choice in the Quebec referendum on sovereignty. *British Journal of Political Science*, 29: 523–39.

Nettle, D. (2005). *Happiness: The Science Behind Your Smile*. Oxford: Oxford University Press.

Neuman, W. R., Marcus, G. E., Crigler, A. N., MacKuen, M. (eds.) (2007). *The Affect Effect: Dynamics of Emotion in Political Thinking and Behavior*. Chicago: University of Chicago Press.

Neundorf, A., Stegmueller, D. and Scotto, T. J. (2011). The individual-level dynamics of bounded partisanship. *Public Opinion Quarterly*, 75: 458–82.

Nie, N. H., Junn, J. and Stehlik-Barry, K. (1996). *Education and Democratic Citizenship in America*. Chicago: University of Chicago Press.

Norpoth, H., Lewis-Beck, M. and Lafay, J-D. (eds.) (1991). *Economics and Politics: The Calculus of Support*. Ann Arbor, MI: University of Michigan Press.

Norris, P. (2010). May 6th 2010 British general election constituency results release 5.0. www.pippanorris.com.

Norton, E. C., Wang, H. and Ai, C. (2004). Computing interaction effects and standard errors in logit and probit. *The Stata Journal*, 4: 154–67.

Norton, P. (2011). The politics of coalition. In N. Allen and J. Bartle, eds., *Britain at the Polls 2010* (London: Sage Publications).

Office for Budgetary Responsibility (2012). *Economic and Fiscal Outlook.* CM 8303. March. London: OBR.

Olson, M. (1965). *The Logic of Collective Action.* New York: Schocken Books.

Oswald, A. J. (1997). Happiness and economic performance. *The Economic Journal,* **107**: 1815–31.

Pacek, A. (2009). Politics vs. markets in the diffusion of human well-being: a cross-national analysis. Unpublished paper, Department of Political Science, Texas A&M University.

Pacek, A. and Radcliff, B. (2008). Assessing the welfare state: the politics of happiness. *Perspectives on Politics,* **6**: 267–77.

Paldam, M. (1991). How robust is the vote function? A study of seventeen nations over four decades. In H. Norpoth, M. Lewis-Beck and J-D. Lafay, eds., *Economics and Politics: The Calculus of Support* (Ann Arbor, MI: University of Michigan Press), pp. 9–31.

Palfrey, T. and Poole, K. (1987). The relationship between information, ideology and voting behavior. *American Journal of Political Science,* **31**: 511–30.

Parkin, F. (1968). *Middle Class Radicals: The Social Basis of the Campaign for Nuclear Disarmament.* Manchester: Manchester University Press.

Pateman, C. (1970). *Participation and Democratic Theory.* Cambridge: Cambridge University Press.

Pattie, C. J., Fieldhouse, E. A. and Johnston, R. J. (1995). Winning the local vote: the effectiveness of constituency campaign spending in Great Britain, 1983–1992. *American Political Science Review,* **89**: 969–79.

Popkin, S. (1991). *The Reasoning Voter: Communication and Persuasion in Presidential Campaigns.* Chicago: University of Chicago Press.

Powell, G. B. Jr, and Whitten, G. (1993). A cross-national analysis of economic voting: taking account of the political context. *American Journal of Political Science,* **37**: 391–414.

Pulzer, P. (1967). *Political Representation and Elections in Britain.* London: Allen & Unwin.

Putnam, R. (1993). *Making Democracy Work: Civic Traditions in Modern Italy.* Princeton, NJ: Princeton University Press.

Putnam, R. (2000). *Bowling Alone: The Collapse and Revival of American Community.* New York: Simon & Schuster.

Quinn, K., Bara, J. and Bartle, J. (2011). The UK Coalition Agreement of 2010: who won? *Journal of Elections, Public Opinion and Parties,* **21**: 295–312.

Radcliff, B. and Pacek, A. (2001). Politics, markets and life satisfaction: the political economy of human happiness. *American Political Science Review*, 95: 939–52.

Raudenbush, S. W. and Bryk, A. S. (2002). *Hierarchical Linear Models: Applications and Data Analysis Methods*, 2nd edn. Thousand Oaks, CA: Sage Publications.

Rawnsley, A. (2010). *The End of the Party: The Rise and Fall of New Labour*. London: Viking Press.

Reinhart, C. M. and Rogoff, K. S. (2009). *This Time is Different: Eight Centuries of Financial Folly*. Princeton, N.J.: Princeton University Press.

Riker, W. and Ordeshook, P. C. (1968). A theory of the calculus of voting. *American Political Science Review*, 62: 26–42.

Riker, W. and Ordeshook, P. C. (1973). *An Introduction to Positive Political Theory*. Englewood Cliffs, NJ: Prentice-Hall.

Rohrschneider, R. (2002). The democracy deficit and mass support for an EU-wide government. *American Journal of Political Science*, 46: 463–75.

Ronis, D. L. and Lipinski, E. R. (1985). Value and uncertainty as weighting factors in impression formation. *Journal of Experimental Social Psychology*, 21: 47–60.

Rose, R. and Mishler, W. (1996). Testing the Churchill hypothesis: popular support for democracy and its alternatives. *Journal of Public Policy*, 16: 29–58.

Runciman, W. G. (1966). *Relative Deprivation and Social Justice*. Berkeley, CA: University of California Press.

Sanders, D. and Gavin, N. (2004). Television news, economic perceptions and political preferences in Britain, 1997–2001. *Journal of Politics*, 66: 1245–66.

Sanders, D., Clarke, H. D. Stewart, M. C. and Whiteley, P. (2007). Does mode matter for modeling political choice? evidence from the 2005 British Election Study. *Political Analysis*, 15: 257–85.

Sanders, D., Clarke, H. D. Stewart, M. C. and Whiteley, P. (2008). The endogeneity of preferences in spatial models: evidence from the 2005 British Election Study. *Journal of Elections, Public Opinion and Parties*, 18: 413–31.

Sanders, D., Clarke, H. D. Stewart, M. C. and Whiteley, P. (2011a). Downs, Stokes and the dynamics of electoral choice. *British Journal of Political Science*, 41: 287–314.

Sanders, D., Clarke, H. D., Stewart, M. C. and Whiteley, P. (2011b). Simulating the effects of the alternative vote in the 2010 UK General Election. *Parliamentary Affairs*, 64: 5–23.

Sarlvik, B. and Crewe, I. (1983). *Decade of Dealignment: The Conservative Victory of 1970 and Electoral Trends in the 1970s*. Cambridge: Cambridge University Press.

Seldon, A. (ed.) (2007). *Blair's Britain, 1997–2007*. Cambridge: Cambridge University Press.

Seldon, A. and Lodge, G. (2010). *Brown at 10*. London: Biteback Publishers.

Seldon, A., Snowdon, P. and Collins, D. (eds.) (2007). *Blair Unbounded*. London: Simon & Schuster.

Seyd, P. and Whiteley, P. (1992). *Labour's Grassroots: The Politics of Party Membership*. Oxford: Clarendon Press.

Seyd, P. and Whiteley, P. (2002). *New Labour's Grassroots: The Transformation of the Labour Party Membership*. London: Palgrave Macmillan.

Sims, C. (1980). Macroeconomics and reality. *Econometrica*, **48**: 1–48.

Skidelsky, R. (2009). *Keynes: The Return of the Master*. New York: Public Affairs.

Sniderman, P. M., Brody, R. A. and Tetlock, P. E. (eds.) (1991). *Reasoning and Choice: Explorations in Political Psychology*. New York: Cambridge University Press.

Soroka, S. N. (2006). Good news and bad news: asymmetric responses to economic information. *Journal of Politics*, **68**: 372–85.

Soroka, S. N., Bodet, M. A., Young, L. and Andrew, B. (2009). Campaign news and vote intentions. *Journal of Elections, Public Opinion and Parties*, **19**: 359–76.

Stewart, M. C. and Clarke, H. D. (1998). The dynamics of party identification in federal systems: the Canadian case. *American Journal of Political Science*, **42**: 97–116.

Stokes, D. E. (1963). Spatial models of party competition. *American Political Science Review*, **57**: 368–77.

Stokes, D. E. (1992). Valence politics. In D. Kavanagh (ed.), *Electoral Politics* (Oxford: Clarendon Press), pp. 141–64.

Tavits, M. (2007). Clarity of responsibility and corruption. *American Journal of Political Science*, **51**: 218–29.

Tett, G. (2009). *Fool's Gold: How the Bold Dream of a Small Tribe at J. P. Morgan Was Corrupted by Wall Street Greed and Unleashed a Catastrophe*. New York: The Free Press.

Thaler, R. (1994). *Quasi-Rational Economics*. New York: Russell Sage Foundation.

Tomz, M., Wittenberg, J. and King, G. (1999). Clarify: software for interpreting and presenting statistical results. Department of Government, Harvard University.

Tov, W. and Diener, E. (2009). Culture and subjective well-being. In E. Diener (ed.), *Culture and Well-Being: The Collected Works of Ed Diener* (Heidelberg: Springer Dordrecht).

van der Brug, W., van der Eijk, C. and Franklin, M. (2007). *The Economy and the Vote*. Cambridge: Cambridge University Press.

Vavreck, L. and Rivers, D. (2008). The 2006 Cooperative Congressional Election Study. *Journal of Elections, Public Opinion and Parties*, 18: 355–66.

Verba, S. and Nie, N. H. (1972). *Participation in America*. New York: Harper & Row.

Verba, S., Schlozman, K. L. and Brady, H. E. (1995). *Voice and Equality: Civic Voluntarism in American Politics*. Cambridge, MA: Harvard University Press.

Vowles, J. (1995). The politics of electoral reform in New Zealand. *International Political Science Review*, 16: 95–115.

Wagner, A. F., Schneider, F. and Halla, M. (2009). The quality of institutions and satisfaction with democracy in Western Europe – a panel analysis. *European Journal of Political Economy*, 25: 30–41.

Walker, I. and Smith, H. J. (2002). Fifty years of relative deprivation research. In I. Walker and H. J. Smith, eds., *Relative Deprivation: Specification, Development and Integration* (Cambridge: Cambridge University Press), pp. 1–9.

Wells, J. M. and Krieckhaus, J. (2006). Does national context influence democracy satisfaction? a multi-level analysis. *Political Research Quarterly*, 59: 569–78.

Whiteley, P. (1995). Rational choice and political participation – evaluating the debate. *Political Research Quarterly*, 48: 211–34.

Whiteley, P. (2012). *Political Participation in Britain: The Decline and Revival of Civic Culture*. Oxford: Palgrave-Macmillan.

Whiteley, P. and Seyd, P. (1994). Local party campaigning and voting behavior in Britain. *Journal of Politics*, 56: 242–52.

Whiteley, P., Seyd, P. and Billinghurst, A. (2006). *Third Force Politics: Liberal Democrats at the Grassroots*. Oxford: Oxford University Press.

Whiteley, P., Clarke, H. D., Sanders, D. and Stewart, M. C. (2010). Government performance and life satisfaction in contemporary Britain. *Journal of Politics*, 72: 733–46.

Whiteley, P., Clarke, H. D., Sanders, D. and Stewart, M. C. (2011). Britain says NO: voting in the AV ballot referendum. *Parliamentary Affairs*, 65: 301–22.

Winkelmann, L. and Winkelmann, R. (1998). Why are the unemployed so unhappy? evidence from panel data. *Economica*, 65: 1–15.

Worcester, R., Mortimore, R., Baines, P., Gill, M. (2011). *Explaining Cameron's Coalition: How It Came About*. London: Biteback Publishing.

Zaller, J. (1992). *The Nature and Origins of Mass Opinion*. Cambridge: Cambridge University Press.

Index